Henry Clay Holloway

A New Path Across an Old Field

Henry Clay Holloway

A New Path Across an Old Field

ISBN/EAN: 9783337254247

Printed in Europe, USA, Canada, Australia, Japan

Cover: Foto ©Andreas Hilbeck / pixelio.de

More available books at **www.hansebooks.com**

Truly Yours,
H. C. Holloway.

A NEW PATH ACROSS AN OLD FIELD.

BY

REV. H. C. HOLLOWAY, A. M.

PUBLISHED FOR THE AUTHOR.

PHILADELPHIA:
LUTHERAN PUBLICATION SOCIETY.

TO THE MEMORY

OF

JOHN BROWN HOLLOWAY,

MY VENERATED AND SAINTED FATHER,

THIS BOOK

IS

AFFECTIONATELY DEDICATED.

PREFACE.

IT was the good fortune of the author of this volume a few years ago to enjoy the pleasure of a visit to the Old World. Whilst abroad, and after his return, he fulfilled an engagement in writing a series of letters for a well-known religious periodical. Unexpectedly to him, these letters were received with general favor. The author has been frequently urged to publish them in book form. After repeated solicitations from many in whose judgment he has more confidence than in his own, he has concluded to comply with what seems to be a general desire. This volume, however, contains much more matter, and in improved form, than originally appeared in public print.

One of the many benefits to be derived from a trip to Europe is the appreciation of our own free institutions, civil and religious. In this country all have the privilege of rising to the highest distinctions in Church and State. With us religion is not hampered by state interference, nor are armies marshaled to uphold the "divine right" of kings. After seeing what we did of Europe, we have learned to love and cherish more sincerely our own land, where freedom in its best form works out the happiest results.

The writer gives his own observations with fairness and candor, so that the reader may see exactly what he saw, and travel hand-in-hand with him. Hoping this unpretentious volume may be kindly welcomed, we send it on its mission, trusting that it may serve a good purpose, and meet with a generous appreciation.

H. C. H.

March, 1886.

CONTENTS.

                                                                        PAGE

CHAPTER I.—The Good-bye—Sea-faring—The Magnificent Ship—The Lord's Day—The Fourth of July—President Garfield—The Great Sorrow—Over the Sea—Lessons of the Sea—On a Foreign Shore   11

CHAPTER II.—On British Soil—The Stranger in a Strange Land—The Scenery along the Way—Chester—Stratford-on-Avon—The Birthplace and Home of Shakespeare—London—British Channel - Ostend—Brussels .   21

CHAPTER III.—In Belgium—Antwerp—An Amusing Incident—Germany—Harvest Scenes—Cologne—On the Rhine—Some of its Legends—Mayence.   30

CHAPTER IV.—Worms—A Welcome Greeting—The Luther Monument   43

CHAPTER V.—Heidelberg and its Environs—The Great Castle—The University—Barbarous Customs.   51

CHAPTER VI.—Harvest Scenes—Rural Life—Military Rule—War Relics—Strassburg—A Vexed Strassburger—Its Wonderful Cathedral—Its Famous Clock—Gutenberg—The Gœthe House   58

CHAPTER VII.—From Germany into Switzerland—An Encounter Between the Conductor (Zugführer) and a Passenger—Bâle—Berne—Its Curious Monumental Fountains—Its Bears—In Switzerland—Interlaken.   65

CHAPTER VIII.—In Switzerland—Interlaken—The Beautiful Sunset—An Excursion—Grindelwald—Its Glaciers—Lauterbrunnen.   72

CHAPTER IX.—Interlaken to Lucerne—The Brunig Pass—Alpine Scenery—Lucerne and its Beautiful Lake . . .   79

CONTENTS.

                                                                                       PAGE

CHAPTER X —Lake Lucerne—William Tell—St. Gothard Pass—Its Passage—Over the Alps Into Italy 85

CHAPTER XI.—Lake Maggiore—Arona—Milan—Its Cathedral 92

CHAPTER XII.—Venice—The City of the Sea—Gondolas and Gondoliers—Its Canals and Bridges—Priests and Females—St. Mark's Cathedral—Its Bronze Horses—St. Mark's Place—Ducal Palace—Bridge of Sighs—The Prisons—Rialto Bridge—The Campanile—Pigeon Feeding—The Streets of Venice—Its Stores—Its Beggars—The Venetian People—A Sail on the Adriatic. 99

CHAPTER XIII.—Over the Apennines—The City of Florence—Pitti Palace—Savonarola—Palace Vecchio—Uffizi Gallery—Church of Santa Croce—Michael Angelo's House—A Funeral Scene 120

CHAPTER XIV.—Rome—The Palace of the Cæsars—Arch of Titus—The Coliseum—The Cathedral of St. Paul. . 129

CHAPTER XV.—More About Rome—St. Peter's—Remains of Pope Pius IX.—The Pope's Unpopularity—The Ticket Agent—The Vatican—The Appian Way—In the Catacombs 137

CHAPTER XVI.—Our Last Day in Rome—Churches and Festivals—Pilate's Staircase—Indulgences—The Pantheon—Victor Emmanuel's Tomb—The Mamertine Prison—Paul and Peter—The Indignant Guide—The Capitol—Emancipated Rome 147

CHAPTER XVII.—From Rome to Naples—The City of Naples—Its People—Pompeii—The Buried City—The Work of Excavation—Old College Friends—The Testimony to the Writings of St. Paul 155

CHAPTER XVIII.—Mount Vesuvius—Its Ascent by Moonlight—The Carriage-way—The Rope Railroad—The Incident at the Battle of Gettysburg—On Foot—The Encounter with Professional Guides—Across the Sulphur Beds—The Burning Mountain—The Final Ascent—Looking into the Crater—The Subterranean Thunders —Our Retreat—The Beautiful Prospect of Land and Sea—What Volcanoes Can Do 164

CONTENTS. ix

CHAPTER XIX.—From Italy into Switzerland—Some Reflections—Pisa—Genoa—Turin—Over the Alps—Mont Cenis Tunnel—Geneva—John Calvin's House—Mont Blanc 174

CHAPTER XX.—From Switzerland into Germany—The Land of Luther—Darmstadt—A Misfortune—Frankfort-on-the-Main—Eisenach—Ursula Cotta—The Luther House—German Hospitality—The Wartburg—The Luther Room—The Famous Inkstand Story 182

CHAPTER XXI.—The Land of Luther—More About Eisenach—Wittenberg—Luther's Home—The Castle Church—Luther's Grave and Melanchthon's—Bronze Statues—Melanchthon's House—The Sleeping Dead about the Stadt Kirche (City Church)—Burning of the Papal Bull—The Wittenberg Seminary in the Augusteum—Dr. Schmieder—Pen Picture of Luther. 192

CHAPTER XXII.—Berlin—The Capital of Prussia—Unter den Linden—The Palaces—Thiergarten—Frederick William and Queen Louisa—Oppressive Military System—German University—Beer and Wine Drinking—The German People—An Incident—Prussian-Franco Love. 205

CHAPTER XXIII.—In France—The City of Paris—Its Cleanliness—Its Stores—The Boulevards—The Inward and Outward—Its Great Public Square—Place of Concord—The Champs Elysées 213

CHAPTER XXIV.—More about Paris—The Triumphal Arch—Bois, or Park of Boulogne—Louvre—The Great Art Gallery—Hotel des Invalides—The Tomb of Napoleon I.—Tomb of Jerome Bonaparte—Luxembourg Palace—Hotel de Ville, or City Hall. 221

CHAPTER XXV.—Paris Continued—A Parisian Sunday—A Pleasant Surprise—The Churches—The Notre Dame—Hyacinthe Loysen—The Madeleine—Sainte Chapelle—St. Bartholomew—The Prisons—Versailles—Marie Antoinette—An Accident—Sympathy for the President 229

CHAPTER XXVI.—From France into England—Rouen—Joan of Arc—A State of Tribulation—On the British Channel—Brighton—Rev. F. W. Robertson—London

CONTENTS.

PAGE

—The Sombre City—Its Streets—The Great Commercial Centre—The March of Improvement. 239

CHAPTER XXVII.—London—St. Paul's Cathedral—The Whispering Gallery—Westminster Abbey—The Temple of Fame—The House of Parliament—The House of Commons—The London Tower—Consecrated Places—The Jewel Tower—The Crown Jewels—The Unfading Crown. 248

CHAPTER XXVIII.—London—The British Museum—Sydenham Crystal Palace—Buckingham Palace—St. James' Park—St. James' Court—Madame Tussaud's Wax Works—Drunkenness. 255

CHAPTER XXIX.—Spurgeon, London's Great Preacher—His Church—The Sermon—Our Impression—The Home of Industry—Miss McPherson—The Dark Side of London —Ecumenical Conference of Methodism—Bun Hill Fields—Bunyan—John Wesley—Daniel DeFoe—Some Reflections on English Character 263

CHAPTER XXX.—From England into Scotland—Edinburgh —The Sir Walter Scott Monument—Calton Hill—The Nelson, Burns, and National Monuments—Holyrood Palace and Abbey—Mary, Queen of Scots—High Street —John Knox's House—St. Giles' Cathedral—Parliament House—Mid-Lothian—Manuscript of Scott's Waverley—The Castle. 273

CHAPTER XXXI.—Something about European Hotels— Languages—Patience and Good Temper—Eating—The Table d'Hôte—Servants and Waiters—Fees and Charities—Improving Opportunities. 282

CHAPTER XXXII.—Things Viewed in the Contrast—The Condition of the Working Class in Europe Compared with Our Own—The Working Women—The Oppressed Poor and Laboring Class—Royalty—The Inequalities of Life—Agrarianism—Solution of the Labor Troubles. 288

CHAPTER XXXIII.—Glasgow—Melrose Abbey—Liverpool —Homeward Bound—Storm at Sea—Ship on Fire—The Great Peril—Death and Burial at Sea—Home Again . 295

A NEW PATH ACROSS AN OLD FIELD.

CHAPTER I.

THE GOOD-BY—SEA-FARING—THE MAGNIFICENT SHIP—THE LORD'S DAY—THE FOURTH OF JULY—PRESIDENT GARFIELD—THE GREAT SORROW—OVER THE SEA—LESSONS OF THE SEA—ON A FOREIGN SHORE.

THE long looked-for day and hour finally arrived, and on the morning of July 2d, we found ourselves on board the magnificent steam-ship *The City of Berlin*, Inman Line, New York. At 9 a. m. she steamed away from her pier with her rich cargo of human freight, bound for Liverpool. Many good-byes had been said, and not a few moistened eyes kept gazing after us as we pulled from shore, and long continued the waving of handkerchiefs to friends on the vessel. Though you are about to realize the pleasure you have so long anticipated in seeing the Old World, yet you now become conscious of a sense of sadness as you stand on deck and watch your native shores as they fade in the distance. You feel that you are leaving home and going to a strange land to be surrounded by new scenes. You cannot be oblivious to the fact that you are about to pass beyond the "great and wide sea" that separates the Old and

New worlds. But the novelty of the situation soon brings with it a contentment as well as courage which help you to say,

> "O happy ship,
> To rise and dip,
> With the blue crystal at your lip."

Among the first things in which you are interested, after having passed out to sea, is the vessel to which you have entrusted yourself for a voyage. In this regard we were soon satisfied that we had made no mistake in selecting the vessel we did—*The City of Berlin*. She is among the largest mercantile steam-ships afloat. Her gross measurement is five thousand four hundred and ninety-one tons. She is five hundred and thirteen feet long, forty-five feet beam and thirty-six feet depth; is five thousand five hundred horse power, and steams sixteen knots. She is supplied with steam by twelve boilers, which are heated by thirty-six furnaces. She consumes ninety tons of coal each twenty-four hours. She has ample accommodations for one thousand seven hundred passengers, of which sufficient space is allotted to accommodate two hundred first-class or saloon passengers. Her saloon is a noble apartment, measuring forty-four by forty-three feet, has four ranges of tables, and provides comfortable sittings for all her cabin passengers. It is lighted with electric light by night, and in day time by an elegant cupola sky-light, the walls of which, like the ceiling of the saloon, are painted and panneled in white, enriched with gold mouldings. The carved work is the finest finish of walnut. Her state-rooms are luxurious, and nothing remains undone in all her apartments that can possibly minister to the comfort of her passengers. She may well be denominated a "naval mansion," a "moving palace." She is also an admirable sailor, rolls but little, but cleaves her way day by day, and night by night, at a grand, steady pace. Of her it may be said in the language of Byron:

> "She walks the waters like a thing of life,
> And seems to dare the elements to strife."

Besides this, her Captain, James Kennedy, is an experienced and most affable commander, having made nearly five hundred passages across the Atlantic, and followed the sea for thirty years. With such surroundings in such hands you cannot feel otherwise than a sense of assurance. You are as well provided for as it is possible to be on sea, and are content to commit yourself to the fate of your noble ship.

As to the rank of our passengers, they are polite, refined and affable, to a degree seldom, if ever surpassed. Our nationality is various—the English, the Italian, the Spanish, the French, and the ubiquitous American. We are also not without a sprinkling of nobility, having on board His Grace the Duke of Sutherland, Major-General Sir Henry Green of the British army, and Lady Green. Then the dozen parsons, representing almost as many different denominations, are not to be despised.

How about sea-sickness? Personally, we escaped. The sea tossed us gently, and what little of this strange tribulation prevailed, was mostly confined to the ladies, whom we pitied very much. The first few days the sea remained almost a perfect calm, the sky being cloudless, and, with the exception of a few small blows and some rain, we had delightful sailing. While our friends at home were sweltering with heat and seeking cool and shady retreats, we were clad in heavy winter robes, and it was difficult to realize that it was July. Some days seafaring was rather monotonous, there being nothing but sea! sea! sea! Other days it was quite to the contrary. Now and then a phantom ship was seen in the far distance, where the sea and horizon meet. Then again the great monsters of the deep, appearing in large numbers on all sides of our vessel, were the occasion of much interest, and frequently of considerable excitement.

The lessons of the sea are many. Perhaps the first and most abiding is its immensity. When on the sea, to a Bible reader the words of the Psalmist at once occur— "This great and wide sea." No plain of earth is so boundless or so beautiful.

> "The eagle's vision cannot take it in;
> The lightning's wing, too weak to sweep its space,
> Sinks half way o'er it, like a wearied bird.
> It is the mirror of the stars, where all
> Their hosts within the concave firmament
> Gay marching to the music of the spheres,
> Can see themselves at once."

You have some sense of the vast extent of the ocean when you stand on the land and stretch your vision across to the farthest horizon; but you have a much profounder sense of its vastness when, from the deck of a ship in mid-ocean, as night is coming on, you gaze around on the watery waste. This is the hour in which you exclaim:

> "How shall pen picture thee, thou lonely sea;
> Awful in thine untracked immensity?"

But every observer of the sea must be struck with its changefulness and unrest. Every atom of it is constantly moving and changing its place, from the depth to the surface, or from the surface to the depth, from the frozen pole to the burning equator, or from the Torrid Zone to the Arctic Ocean. No wonder that in Scripture and in the poetry of all nations the sea is the emblem of endless unrest. Its waters — those barren, wandering fields of foam going moaning round and round the world with apparently profitless labor — seem at first to speak of nothing so much as unbridled power, tumult and strife, anarchy and rebellion. Who does not see in them the picture of an evil soul — a soul unreconciled to God — a soul across which strong gusts of temptation drive, and which is tossed by its own boiling passions? Truly saith the prophet, "The wicked is like the sea, which cannot rest."

Much might be said on the mystery of the sea. We feel as we pass over it and look at it, that it is a great secret world of wonders. Oh, secret and mysterious sea:

> "Thou hast pearls of price untold,
> To light thy ruby cells;
> And splendid wrecks, and mines of gold,
> 'Mid rainbow-colored shells."

Life itself is not unfrequently spoken of as a sea, and surely the sea mirrors the life of a man. And all are on this great and wide sea. Some have only moved their boat a little way from the sunny shores; others are well out in mid-ocean, riding over its billowy waves amid storm and tempest; while others are well nigh over, and are rapidly approaching their "desired haven." Though all are on this sea of life, not all are on it in the same manner. Not all have taken Christ with them. Some refuse His companionship, and in the joyfulness and gayety of their hearts, seem not to need the presence of such a Friend. Now hope is bright, and the spirit free and buoyant. While the sun shines and the wind is low and the sea calm, they drift away on the wide waste of waters, dreamily watching the silvery foam hills, or are looking onward over the bright expanse. No sad forebodings oppress the soul; the dark and lonely shores of death are unseen, and the roar of the breakers unheard; and if, at times, the cry of some shipwrecked one comes fitfully on the breeze, it soon dies away in the great space above, and they dream on and on; and thus they sing and float purposelessly on, and fancy they are sailing, and Hope pointing their barque to the land of prosperity and happiness. But the tide sweeps on to the gloom of eternity, and all the while they are drifting, drifting away,

> "Gliding away, away,
> To the throne, to the Judge, to the awe,
> To the book of the broken law."

Then there are those who are on this great and wide sea of life in close companionship with Jesus. He is on the vessel with them. His word the winds and the sea obey. Amid storm and calm, sunshine and cloud, He is their refuge and strength. The fair haven beyond awaits them. Their vessel can never sink nor be destroyed; it carries Him who is greater than the sea and mightier than its storms. They are carried forward to the future times, the period when the earth shall be "full of the knowledge of the Lord as the waters cover the sea;" to the "sea of glass, mingled with fire," on which shall stand the victors over the beast, having the harps of God; to the day when the sea shall give up the dead that are in it; and to that yet more glorious day, when in the new heaven and the new earth there shall be "no more sea." O the glad day to every anxious, struggling soul to get home to God!—that after having been tossed and rocked on the high waves of the sea of life; having braved its mighty perils, and endured hardness as good soldiers of Jesus Christ, and for many long days and weary years looked anxiously for the shores of the better land, they shall behold its peaceful haven, and anchor safely in its protecting care! Then,

"Calmly rest! where every storm is hushed
To peace, and cloudless skies are beautified
With everlasting day! Soft is the light
That glances on their brows, and pure the gales
That breathe their music there—the light, the breath,
The melody of Heaven."

The amusements on board the ship were various — some innocent enough, and others sinful. The gambling and drinking were bold and disgraceful. We were glad to know, however, that the Christian sentiment among our passengers was so strong and positive in its condemnation of these evils that the gaming was not allowed on the second Lord's day we were at sea.

The religious services on ship-board were impressive and well attended. Though a number of clergymen were on board, there was no sermon, the captain reading the service of the Church of England. In the evening there was a preaching service on the deck of the vessel, which was greatly enjoyed by all present. How natural that as our hearts communed with God on the far-off sea, we should also think of loved ones at home. These also worshiped the same Almighty Father who has made both the land and the sea. How many devout and earnest prayers ascended up to Him who "holds the winds in His fist and the sea in the hollow of His hand," that He would give us a safe voyage, and bring us into our "desired haven."

Though out on the broad Atlantic, we had a "glorious Fourth of July," even on a British steamer. At 7 A. M. the "Stars and Stripes" were unfurled to the breeze at the main-mast of our vessel, and almost simultaneously the "Union Jack" on the mizzen. Then went up a hearty cheer for both by the passengers on deck, declaring very decidedly and beautifully the friendly relations existing between the two countries. One countryman who possibly lived too much in the past refused to mingle his voice in a cheer that included the British flag, on the ground that that flag had done his country an injury. Besides flying the Stars and Stripes, we had Fourth of July speeches and appropriate recitations in the saloon at night. It was something to be an American on the sea, and even on board a British vessel. All that was wanting to make this a perfect Fourth of July celebration were the fire-crackers. The wonder was that no one of our number was thoughtful enough to bring some along.

On the eighth day of our voyage, in the afternoon at four o'clock, the cry went up, "Land in sight!" All below rushed on deck, and there to the larboard in the far distance loomed up the cliffs of Skelly, on the coast of Ireland. An hour later and we see Cape Clear, Brown Head Signal Station, and Rochie Point. Soon came in sight the beautiful green fields and hills, and an unbroken view of the coast of Ireland. How welcome the sight of land! How lovely the scenery on which we now gaze!

The shades of night now gather over us, and darkness covers sea and sky. In an hour later we are safely brought into the harbor at Queenstown. How soon our joy is turned into sorrow by the sad news that reached us that the *Brittanica*, of the White Star Line, was lost in the Irish channel. But almost in the same moment still sadder news comes—the report of the assassination of President Garfield. The sorrow was universal on our ship. The moaning sea seemed to mingle with the sad hearts that wept over this great sorrow. All on board were deeply touched by this calamity, and few retired until after midnight. We sought comfort in the hope that the President would survive and be spared to the American nation.

In the afternoon of the ninth day of our voyage we were safely landed in Liverpool. With good will to the noble ship that brought us safely over the deep, and with gratitude to a kind Providence that guided it in its watery path, we went on shore. After going through the formality of having our luggage examined in the Custom House, we were ready to take the train, on the Great Western Railway, for Chester.

CHAPTER II.

ON BRITISH SOIL—THE STRANGER IN A STRANGE LAND—THE SCENERY ALONG THE WAY—CHESTER—STRATFORD-ON-AVON—THE BIRTHPLACE AND HOME OF SHAKESPEARE—LONDON—BRITISH CHANNEL—OSTEND—BRUSSELS.

AT once things began to appear strange to us, and we were introduced to things both new and old. For instance, we looked for a ticket office, and upon inquiry no one could tell us what that was. One gentleman said he never heard of such a thing. Above a door we saw in large letters, "Booking-House." We thought of a book store, and seing a good many people going into this place, we followed suit, and soon found that this was the *ticket* office, but in England is known as the "Booking-House." So we had ourself "*booked*." This is the old phraseology still retained of former stage-coach days, well remembered by our older citizens; and the English people being very tenacious of old customs, prefer the "good old" term "booking." In the days of public travel exclusively by stage coach, and before railroads were built, the name and destination of each passenger were written in what was called the "way-bill," being in a small book form, with black cover, and generally carried in the driver's side pocket. Thus a passenger was "booked" from M. to H. We had ourself "booked" from Liverpool to Chester.

The next new thing to us in our "New Path" was the construction of the railway cars. They are much smaller than ours, and made into compartments, two seats in each, and facing each other, having capacity for eight persons. There are three such compartments in each car, which, in all, carries twenty-four passengers, being about half the capacity of one of our cars. Then there are first, second and third classes, and you pay according to the class you take. There is a *saying* that "fools and Americans travel in *first* class;" we took the *second*, and sometimes the third. It is said that Gladstone, the great English statesman, being asked why he rode in third class cars, replied, "Because there isn't a fourth." Whilst all the cars which we occupied were comfortable, yet none of them had the comforts and conveniences of our American coaches. Ours are much to be preferred. Think of it—locked in a small compartment, with low ceiling, one small window for air in the upper half of the side door by which you enter the coach, no bell-rope to pull in case of need, and no water in the hot days of July. These are only some of the luxuries you enjoy on the coaches of the English railway. The precaution with which railroads are constructed in some parts of the Old World is much to be commended. Thus, in England the tracks are never laid across the country roads, always either over or under. In Germany every highway, across which a railway track is laid, is guarded by a gate, and has stationed by it a watchman to open and close the gate as trains approach and depart. This is protection against accident and loss of life.

Then, too, the conductor's duties are performed amid the greatest perils. He cannot pass through the cars in collecting tickets, but is obliged to pass over a narrow platform ten inches wide, which encircles each car outside, and thrust his head through the window of the coach. The wonder is that not many more of these officials lose their lives in the performance of their duties.

It gives us pleasure to mention the gratifying fact of the extreme politeness, both in England and Germany, of all railroad officials, and especially so that of the ticket agents and conductors. At an English railway station, or booking-house, you ask for a ticket—in Germany, for a "billet," i. e., a ticket also—and the agent heartily thanks you for your money. Did any one ever know of such a thing in our country? So you show your "billet" or ticket on the train, and the conductor thanks you in the politest manner. We have met with railway conductors in our country who might learn a good deal in this particular. Politeness costs nothing, but shows good breeding, and goes a great way in smoothing life's rough path. Never does one feel this more keenly than when wandering "a stranger in a strange land." But kind treatment and polite attention, whether there was money involved or not, were not confined to railroad officials, but we found the same to be true of all classes of people we met. We mingled freely with the people in order to learn the manners and customs of the countries, and, with but two exceptions, received not a single incivility. The English and German people seem specially anxious that foreigners shall think well of their respective countries.

So courteously were we treated by all, that we were almost vain enough to believe that the reason for this was the fact that we were Americans. But, while an American is not at a discount abroad, yet the right solution of the matter is, that the people among whom we traveled were by nature well-bred gentlemen. As for ourself, we were not quite sure to what nationality we belonged, for when in Germany, where we filled the office of spokesman and interpreter for our party of three, we were taken once for a Dutchman, another time for a German from Wittenberg, and again, when attempting to speak English, it was presumed we were something of a Frenchman. This was not a little confusing, and was enough to put us on the way of studying our ancestry.

The scenery from Liverpool to Chester, on the Great Western Railroad, is very beautiful. The mossy green of the fields, and hedge rows so carefully trimmed, the sodded and cultivated embankments on both sides of the road, the beautiful flower gardens at almost every station, the stately mansions and open lawns which stretch far around them, all contribute greatly to enhance the pleasure of the wayfarer. The day from Liverpool to Chester was all that we could wish. In the evening we found ourselves resting at the Queen's hotel.

At twilight we took a stroll through parts of this quaint old town, but gave it a more thorough inspection the next day. It is a town full of historic events. It was one of the chief military stations of the Romans, and the last city in England to hold out against William the Conqueror. The walls, built by the Romans, completely surround the city, a circuit of nearly two miles. As we took an early morning walk over these walls, history at once began to crowd upon us. There we see, among the first historic marks, the Phœnix Tower, which bears the inscription: "King Charles stood on this tower, September 24, 1645, and saw his army defeated on Rowton Moor." In walking through this city, one is at once struck with the curious and unique features of what are called the Rows or Arcades. Besides the ordinary pavements of the streets, there is a continuous covered gallery through the front story of the houses. On this "upstairs street" all the better class of shops are situated. We found it to be true, as one had said about this feature of the town: "Great is the puzzle of the stranger as to whether the roadway is down in the cellar, or he is upstairs on the landing, or the house has turned itself out of window." Everything looks old; the castle, the houses, the cathedral, all things were full of interest to us. In this old but beautiful cathedral Dean Howson, whose learned works are well known to all scholars, has long preached the pure Word of life. Within its ancient walls we stood by the side of the tomb of John Pearson, who is the author of the well-known work, "Pearson on the Creed." But I dare not detain you with these things and many more which I saw, and that were so full of interest to me.

The next day we continued our journey, and came to Stratford-on-Avon, the birthplace and home of Shakespeare. The home of the famous dramatist is an antique-looking stone house, two stories high, with picturesque gables fronting the street. The custodian of the house is a quaint, pleasant, elderly lady, who admitted us, and talked as familiarly about Shakespeare as if she had known him personally for a lifetime. Before the door is unbolted for your exit, you are plainly reminded that you are expected to pay for the lecture you have received. And who would not wish to pay? No tourists patronize Stratford more generously than Americans, no less than fifteen thousand having visited this famous house in one year; and just that many shillings were taken in from these alone.

In the room in which Shakespeare first saw the light of the world which he was to enrich with his thought, there is a cast of his face taken after his death, and a portrait painted in the prime of life. The latter showed a truly noble brow; it was such a face as fancy itself might paint, so royally did it seem endowed with genius. In this room Sir Walter Scott inscribed his name on a pane of glass with his diamond ring. And Wordsworth once wrote a stanza, which is still preserved under glass in this room, and it reads thus:

> "Of mighty Shakespeare's birth the room we see;
> That where he died, in vain to find we try.
> Useless the search, for all immortal he;
> And those who are immortal never die."

In the rear of the house is a garden, in which grew the old English flowers that are portrayed by the poet in his dramas. Not far from the house stands the cottage of Ann Hathaway, Shakespeare's wife, whom he loved in youth when life's bright days lay before him. It is a

cottage which is mainly noticeable for its simplicity.
"There is the place where he sat when he came to see
his sweetheart," said the good lady who showed us the
house.

Shakespeare and his wife sleep in the same beautiful
church, amid the bowery town of Stratford-on-Avon.
His tomb is within the chancel of the church. The Avon
runs but a short distance from the walls, and the cool
boughs of the summer trees wave before the windows.
A flat stone marks the place where the poet is buried,
on which are inscribed the oft-quoted lines, said to be
written by the poet himself:

> "Good friend, for Jesus' sake forbear
> To dig the dust enclosèd here!
> Blest be the spade that spares these bones,
> And curst be he that moves my bones."

Over the grave, in a niche in the wall, is a bust of the
poet. The inscription mentions his age as fifty-three
years. The town of Stratford is a charming, cleanly and
inviting town of eight thousand inhabitants, all of whom
take special pride in the privilege of living in so noted a
place.

The evening of the same day found us in the great city
of London, where we rested for the night. The next day
we arranged our affairs for a tour over the Continent, and,
without attempting to "do" this wonderful city *then*, we
departed in the afternoon, and came by rail to Dover, a
British military post on the banks of the English Channel.
On the white cliffs yonder we saw the red-coats in their
evening dress parade. After a good night's rest, in the

morning we took ship for Ostend, which is in Belgium. From the smooth, placid waters of the Channel that morning, we were slow to believe that ours should be anything but the smoothest sailing; and sure enough, these waters which are so much dreaded by many tourists, and that, too, for the best reasons, afforded us a most delightful trip across. There was scarcely a ripple on their surface. The day was bright and sunny, and the distance of sixty-eight miles was made in four hours. Here we found ourselves in a still stranger country than when in England. Now again the money has changed, and the language. We hear the French language, but little German, and no English. We now feel that we are foreigners, for things are very foreign to us. We had to depend altogether upon the honesty of the people for fair dealings with us, and we had no reason to think that our trust was betrayed.

The people seemed also to trust us, for in the examination of our luggage, the inspectors simply *asked* us whether we had anything dutiable. It was enough for us to say "No." They took it for granted that we were honest.

The same evening we reached Brussels, the Paris of Belgium, and certainly a charming city of 180,000 people. Its cleanliness is remarkable. Its streets generally are wide, and the houses have the appearance of having just lately been scoured. Some of its boulevards are magnificent, and at night are brilliant with beauty and fashion. The city is full of enterprise, and is the centre of thrift and industry. Its people generally are refined in manner, and have an air of intelligence that is striking.

In the evening we attended a concert, given in one of the open gardens, and saw for the first time what such things are. One franc admitted us within the enclosure. At first sight there burst upon us a scene of gayety and brilliancy that were marvelous. The music from the central pavilion was delightful. Many thousands, intent upon beer and wine, were seated in groups around small tables. The husband does not go alone, leaving his wife and children at home; but brings them along, that they with him may enjoy the evening. There was much drinking of wine and beer, but an absence of all disorder, even of loud talking. Among all that vast multitude we saw no drunkenness, but the most decorous deportment on the part of all. We concluded these people enjoyed life, and for good behavior were an example to many others.

CHAPTER III.

IN BELGIUM—ANTWERP—AN AMUSING INCIDENT—GERMANY—HARTEST SCENES—COLOGNE—ON THE RHINE—SOME OF ITS LEGENDS—MAYENCE.

IT was with regret that we took our departure from the delightful city of Brussels, there being so many things to invite and interest us. But one of the many delightful experiences in travel is the pleasure of anticipation. You reluctlantly leave one place, but immediately become interested in another to which you are going.

It is but an hour's ride by rail from Brussels to Antwerp, the chief sea-port of Belgium, whither we came to see some of the fine paintings of Rubens in the great cathedral. We were well repaid for our trip. No matter how well portrayed, a description of "Ruben's Descent from the Cross" could very imperfectly present to the reader a true conception of this piece of art. It deeply impresses both the mind and heart, as one sees the blessed Saviour in the strong arms and gentle hands of His loving friends, who lift Him from the cross, preparatory to his burial in Joseph's tomb. Great indeed the genius that can conceive, and the skill that can execute, such a picture. Consecrated talent thus employed continues to teach and bless the coming ages.

There were many street scenes in Antwerp that interested us by reason of their novelty. Among these were the open markets. For many squares you see goods of every description displayed on the paved streets, the only protection being an underlaid canvas. Here you could purchase almost anything, from a row of pins up to a silk dress.

Another novelty was the use made of dogs. The people make them work and earn their living. They are hitched to small carts used for transporting goods, and pull them through the streets with remarkable skill. You see none of the canine species running at large by day, neither do you hear their hideous howling by night. They work, and therefore are too busy " to bark and bite." They also are very helpful in bringing marketing from the small neighboring farms to the city, and thus serve in place of the horse.

To see people of both sexes wearing heavy wooden shoes was still more of a novelty than previous sights. These shoes are actually constructed of wood, and are very clumsy. The soles are fully half an inch thick and turned up in front, reminding one of skates. They do not present a neat appearance, and come far short of being a good fit. No matter how handsome the foot might be, the owner must give up in despair any idea of exhibiting it with such shoes. We were, however, surprised to see how quickly, and even gracefully, the people move about in these timber shoes. They do not seem to be incommoded in the least by them. The constant clattering noise they make as their owners move about the streets, attracts a stranger's attention. The shoe does not come above the ankle, and the children wear them in the form of slippers, and run or walk as nimbly with them on their feet as our children in leather slippers. But why will people, you ask, wear wooden shoes when leather is so cheap and makes a much more comfortable and neater shoe? This question we are not able to answer, unless with some of the people it is on the ground of economy.

In the evening of the same day we retraced our steps and came back to Brussels and immediately started for Cologne. An amusing incident occurred at a way station some miles beyond Brussels where we had to change cars and take the train direct for Cologne. There were three of us and the compartment we entered had no passengers. But just as the train was about to start, three gentlemen entered, one quite a young man. He at once began showing his displeasure at our presence by alluding to us in not the most respectful manner. He spoke in German and remarked to his frends that we were some more of these "American tramps," and for aught he knew might be "jail birds, or candidates for the American presidency." After the youngster had well spent himself on us, to the great merriment of his companions, it came our turn to say something, and we said it. We addressed him in German, at which he was startled; and he at once began to beg pardon in the most agitated manner. But we reminded him that as we had not interrupted him in his comments on us, we would allow no interruption on his part, and he must now keep silent until we were done. He saw the dilemma he was in, and accepted the situation. We told our critic that we were Americans and were proud of it, and withal were gentlemen, and that he was the first man we had met in our journey who failed to prove himself such; that if he continued to show his bad manners, he would, before very long, know from personal experience what a "jail bird" was; reminding him at the same time that the office of President in our country was open to all who might seek it, excepting such as himself. He begged pardon for his conduct, and it was granted—not, however, until reminding him "how golden is silence," especially in regard to those whom we do not know.

As we journeyed through the country, we saw the farmers busy cutting and gathering the grain crop, which was good and promised a large yield. Fences now disappeared, save here and there a hedge. The country is beautiful, and with here a golden grain field, and there a green meadow, and yonder a waving hill of rye, we have an animating and delightful picture. We could not help but wonder at the old-time method of cutting grain. Instead of the reaper, they use the sickle and a small three-fingered cradle, or a short scythe, all of which reminded us of our earliest boy-hood days. Then, we saw more women than men in the fields, and these working in the hot sun with nothing but a blue cloth tied over their heads as a protection against the heat, and many even without this. Things go slow, but with care; and every farm place is cultivated as carefully as we Americans cultivate a flower-garden. The Germans teach us economy. Every spot of ground is utilized. The most common or universal products are rye, wheat, barley, oats, hemp, hops,

Indian corn, tobacco and flax. The working class in Germany work very hard, and severely feel the oppressive military rule. A German said to us: "We work most of the time for the government, taking nearly all we make for taxes." We said to him: "Your army is too large." "Yes, my friend," he answered, "but self-protection requires that we have a large army, for our neighbors would come in on us from all sides and steal our government and all we have." No doubt this is the truth. Among the many things that are easier in America than in Germany, is farming.

After a long and hot ride we reached Cologne late in the night. The next day we spent in sight-seeing in this famed city. Its streets are remarkable for narrow pavements and crookedness, at some points almost running zig-zag. The public and private edifices are generally well built, and the city is decidedly clean, although Coleridge many years ago wrote of it:

> "Ye nymphs who reign over sewers and sinks,
> The river Rhine, it is well known,
> Doth wash your city of Cologne;
> But tell me, nymphs, what power divine
> Shall henceforth wash the river Rhine?"

Since Coleridge wrote these lines, certainly a great change has taken place in this city, for it is now a place of sweet odors, and worthily has become "the great depot for the manufacture of *eau de Cologne*, the liquid of Christendom." The city has a population of one hundred and forty thousand inhabitants, and is walled and strongly fortified. The chief attraction of Cologne is its magnificent cathedral. It is of Gothic architecture, and looms up over all surrounding buildings. Its beginning dates back over six centuries, and it is not yet fully completed. Several millions of dollars have been spent on it during the past forty years by the kings of Prussia. All the pictures we had ever seen of this world-wide known building, and descriptions we had read of it, did not seem now to have been exaggerated. One is over-awed with its largeness and its indescribable beauty. While it does not contain as many paintings of historic note as the cathedral at Antwerp, it has much finer windows and better and finer architecture.

Behind the high altar is the chapel of the Magi, or the three kings of Cologne. We were assured by the custodian that the silver case contains the bones of the three wise men who came from the East to Bethlehem to offer their presents to the infant Christ, and that the case, which is ornamented with precious stones, and the surrounding valuables in the chapel are worth six million dollars. The remains of the wise men are said to have been presented to the Archbishop of Cologne by the Emperor Barbarossa when he captured the city of Milan, which at that time possessed these wonderful relics. Surely, to believe all this requires faith greater than that which would remove mountains.

Being too late to catch the boat, we took the train to Bonn, where we overtook the boat, and steamed up the Rhine. At Bonn we thought of the great and good Christlieb, and passed through the grounds of the University buildings. The eminent Christian and theologian was not at home, or we certainly should have called to see him.

And now we are on the boat up the Rhine, the beautiful Rhine, a full history of which will never be written. At first there seemed to be some disappointment experienced, as we started on our way with a trip of pleasure and fine scenery pictured in our minds, such as we only hoped now to realize. There was neither that grandeur nor the beauty we expected to see, and there seemed an absence of all special interest. But we were not long in waiting until we were relieved of all disappointment, and to attempt to express our supreme pleasure and delight, as view after view of sublime scenery burst upon our vision, would be entirely impossible. We begin to think of the stories and legends connected with the numerous castles that tower high up on the mountain sides and tops, on both sides of this historic river. We think of the many bloody wars waged on its banks, and the glories of Fatherland connected with its long and eventful history. We think of the effort by many to celebrate in song what we are now permitted to gaze upon in a beautiful, quiet July day. As we go on our way, we see many beautiful towns and villages dotting its banks, vine-clad mountains and mossy green, and waving fields of golden grain; and one almost wearies of the perfect panorama of enchanted beauty which constantly rises to view. Well could Longfellow say: "O, the pride of the German heart, this noble river!" And right, it is; for, of all the rivers of this beautiful earth, there is no other so beautiful as this. There is hardly a league of its whole course, from its cradle in the snowy Alps to its grave in the sands of Holland, which boasts not of its peculiar charms. If I were a German, I would be proud of it too, and of the clustering grapes that hang about its temples, as it reels onward through vineyards in a triumphal march, like Bacchus crowned and drunken.

And now we have reached Bingen, which the poets have described as "Sweet Bingen on the Rhine." It is a town of about six thousand inhabitants; and, as viewed from the river, has a very ancient appearance. Opposite this town, on an immense rock, in the middle of the Rhine, is the famous Mouse-Tower, a monument of the sordid avarice of an Archbishop of Mentz, called Hatto, and at the same time the scene of a dreadful catastrophe which is said to have happened this dignitary of the church. Erected by Hatto, in order to exact a heavy tax from the Rhine boats that passed, it one day became the refuge of the Archbishop, but did not save him from an awful death.

The legend runs as follows: The diocese of the Archbishop was visited by a terrible failure of the crops; when winter came, the people were starving, the price of corn was exorbitant, and incessantly rising. The Archbishop had bought up all the corn remaining from previous harvests, and retailed the contents of his full granaries at usurious prices. The people begged and implored for bread, and hinted that they would take it by force if he did not give them some. But the merciless man only sneered at them and said: "I will procure them bread; let the people go into the empty barn, there they shall have warm bread enough."

The people rushed into the building, and, when it was full, the doors were securely fastened, and it was set on fire on all sides. A heart-rending cry of terror was heard, piercing the heart of every one to the quick, but did not move the Bishop. He stepped on the balcony of his house near by, and cried out, "Listen to the piping of the mice! I treat rebels as I do mice; when I catch them I burn them." The shrieks soon ceased, and the roof and walls buried the poor wretches in the ruins.

But ere long they were fully avenged. The legend goes on to say that out of the ashes of the barn crept innumerable hosts of mice. They filled the streets leading to the Archbishop's palace, covered the steps of the splendid edifice, penetrated into every opening in the interior, and the apartments. He sent out his servants to destroy the troublesome guests, but in vain; as many as were crushed under their blows and feet, so many more appeared in fresh swarms. There was no more help; the servants fled from the palace. Hatto escaped to the remotest apartments, for already the mice were pulling at his robes and gnawing at his shoes. He fled from the palace, but the inexorable mice followed him. He rushed into a boat; the Rhine was high, and now he thought himself free from the vile intruders. He landed at the tower, and shut himself up in the uppermost apartment.

But the mice were not to be daunted by the roaring element; myriads, gnawing at the doors, climbed up the walls and steps and rushed into his hiding-place. There a dreadful cry was heard, when all again became still. A few days afterwards some courageous boatmen found the skeleton of the Bishop that had been gnawed by the mice.

This is a sample of the Rhine legends connected with the many castles that crown the heights of this eventful river. There stand the ruins of the tower, and if the story be true the old fellow deserved to be eaten up by mice, even if he were not.

And now we have reached *The Drachenfels*. (The Dragon's Rock.) Here seven summits arise, like so many crowns on the mountain; demolished by the storms of time, stand ruins of castles and chapels which, mirrored in the waves of the Rhine, proclaim to the tourist the magnificence of bygone times.

The Drachenfels tower, majestic in front, close to the flowing river, seems to be addressing with a warning and prophetic voice the peaceful world below: "Thou also hast still to combat with the Dragon, which, in a future paradise, guards the entrance to freedom's glorious kingdom, where all shall be equal in fraternal love."

On the side of the Drachenfels is a deep and gloomy cavern, which, according to tradition, was long the den of a dragon, the terror of all the country round. Neither exorcism nor arms could free the pagans who lived thereabout from the monster. To propitiate it, the people sacrificed to it their criminals and prisoners taken in war, who were ravenously devoured.

During one of their battles with a foreign tribe, a virgin fell into their hands. Her beauty was so transcendent that it kindled a flame of intense love in the breasts of two of the heroes. These, who were chiefs, disputed with each other the prize. A third, however, to terminate the dispute, ordained that the virgin should be delivered over to the dragon.

Clothed in purest white, her hair adorned with bridal flowers, and around her neck a golden chain, which had been worn by her in her happy days, and was now left in her possession, she was condemned to the sacrifice. She advanced to meet her fate; no pallor, caused by fear, overspread her cheek. Courageous and collected she stood in the circle which surrounded her.

As she approached the cavern and the dragon's fiery breath fell on her, she lowly murmured a pious prayer, and sang a hymn like one of the celestial choir. She drew from her bosom, attached to the golden chain, a cross, her greatest treasure in all her tribulations.

She held it towards the dragon, which, gazing wildly at it, shuddered in its scaly armor, closed its jaws, turned and fled — fled before the unarmed maid, and dashed down into the flowing Rhine, its scaly carcass crashing against the rocks, and at once the monster is annihilated and the heavens are o'ercast with a fiery glow. A golden halo surrounded the garland of flowers in the virgin's hair; her countenance beamed with a celestial expression when she had overcome the threatened danger. The pagans standing around and seeing the wonder, were seized with a fear hitherto unknown, sank down before the divine glance of the maiden and the cross, and were converted thereby to the faith of pure brotherly love, and became worshipers of the meek Deity of the Christians.

Similar stories and legends are connected with every town and castle on the Rhine, but time and space forbid their mention.

As regards the beauty and attractiveness of the Rhine, according to our judgment, the finest scenery lies between Coblentz and Mayence. As if Providence meant to give us a specially favored day to see the Rhine and its charming scenery under a variety of circumstances, there came down upon us a fearful thunderstorm, accompanied with much wind and a great rain. But an hour before we left the boat the clouds broke away, and we saw the Rhine and mountains arched with a beautiful rainbow, and the day closed with one of the most beautiful sunsets we ever beheld. The picture of the Rhine and its charming scenery we now hold in our mind is fixed as a thing of childhood, never to be blotted out.

The evening found us safely in Mayence, or Mainz. We saw all of the most interesting sights the next day. It is, like everything in this part of the world, very old. There was a Roman camp here as early as 38 B. C., and the foundations of the city walls were laid even earlier. In the citadel, which Drusus built, there is an interesting monument, erected by the soldiers, in honor of Drusus. Outside the city there are extensive remains of a Roman aqueduct. The cathedral, founded in A. D. 978, but six times burned and restored, is one of the grandest in Germany, and no other is so rich in monuments. We were present during the morning service. The singing was truly fine and to hear the peals of the great organ as they rolled and reverberated through the grand arches, was impressive. In these cathedrals one is overwhelmed with demonstration and show, all appealing to the senses more than to the affections. There is, no doubt, true worship on the part of the many thousands who gather here, but the people receive no instruction. There is an immense amount of superstition connected with nearly everything that is done in the way of service. Our heart went out in deepest sympathy for these benighted people. No wonder Martin Luther's soul was set on fire with heavenly zeal, when he saw still much more of this than now exists in the Romish Church.

CHAPTER IV.

WORMS—A WELCOME GREETING—THE LUTHER MONUMENT.

THE site on which the ancient city of Worms reposes is consecrated to legend, history and art. It is the scene and perhaps the home also of the German *Nibelungen Legend*, the place where *Luther* for the first time spoke before the Emperor and the Diet, as the emancipator of conscience, as the hero of the first war for the liberties of the German nation; and the fact of its now being adorned with a magnificent *Monument of the German Reformation* and its forerunners, is sufficient to stamp it as classic ground.

As we attempt to write from so historic a place as Worms, in Germany, we wish we could command the inspiration needed to write in a befitting manner. We wish also we could give expression to the supreme pleasure it afforded us to visit the place where were enacted such deeds of heroism in the interests of truth and righteousness. While every Christian heart must be touched in wandering amid places like Worms, yet to a Lutheran this is thrillingly interesting, and he glories afresh in the man who, under God, glorified the ages, and lives anew in history, as do but few.

We reached Worms from Heidelberg in the evening, after dark; but so great was our desire to see something of the town, that we took a stroll through some of its streets by gaslight. The impressions made upon our mind were quite favorable. Its streets are clean, well paved, and well lighted. It has a population of about fifteen thousand, nearly two-thirds of whom are Protestants. In the time of Frederick Barbarossa it had a population of seventy thousand; but at the beginning of the seventeenth century the number had dwindled to forty thousand. The thirty years' war proved very disastrous to Worms, which was repeatedly occupied and laid under contribution by Mansfeld and Tilly, the Spaniards and the Swedes.

We were kindly shown through the churches (three of which are Lutheran and very large) and in one case the sexton's wife got up at 6 o'clock in the morning to show us the interior of the *Driefaltigkeit's Kirche*, or the Church of the Trinity. This contains a painting of the Diet of Worms, which was held in 1521, at which Luther defended his doctrines before the Emperor Charles V., six Electors, and a large and august assemblage, concluding with the words: *Here I stand; I cannot do otherwise; God help me! Amen.*

After having seen the interior of the Church of the Trinity, we inquired of the sexton's wife the pastor's name, which she gave us as Pastor Müller. We had a desire to see him, and yet from the representation made to us by some of the Lutheran divines in America, we felt a hesitancy in calling on him, it being also so early in the morning. But we concluded to try, as certainly no harm could result from simply calling on him. We pulled the bell at the parsonage door, were invited in, and on inquiry found that the pastor was at home, and after a moment's waiting he made his appearance; and upon introducing ourself, we were most cordially welcomed into his study. No one, to whom we were a stranger, could have received us more cordially or treated us with more consideration. Pastor Müller reminded us much of some of our genial German pastors at home. He inquired very particularly about the Lutheran Church in America, both as to its form of worship and prospects for the future; where were located our colleges and theological institutions, and about our synods. He said he heard of Dr. Krauth being in Worms last summer, and was sorry he did not enjoy the privilege of meeting him. We found Pastor Müller so pleasant and entertaining that we regretted our stay with him was so short. When we left his door he shook us heartily by the hand, and invited us to come and see him again before we left Worms. Whatever others may have experienced, surely our visit to a Lutheran pastor in Germany was a most pleasant one, and we carried away with us pleasing recollections.

The chief attraction, however, at Worms, is the Luther Monument, which of itself is worth a long journey to see. It stands in a square in the city, and is surrounded with tasteful pleasure-grounds and flower-beds. It is most imposing in appearance. The monument is of bronze, and rests on a square substructure; the latter being of granite, and measuring forty-one feet. At the four corners stand, on pedestals of polished syenite eight feet high, the statues of the mightiest supporters and promoters of the Reformation. In front that of Frederick the Wise, elector of Saxony, nine feet high, also Philip the

Magnanimous, Landgrave of Hesse. At the back, Philip Melanchthon and John Reuchlin. The front of the quadrangle is open, and two steps, between the statues of the first two, which are thirty feet apart, give access to the inner area. The three remaining sides are inclosed by battlemented walls, three feet high, also of polished syenite, in the middle of each of which is seated, on a syenite pedestal six feet high, a female figure emblematic of the cities—first of Augsburg, with the palm branch, six feet high; second Magdeburg, lamenting the desolation of her hearths, five feet high; and of protesting Spires, five feet high. On the inner faces of the battlements are the arms of the twenty-four cities which fought and suffered for the Reformation. The Luther Monument is, strictly speaking, in the centre of the enclosure. On the four pillars jutting out from the richly ornamented chief pedestal, are seated the statues of the four earliest champions of the Reformation, namely: Peter Waldus, 1197; John Wickliffe, 1397; John Huss, 1425; Hieronimus Savonarola, 1498. These are surmounted by the colossal statue of Luther (eleven feet high, with the pedestal twenty-eight feet), towering above and crowning, as it were, the whole. In front on the chief pedestal we read the bold, decisive words, which were perhaps the direct cause of the monument at Worms being erected: "Here I stand; I cannot do otherwise; God help me! Amen!" Underneath are the portraits of the two Saxon Electors, John the Constant and Frederick the Magnanimous. At the back is the passage: "The gospel that the Lord hath put into the mouths of the

Apostles, is His word: with it He strikes the world as if with lightning and thunder." On the lateral face to the right of Luther we read the two passages: "Faith is but the right and true life in God Himself." "In order to understand the scriptures rightly, the spirit of Christ is required."

Underneath are the likenesses of the faithful companions and disciples of Luther, Justus Jonas to the left, and John Bugenhagen to the right. On the lateral face to the left of Luther are the words: "Those who rightly understand Christ, no human ordinance will be able to captivate: they are free, not according to the flesh, but according to conscience." Underneath are the two Swiss Reformers, John Calvin and Ulric Zwingle—the former on the left, the latter on the right of the spectator.

The lower *cube*, as it is called, is adorned with bas-reliefs illustrating prominent deeds and incidents in Luther's life. In front, we see Luther before the Diet at Worms (1521). At the back, Luther affixing the Theses to the gates of the castle church of Wittenberg, October 31, 1517. On Luther's left, the translation of the Bible and the Luther-sermon. On his right, the communion in both kinds, administered by Luther, and the marriage of the clergy—Luther joined in marriage by Bugenhagen. Besides these, there are many other designs, giving the history of the great events which transpired in the days of Luther as connected with the Reformation.

It is in every way a grand and glorious monument, most befitting in every design, and executed with that skill and genius so common to the German mind. It is erected to the memory of the greatest man since the days of the apostle Paul, and in commemoration of the greatest event in all modern times. The execution of the monument occupied nine years, and cost nearly a hundred thousand dollars. It was designed by Rietschel, partially modeled by him, and completed after his death by Kietz and Dondorf, of Dresden.

For a long period of time, Germany has not seen such stirring days as those in June, 1868, when the monument to Luther was unveiled. We can scarcely conceive the enthusiasm with which the thirty thousand spectators were filled, when the covering fell from the tall figures of that majestic group, as the solemn chorus "Ein' feste Burg ist unser Gott," in which the general inspiration involuntarily resounded through the air, was the true salutation to the glorious countenance of that plain priest, whose gigantic figure towers far above his predecessors, Waldus and Wickliffe, Huss and Savonarola, his fellow champions Reuchlin and Melanchthon, and his princely protectors, Frederick of Saxony and Philip of Hessen. It was he who spoke the memorable words, before the imperial Diet, "Here I stand, I cannot do otherwise." And this is just the moment the artist has seized, and carved it in solid granite, in honor of the great Reformer, who was invincible in his rock-built faith, and inflexible in his will.

German sculpture is now beginning to become national. Ernst Rietschel is the greatest master of this new style, and his *Luther* is his greatest production. Uninstructed people are the best judges of art in these matters. The impression which this mighty work produces must be seen and read upon the faces of those plain country people, who every Lord's day perform their pilgrimage in crowds to the monument, in order to comprehend the power of a national production. The word of the peasant, in his coarse apparel, looking up to Luther and exclaiming, "Thou wert obliged to come; without thee we should have eaten naught but hay and straw," weighs heavier in such a case than many a well-turned opinion of technical criticism, which is the privilege of the connoisseur, but does not affect the multitude.

Worms boasted of another monument of Luther, which legend had created, before Rietschel and his distinguished pupils Kietz and Dondorf made themselves masters of Luther's history.

When Luther, in April, 1521, in a little cart, and with his lute at his side, the imperial herald preceding, was driving towards Worms, the valiant knight, George von Frundsburg, is said to have asked him, " Well, my little monk, dost thou believe in the victory of thy doctrine?" to which Luther is said to have answered, " Look at that little sprig just now sprouting from the earth. As sure as that tender little plant will become a gigantic tree that will o'ertop the towers of the city, so sure will my doctrine obtain the victory." And out of that little plant sprung the mighty elm which for so many scores of years was called " the Luther tree." A few summers ago it succumbed before a heavy storm. An enterprising German in Worms secured this tree, had it sawed into blocks, and stored it in his relic establishment, where now he is making a fortune out of it by carving all sorts of curious as well as useful articles out of the wood. Almost every tourist who visits Worms purchases a relic carved out of the famous Luther tree.

A short distance from the great cathedral, where the fine Heyl'sche Haus now stands, was formerly the Episcopal Palace, in which met the famous Diet, and where Luther made his ever memorable defense before the Emperor Charles V. The garden surrounding this mansion, which now belongs to an English gentleman, is open to the public, and is very attractive. With many regrets we took our departure from Worms, the memorable spot of such thrilling scenes, and so important to the centuries past and those to come. Our visit to this consecrated place was entirely satisfactory, and we continued our journey with new inspiration, and rejoiced in the privilege of preaching the pure gospel which Luther preached, and for which he imperiled his life, and was so ready to yie all for Christ's sake.

CHAPTER V.

HEIDELBERG AND ITS ENVIRONS — THE GREAT CASTLE — THE UNIVERSITY — BARBAROUS CUSTOMS.

ON our way from Worms to Heidelberg, we passed through some fine rural districts, and also some large and attractive towns, such as Speyer and Manheim. The former was a Roman station, and often the residence of the German Emperors. The only real attraction is the cathedral, dating to the tenth century, which is a fine specimen of Romanesque churches. Manheim is a modern town, and remarkable for the regularity with which it is laid out, having some fine squares, fountains and statues.

To tell about Heidelberg would require more time and space than one chapter. There are few places in Germany that possess more historic interest than this old university town and its surroundings. It is a favorite place of resort for nearly all tourists, and is thronged by large numbers of visitors every season. The town itself, apart from its famous university and wonderful castle, is not so attractive; still it contains some beautiful homes, and a goodly number of modern dwellings. It forms the key of the mountainous valley of the river Neckar, which below the town opens into the plain of the Rhine. It has a population of twenty-three thousand inhabitants, and gives signs of considerable thrift and industry.

We spent three days in and about Heidelberg, stopping at the inn *Zum Ritter*, erected in 1592—a quaint old house, indeed, and one of the few which escaped destruction during the terrible devastations of 1693.

The castle, which towers sublimely on a wooded spur nearly four hundred feet above the town, is to many the chief attraction of the place. In this respect it certainly is one of the wonders of the old world; and, perhaps, of all the numerous castles for which Germany is so famous, there is none superior in magnitude and historic interest to the well-known Heidelberg castle. The walls are of vast extent, and form the most magnificent ruin in Germany. The ivy-clad ruins are moreover linked with innumerable historical associations; and the striking contrast here presented between the "eternal rejuvenescence" of nature and the instability of the proudest of human monuments, has called forth many a poetic effusion.

The castle dates back to the fourteenth century, being founded by the Count Palatine Rudolph I. (1294), and combined the double character of palace and fortress. In its day it served as an immense and powerful fortification; and judging from its ponderous walls, solid masonry twenty-one feet thick, its extensive towers, etc., it must have done good service to those who were sheltered within its enclosure during the shock of battle which so often raged around it in earlier times.

On a beautiful July morning we started on foot to "do" this wonderful castle. On our way we fell in with a university student, who, by his familiar knowledge of the place and readiness to communicate all necessary information, proved a very pleasant and profitable companion.

The road leading up to the castle is quite steep, but well constructed and smooth, and leads through delightful shade and romantic scenery. For a time the castle is hidden from sight by reason of heavy groves of trees that cover the hill-side; but one is charmed with the wonderful panorama of beauty that rises to view in the deep valley and extended plains below. One is glad to linger on the way, in order that he may feast his eyes on the lovely views which meet his gaze at every spot in the advance upward.

At last the entrance gate is reached, and one more long and steep ascent and you pass under an immense arch-way which brings you within the inner court, or yard. For a small fee you can visit the chapel, and cellar, and other parts of the interior, including a collection of pictures, coins, relics, etc. The longer you wander amid this distinguished ruin, the largers it appears to grow, for you seem all the while to be making new discoveries; and you are puzzled to know which to wonder at the more —the genius or the folly which led to such expenditures of time and money as were required to construct so vast a monument of stone in walls and towers. The royalty of the early times had an eye to vastness and permanence; they built for the ages, yet their labors were but temporary. There are, however, yet remaining many magnificent specimens of architecture, richly adorned with beautiful sculpturing. In the niches of the walls facing the inner court, or yard, are a large number of statues, all having a symbolical meaning. In the lower niches are Joshua, Samson, Hercules and David; in the middle niches are placed allegorical figures of Strength, Justice, Faith, Charity, Hope; in the upper, Saturn, Mars, Venus, Mercury and Diana; most of these being in a good state of preservation. Besides these are many more, and almost countless, forms of sculpture are wrought in the massive walls and towers that loom up on every hand. That portion called the English palace, was built by the Elector Frederick V. as a residence for his bride, daughter of James I. of England.

The cellars of the castle are very extensive; in one of them is the celebrated Tun, said to hold 283,200 bottles of wine or beer when full, or eight hundred hogsheads. It's a monster cask, and is said to have been full only three times since its original construction in 1664. The old royalists who inhabited this castle and palace, it would seem, were good providers, and probably had immense drinking capacities. It certainly took some considerable coopering to build this Tun.

Besides these, there are numerous objects of interest, such as vaulted passages, chapels, shady retreats, beautiful groves, fountains, banquet-halls, terraces, gardens, ivy-clad walls, every one of which has a thrilling historic story of the olden times connected with it. The folly and simplicity of kings are pointed out to the visitor in such things as the representation of the twins whose occupation was wine drinking, and the fox-tail attached to a clock for curious movements, these things serving as amusements for the court people.

The *Grainberg gallery* contains an extensive collection of portraits of princes, chiefly of Palatinate, documents, manuscripts, coins, relics almost innumerable, all more or less connected with the history of the castle and town. Among the many things of interest in this connection, we saw two fine oil paintings of Luther and Melanchthon, by Cranach; also Luther's ring, beautifully mounted on a rich-colored velvet case. It was a gift to the castle by Prof. Paulus, at one time a professor in the Heidelberg University, and who died in that place. In a large glass case we saw, with other documents, a book by Rev. Dr. Kiefer, of the Reformed Church, with the title: "Ter-centenary Monument in Commemoration of the 300th Anniversary of the Heidelberg Catechism."

After inspecting the inner parts of the castle we rambled amid the grounds and shady walks without, which are charming, with lovely views that tempt one to linger. We still have pleasant recollections of the delightful dinner under the shady trees, in front of the excellent restaurant on the grounds. By climbing the hill towering three hundred feet above the castle, you have a still broader view; and the tower on the Königsstuhl (nine hundred feet above the castle, and nineteen hundred feet above the sea) commands a magnificent prospect of the valleys of the Rhine and Neckar, the Odenwald, the Black Forest, etc. Besides these there are many shady foot-paths, mostly through vineyards, with views of indescribable beauty.

But we must leave the beautiful mount and castle of story and song, and come down and see more of the town and its distinguished university. This, with one or two exceptions, is the oldest university in Germany. As is known to the reader, it is hence that comes the Heidelberg Catechism; and in the seventeenth century, it was the chief seat of Reformed learning in Germany. We found many things of great interest in our visit to this famous university. Its libraries are very extensive, containing over three hundred thousand volumes, eighty thousand pamphlets, nineteen hundred MSS. and fifteen hundred diplomas. There are many original MSS. of distinguished persons here, among them some of Luther's.

In the afternoon we gained admittance to the lecture (forlasung) rooms, and heard the distinguished Dr. Bluntschli* lecture on International law. Of course it was German, yet we could follow the doctor in his argument. We had hoped to hear a theological lecture, but in this were disappointed. Prof. Bluntschli is probably sixty-five years old; has a pleasant round face; is heavy set, of medium height, with a pleasant address; speaks fluently, standing behind a small desk with his hands folded in front of him throughout the lecture. He had some notes, but seldom referred to them. There were present thirty-three students; some took down the lecture in full, others only taking notes, and some merely listened. On the Professor's entrance and departure,

---

*Since the above was written we were pained to learn of the death of the distinguished Professor Bluntschli. He is the author of a number of ponderous volumes well known to the legal profession. His valuable library has been willed to the Johns Hopkins University, Baltimore, Maryland.

the young gentlemen applauded with a shuffling of their feet. The number of students is seven hundred at present. The faculty is now about equally divided between Protestants and Roman Catholics.

Many of the students bear scars of different sizes on their faces, the results of dueling, which is still in vogue here and at other universities in Germany. These scars are considered honorable, and one is not regarded as a full-fledged student who has not gone through this barbarous practice, and received or given a good slashing with the sword; and even though he be minus an eye or part of his nose, his beauty is by no means considered diminished. It, however, does not always remain a mere scar, but now and then this barbarous practice results in death—murder. We were glad to know that the American students, of whom there are not a few in Germany, do not engage in this shameful practice.

The three days spent in and about Heidelberg were among the most pleasant and enjoyable of our whole trip in Europe; and now memory lingers with delight about the beautiful Neckar, the grove-crowned heights of the castle, the shady foot paths, the terraces and beautiful gardens, the many sublime and lovely views, the rest and sweet repose, that so pleasantly and profitably ministered to us during our sojourn there.

CHAPTER VI.

HARVEST SCENES—RURAL LIFE—MILITARY RULE—WAR RELICS—STRASSBURG—A VEXED STRASSBURGER—ITS WONDERFUL CATHEDRAL—ITS FAMOUS CLOCK—GUTENBERG—THE GŒTHE HOUSE.

THE day from Heidelberg to Strassburg was excessively warm, and we suffered a great deal from the heat. The people told us that it had not been so warm in Germany for ten years as during that week. For a change, but more especially that we might learn more about German life among the masses, we took third-class cars, and found them quite comfortable. Our subsequent experience proved that in Northern Germany third-class cars were even better than second class in some parts of France, or England, or Italy. With all the heat, nevertheless our ride to Strassburg was full of interest, and very enjoyable. The farmers were busy cutting their grain, which consisted mostly of rye. There was some wheat and barley. A man from the States is surprised at two things when he views a harvest scene in Germany: one is, the use of the small hand sickle in cutting grain; the other, that so many women work in the harvest field, almost bare-headed, and exposed to the broiling sun. We did see in a few instances the use of reapers and some small cradles. Upon inquiry we were told that most of the farms in Germany were small, and that in the majority of cases farmers could not afford the expenditure involved in such modern machinery as reapers and mowers. The wages paid, including board, for a day's labor in the harvest field, is one and a half mark, which is equal to thirty-six cents of our money. We wonder how many harvest hands our farmers could employ at such wages? The Germans, however, do not seem to work hard, but take it very leisurely, and are very unlike in this respect to our people. Their manner of living in villages, instead of farm-houses scattered here and there, is a striking feature to one not accustomed to German life. These villages and towns are from one to three miles apart, and from these the farmers go out and do their work in the fields. The dwellings of these towns are built of red brick, and present an inviting appearance. This way of living has its advantages. It is more sociable, presents better opportunities for church-going, brings the school-house about equally near to all, and subjects the children to less exposure in the winter season.

On our way to Strassburg we met with a number of people who were soon expecting to emigrate to America. As might be supposed, they were anxious to hear our answers to the many inquiries they made in reference to our country. We sincerely hope all their sanguine expectations have been realized in regard to the perfect felicity they hoped to enjoy when once they reached these happy shores. Just passing through Germany, as well as other countries in Europe, and looking out upon their beautiful and well cultivated fields, their well built towns and cities, and the home-like appearance of the country, one would suppose that none of their people would care to leave such a land; yet many thousands annually take their departure. So vast have been these numbers, that Germany is about passing stringent laws looking toward the regulating of emigration from their country. In some of the rural districts there is beginning to be real depletion in population, especially of young men. "It is not all gold that glitters," and the fact is, the military system, not only in Germany, but all over Europe, is becoming almost unendurable; and yet, under the existing state of things, it is a necessary evil to the very existence and maintenance of their different forms of government. There is naturally a growing disposition to get away from so oppressive a system, for it imposes an enormous taxation, and its people are plagued with a feeling of insecurity even in the small possessions they may have.

As we approached Strassburg we had numerous and very marked indications of war times, in the many and extensive fortifications which girdle the entire city. It is the ancient capital of Alsace, and was in possession of France from 1681 until 1871, when it was restored to Germany. There are few cities in Germany that have suffered more from the scourge of war than Strassburg. In the middle ages it was one of the most prosperous and powerful of the free cities of the German Empire. Their love of independence and skill in the arts of war often brought its people in deadly conflict with other nationalities. They have always been distinguished as a brave people of almost unlimited endurance. The city has a population of one hundred thousand people, more than half of whom are Roman Catholics. It is situated on the river Ill, about two miles from the Rhine, with which it is connected by a small and a large canal. In the late siege (1871) parts of the city suffered greatly, some of its finest public buildings being entirely destroyed; but it was the pride of the Strassburgers to remove every mark and trace of the war inflicted upon them by the German army. The city in many parts presents a dilapidated appearance, and has many quaint and most singularly constructed buildings. The streets generally are narrow and crooked. Many of the houses have gothic gables, embellished with wood carving, the roofs being very steep and of immense proportions, with as many as four rows of dormer windows, ranged one above the other. In many cases the roof portion of the house is larger than all the other parts. While there are some fine buildings and beautiful streets, yet, taking it all together, we hardly think the epithet of "most beautiful city" applied to Strassburg in an old "Volkslied," which we learned to sing when a boy from an old Prussian soldier, would be applicable now. The city contains an unusually large proportion of poor people; and the masses of the population are far from being satisfied under German rule. They are quick, too, in expressing their dissatisfaction. Having formed the acquaintance of an intelligent book dealer, we enquired how they were pleased under German rule (regierung) and his reply was, "Not at all, we are oppressed with fearful (furchterlich) taxation, and only beggars and office-holders come here from Germany; and we wish '*das der Teufel*' had all the Germans." When we said to him, "Well, but that might include yourself, for we infer from your speech that you are a German," he replied, "No sir, I am a *Strassburger*."

In our strolls through the streets we noticed a great many storks perched on the chimney-tops of the houses, where they build their nests, seeming to be well satisfied with their lofty habitations. These birds come in the spring of the year, lay their eggs and hatch their young, and in the fall go south again. They are protected by law. They destroy insects of all kinds, and eat snakes and frogs, and are regarded as very beneficial to the farming community.

One of the chief attractions of Strassburg is its great cathedral. A description of this in detail would be a useless effort, if one meant to present a true representation of it. It must be seen to be properly appreciated. It was founded in 1015, on the site of the church built by Clovis in A. D. 510, and the interior was not finished until the thirteenth century. There is some very beautiful work in sculpture, and a great variety of architecture to be seen here. Its pillars and columns are wonders of beauty, as well as its stained-glass windows, dating to the fifteenth century. The subdued light of the morning sun entering through these windows presents pictures of unsurpassed beauty in brightness and delicacy of color. Its carved pulpit is a wonder in itself, and is regarded as the finest, perhaps, in Europe. The entire building abounds in exquisitely wrought sculpturing and painting, symbolizing different forms of Christianity. One almost becomes bewildered amid the many and imposing attractions which everywhere meet the eye in these cathedrals. They do appeal to the senses wonderfully, and yet we are not prepared to say that, *therefore*, they are all useless or of no good.

In the Strassburg cathedral we find the wonderful astronomical clock, constructed by a fellow townsman. This has greater attractions, especially at the hour of noon (for then it performs), for many visitors, than all the glories of the cathedral. It certainly is a very interesting and curiously constructed piece of mechanism. The exterior attracts spectators at all times, especially at noon. In the summer months, from fifty to one hundred persons daily stand before the clock at noon when it strikes, and gaze in wonder at its performance. On the first gallery an angel strikes the quarters on a bell in his hand, while a genie at his side reverses his sandglass every hour. Higher up, around a skeleton which strikes the hours, are grouped figures representing boyhood, youth, manhood, and old age (the four quarters of the hour). Under the first gallery the symbolic deity of each day steps out of a niche, Apollo on Sunday, Diana on Monday, and so on. In the highest niche, at noon, the twelve apostles move round a figure of the Saviour. On the highest pinnacle of the side-tower, which contains the weights, is perched a cock which flaps its wings, stretches its neck, and crows, awakening the echoes of the remotest nooks of the cathedral. The mechanism also sets in motion a complete planetarium, behind which is a perpetual calendar. The most wonderful feature of this piece of mechanism is that it is calculated to regulate itself, and adapts its motions to the revolutions of the seasons for an almost unlimited number of years. The exterior of this cathedral is equally as much a wonder for beauty and massiveness. It has a spire four hundred and sixty-eight feet high, perhaps the highest in the world.

The city is also graced with quite a number of fine statues. The one erected to *Gutenberg*, the inventor of printing, who made his first attempt at Strassburg in 1435, is very beautiful. The site where in the fourteenth century two thousand Jews were burned to death, accused of having poisoned the fountains and wells, which gave rise to the plague that so desolated the city, is still pointed out to the stranger.

We visited the house in which Gœthe lived when a student at the university located here. It is a plain three-story house, with smooth white walls, and externally finished in plastering. On a white marble stone, set in the wall above the first-floor windows, facing the street, is seen the following inscription: "The Gœthe house —1770–1771." Time and space forbid to speak of the many more interesting things in this historic city.

CHAPTER VII.

FROM GERMANY INTO SWITZERLAND—AN ENCOUNTER BETWEEN THE CONDUCTOR (ZUGFUHRER) AND A PASSENGER—BALE—BERNE—ITS CURIOUS MONUMENTAL FOUNTAINS—ITS BEARS—IN SWITZERLAND—INTERLAKEN.

AFTER enduring the great heat in Strassburg, it was a relief to even think that we were going into a locality where it would be cooler and more comfortable. Only one who has experienced it can really know how wearisome and exhausting it is to travel and be sightseeing in hot weather. You remember how you exhausted your physical powers at the Centennial; well, seeing Europe is a second Centennial, only on a larger scale. On our way to Switzerland we passed through some very attractive country and picturesque scenery. The land, generally, is fertile and well cultivated, tobacco being one of the principal products. We sincerely hoped it might be good tobacco, if such there could be, for of all such weed none has been so offensive to us as the European. The hill slopes and mountain sides are covered with vineyards. The banks of the Rhine between Bonn and Bingen are not more thickly studded with castles than the eastern slopes of the Vosges, which loom up so sublimely in the distance.

Now we pass by Colmar, Rufach, Bollweiler, and Mühlhausen, large and important towns. The well-known

Arbeiterstadt, or artisan's colony, founded in 1853 by Dollfuss, to improve the condition of the working classes, lies in close proximity to Mühlhausen, and is a most worthy and useful institution. It has been helpful in developing among artisans talent which otherwise would never have been brought to public notice. An hour more and we approach Bâle, or Basel, the first city of special interest in Switzerland. It is the capital of the Canton Basel-stadt, has a population of fifty thousand people, and is a busy commercial city. Here, just as the train had stopped, our attention was attracted by the conductor (Zugführer), who was earnestly engaged in what seemed a dispute with our fellow-passenger and traveling companion. They both gave evidence of being in earnest in the dispute, and yet neither of them understood a word the other said—the one presenting his case in English, the other in German; and you might know how plain they would make things to each other! The dispute between them, though very amusing to one who understood both languages, became warmer and still warmer, until it threatened to become really serious. The Teuton would not yield, and the American, just as true to his well-known characteristic, was equally determined. It was now time to interfere, and so the writer ventured to act as interpreter and avert serious trouble. The difficulty was, the passenger had stepped off the car on the left-hand side, which is a violation of their railroad regulations, instead of the right hand, and the conductor (Zugführer) interfered with the man as he endeavored to make his way from the train in that direction, telling him he must go over to the other side, as he subjected himself to both danger and a heavy fine. The passenger was determined not to be interrupted, and looked upon the conductor as interfering with his liberties. The passenger was wrong, and the conductor was right. We were able to explain matters, and the parties became reconciled. The knowledge of some German that afternoon, as on so many other occasions, served a good purpose; for without this help there would have been serious trouble. The railroad regulations, in Germany, and Switzerland especially, are very strict, and remind one of military rule. This is as it ought to be; it is a mutual advantage.

Bâle, like all the cities in the old world, is not without its cathedral, picture galleries, monuments, and concert gardens and statues. From the terrace in the rear of the cathedral there is a beautiful view of the Rhine and the heights of the Black Forest in the distance. But we have not more than a few hours' time, and are off again.

Now the atmosphere is growing perceptibly cooler, and in the evening we rest comfortably at the hotel *Pfistern*, in Berne, right opposite the old tower which contains the curious clock, something like the one at Strassburg.

In the evening, after returning from a stroll, we were reminded of the time when in our boyhood days, in the old academy at home, we used to join heartily in singing, from Pelton's outline maps, the geography of the old world and the new, and with what emphasis we used to sing: " Switzerland, Berne, Lucerne, *Zurich*." In those days Berne was too far away to be even thought of as probable for a visit. Time does wonders, however, and we never had sweeter sleep than that and succeeding nights in Berne. Here also, for the first time, was brought forward regularly the well-known (over there only) Swiss honey. There is none like it, for superior quality, in the world.

This is certainly a beautiful and interesting city of forty thousand people. Many of its streets are as clean as if newly scrubbed, and are of peculiar structure. They are provided with arcades—that is, the second story of the houses extends over the sidewalks and rests on heavy masonry, pillar-shaped, placed on what we call the curb. These extensions are usually of white stone, and beautifully arched. At night especially, when the many attractive stores, in which Berne greatly excels, are lighted up, these streets present a brilliant appearance. You can walk over a great part of the city under these magnificent archways, needing no umbrella for protection against rain or sun.

We are also introduced to strange street scenes—dogs hitched to carts on their way to market, women in company with men sawing and splitting wood, immense wooden milk cans and willow baskets carried by women from door to door, selling their wares. Among the strangest scenes was that of a woman hitched in a wagon side by side with a cow. One is also struck with the peculiar dress, especially of the females—the large butterfly-shaped head-dress, the white linen bodies, adorned with fine silver chains, and beautifully pleated sleeves.

Numerous quaint and monumental fountains decorate he streets. As the city derives its name from the word *Bären*, the German name for bears, so it is famous for its *bears*, sculptured, automatic, and living. The figure of that interesting quadruped is conspicuous everywhere: in the armorial bearings of the Canton, on the fountains, on the city gates, its houses, and even jewelry. Everything is decidedly *bearish*. Especially of note is the *Kindlifresser* fountain, or child-devouring one. This is a fountain, surmounted with some sort of statuary, representing a man who has gathered a number of children in his arms and side-pockets, and is in the act of devouring one of the innocent ones. From the little progress made in his efforts to eat this one, the rest, though doubtless suffering from fear that their turn will come next, need not be distressed that it will come very soon, for the *fresser* has been gnawing at the first one for several centuries.

But if Berne has sculptured and automatic bears, it also has living ones. For many centuries living bears have been kept in a very liberal manner at the expense of the city, and a fund is still devoted to that purpose. The bear-den or Barengraben is among the things to be visited here; and of course we paid our respects to Bruin, who has extensive and substantial quarters. These quadrupeds give one a friendly greeting, sitting on their haunches and extending their forepaws, with their mouths open; they look very innocent and harmless, but they are nevertheless really ferocious and deceitful bears. This was tragically demonstrated in the case of an Englishman who a few years ago accidentally fell into one of their dens, and was almost devoured by the ferocious beasts before he could be rescued.

Berne also affords a fine cathedral, once Roman Catholic, but since Switzerland's independence converted into a Calvinistic church. It is now very plain, and stripped of everything that looks Romish. It however contains a number of beautiful monuments and memorials in honor of the soldiers who fell in the war for Swiss independence. From the *Terrace*, in the rear of the Cathedral, one has presented a glorious panorama of mountain scenery.

But we must leave Berne, yet not without regret, for still further advances into Switzerland. By rail we reach Thun, a picturesque and delightfully situated town, washed by the river Aar. Here we took the boat and passed from the river into Lake Thun. This is a charming sheet of water, commanding some sublime scenery. It is nestled between steep and towering mountains. Its shores are dotted with beautiful villas and towns, green fields, and pleasant summer resorts. As we glide quietly over its waters, the Alps begin to loom up grandly on every side. The water is of a peculiar soapy-green color, caused by the melting of the snow and ice from the Alps; later in the summer it is very clear. The lake contains many varieties of fine fish, among others the speckled trout.

An hour's sail brought us to Darlagin, where, amidst

a rain-storm, we passed from the boat to the railway train, which consisted of three two-story cars. One hour more, and we were domiciled comfortably in the *Hotel Oberland* at Interlaken, of which we shall hear again.

CHAPTER VIII.

IN SWITZERLAND—INTERLAKEN—THE BEAUTIFUL SUNSET—AN EXCURSION—GRINDELWALD—ITS GLACIERS—LAUTERBRUNNEN.

WE are now in one of the most lovely spots in the Alps—the quiet vale of Interlaken. As the name implies, it lies " between the lakes" of Brienz and Thun. There is perhaps no place in Switzerland more popular with tourists than Interlaken. It is a place, above all others, that meets the wants of those who seek rest and quiet, and yet is full of interest and pleasant inspiration. Its situation is lovely, resting at the feet of the snow-clad Yungfrau, the famous mountain, towering nearly fourteen thousand feet into the sky—a form of beauty as well as awful majesty. There is also a range of high and steep mountains immediately behind the town, which is separated from them by the Nare, a narrow but deep and rapidly flowing stream.

The town, though having many lovely shaded walks, has but one principal street, which is wide and beautiful. In this are situated the large and well-kept hotels and boarding houses. These places are profusely decorated with the richest flowers and flower-beds artistically arranged. On this broad street great numbers gather for the evening promenade, and also to witness the beautiful sunsets, which are of rare splendor and attraction. From many points on this street there is an open, full view of the splendor of the Bernese Oberland. But of all the mountains in view, there is none equal to the wonderful Yungfrau. It stands in quiet, sublime grandeur, robed in its perpetual snowy vestments—the becoming dress of a bride—the highest of the numerous peaks that lift their lofty heads into the clear blue sky. Indelibly fixed in our mind is the glorious sunset which one July evening enraptured us all, as we walked in view of the mountain range. The picture was more beautiful than any human skill can paint—it was the painting of the great Artist of the universe, who, that evening, glorified the snow-white mountain with a heavenly glow of beauty. The surrounding mountains were covered with a dark green foliage, and shaded with the still darker shadows of evening that were falling on them. The sky was cloudless. The white-robed Yungfrau alone caught the golden light of the setting sun, kindling brighter and brighter on its summit and massy side, till it seemed lost in glorious lustre. It was a mountain transformed into glowing beauty of purple, scarlet and gold, so brilliant that it seemed almost like a second sun rising to dispel with its flood of light the evening shades that were gathering over surrounding mountains and valleys. With rapturous delight we beheld the fading glories of that splendid sunset over the Yungfrau.

The town contains many beautiful shops and fancy stores. In these are found large varieties of articles to tempt the fancy of visitors. Artistic carvings in wood and ivory and precious stones are numerous. These can be bought for various prices,

In common with other resorts for tourists in Europe, Interlaken also boasts of its Kursaal, where the finest music may be enjoyed at regular hours of the day and evening. You pay for this, whether you attend the splendid concerts or not. You will be sure to find on your hotel bill a charge for music. This may be properly considered an imposition, and is *vehemently* so regarded by a stray one who now and then comes along as a non-lover of music. But the illuminated grounds are so beautiful, the music so charming, the accommodations so excellent, and the tax to each visitor so small, that one becomes easily reconciled to the paying part. But even so good a thing as sweet music, like the gospel, some people would enjoy without paying for. A good thing is always better when paid for than otherwise.

There are a number of delightful excursions which may be made from Interlaken into different parts of the neighborhood; among these Grindelwald and Lauterbrunnen are the favorite ones. Four of us arranged to visit these renowned places. Six o'clock in the morning found us on our way, seated in a good carriage, drawn by a span of excellent horses, in the hands of a good driver. The morning was bright and the air bracing. We took a seat alongside of the driver, who was genuine Swiss, and took pleasure in pointing out to us the places of note and historic interest. The road soon leads from the valley into the mountains, and we rapidly approach the snowy and ice-crowned peaks, towering in sublime heights around us. Now we are amid genuine Alpine scenery, majestic mountains, snow and ice, the roaring of cataracts, and the rumbling noise of distant avalanches. All along the steep ascent we note the Swiss cottage perched amid the grassy slopes of the mountain side, the goats feeding amid the rock cliffs, the busy farmer gathering the grass and grain of the season, and laying in store for the coming winter. Now and then we hear the sounds of the Alpine horn, and then at long intervals we pass the Swiss sitting by the roadside, blowing in solemn mood into his horn twelve feet long, and waking the sweetest echoes amid the everlasting peaks. At every turn we are met by the flower girls coming out of their little booths, urging us to buy their small bouquets and dishes of goats' milk. The boys put us under obligations by whisking the flies from the horses, and placing large wooden blocks under the carriage wheels when we stop to rest the horses in their long and weary pull. Thus in the most secluded spots you have bids made for your money, and plenty of opportunities to spend it.

But now Grindelwald is reached. This is a scattered town of three thousand people, and the centre of all that is grand and majestic in Swiss scenery. It is overlooked by almost all the great Oberland giants, the Yungfrau, the Mönch, the Eiger, the Wetterhorn or Peak of Tempests, the Schreckhorn or Peak of Terror, Finsteraarhorn or Peak of Darkness. All range in height from twelve to fourteen thousand feet above sea level, their summits crowned with perpetual snows, and forever bearing the seal of their appointed symbol; "Thy *righteousness* is like the great mountains," "Who by His strength setteth fast the mountains; being girded with power." From the vast snow-fields above, two large glaciers descend into the Grindelwald valley. The chief attractions of Grindelwald are these glaciers, the upper and the lower. The latter is much the larger, but the ice of the former is far purer, and the *crevasses* more beautiful. These glaciers are wonders, being immense fields or masses of ice, or snow and ice, formed in the region of perpetual snow, and moving slowly down mountain slopes and valleys, at the rate of from ten to twenty inches a day. The stones which are caught between them and the rocks over which they pass, or which are imbedded in the ice and dragged along by it over those rocks, are subjected to a crushing and grinding power altogether unparalleled by any other force in constant action. The dust to which these stones are reduced by the friction, is carried down by the streams which flow from the melting glacier, so that the waters are whitened with dissolved dust of granite, and this in proportion to the heat of the preceding hours of the day, and to the power and size of the glacier which feeds them.

We started on foot, a distance of three miles, for the upper glacier of the Grindelwald, and a good, long, steady tramp brought us to the foot of the Wetterhorn glacier. Here we stand in the presence of matchless beauty and sublimity of scenery in nature. The running and rushing of the floods from beneath the glacier, the noise, like the voice of many thunders, produced by the avalanches of snow and ice, falling thirty miles away, the glare of the noonday sun on the ice-fields, giving them a beautiful tinge of blue, much like that which one sees in the wake of a vessel at sea, all contributed to make this the most sublime and wonderful spot we had yet visited. We were on the glacier, and in it—having entered by a grotto cut through a solid bed of ice for a long distance. After having climbed and walked ourselves weary, and having a better idea of what a glacier is than ever before, we retraced our steps and rested at the foot of its ascent. Here we had a refreshing lunch, which in part consisted of strawberries and cream, nicely prepared by a Swiss maiden, who informed us that the berries were gathered near the place where we were eating them.

We find ourselves back again in the town, and an hour later we are on our way to Lauterbrunnen, twelve miles distant. It is situated on both sides of the Lutschine, in a narrow valley so shut in by rocky walls that in the winter the sun is hardly seen at all, and even in July not before seven o'clock in the morning. As its name indicates, Lauterbrunnen—" nothing but springs"—is nestled amid these giant mountains. In the vicinity fountains are very numerous, chief of which is the Staubbach, the highest fall in Europe, the water having a perpendicular fall of nearly nine hundred feet. It is but a short distance from the inn. The body of water is not large, which gives it the appearance of spray or dust long before it reaches the bottom; hence its name. Byron, in his Manfred, compares its appearance to the tail of the white horse on which death was mounted in the Apocalypse. Not far off is the Wengern Alp, from which point are seen and heard the mighty avalanches of the Yungfrau and the greater and lesser Scheideck. Here it is said Lord Byron wrote his "Manfred."

> "Ye avalanches, whom a breath draws down
> In mountains overwhelming, come and crush me.
> I hear ye momently, above, beneath,
> Crush with a frequent conflict."

The village abounds in large lace shops and carving establishments. The sides of the streets are lined with small and large booths, where a great many Swiss women and girls are busy knitting the finest laces, which are marvelously cheap. But the lateness of the hour admonishes us to be getting down the mountain, and at sunset we are again in the village of Interlaken, delighted with our excursion, and with appetites well sharpened for the rich and well-prepared Swiss meal that awaited us at the Hotel Oberland.

CHAPTER IX.

INTERLAKEN TO LUCERNE—THE BRUNIG PASS—ALPINE SCENERY—LUCERNE AND ITS BEAUTIFUL LAKE.

THE last day spent in Interlaken was the Lord's day, and a profitable day it proved to be. In the early morning the church bells sent forth their rich peals, reminding all of the privileges the day affords, and inviting the people to the house of the Lord for worship. At 9 a. m. I started in search of a German church to which I had been directed, and soon found it, and at once gained admittance. The church edifice, both externally and internally, gave many striking proofs of great age, and need of repairs. The people attending service, with a few exceptions, evidently were of the hard-working class. They seemed much interested in the service, and gave evidence of great devoutness. Children constituted a large portion of the congregation, and here, as elsewhere in Switzerland, the children have a peculiarly oldish look the reason for which I am not able to give, unless it be their almost constant exposure and hard work in those elevated regions.

The congregation was of the Swiss Reformed faith, and the pastor preached an earnest good, gospel sermon (of course in German) on "the God of all comfort." The large stone edifice was well filled with devout hearers. The services reminded me somewhat of our own, only during the reading of the Scripture lessons the congregation remained standing. The closing prayer the pastor read. There was no doxology, the benediction immediately following the Lord's Prayer.

As far as I could learn, the different churches of the town were well attended in the morning. The stores were mostly closed, and the place had settled down to a quiet Lord's day, much like in our own country. In the afternoon, however, the town presented a strikingly different aspect—all the stores being open, and many people busy making purchases, the Kursaal, with its restaurant, billiard halls, and band of music, all in full blast—and Sunday seemed to be entirely set aside during the after part and evening of the day.

There is perhaps not another town that can boast of so much external union in the matter of churches as Interlaken. Here is a Roman Catholic church, a Scotch Presbyterian, and an Episcopal church, all worshiping in one edifice under one roof. It happens to be an old convent building, which was disbanded many years ago. The doors of the Catholic and Episcopal congregations are alongside of each other, each designated by a tin sign, while the Scotch congregation worships in another wing of the building. This is coming close together, and yet, when one thinks for a moment, there is no organic union among these different churches. though perhaps as much of an approximation toward it as some who worship far apart, but make great demonstrations to the world of their oneness with other denominations.

But the time has come for us to bid adieu to Interlaken;

and accordingly, on Monday morning, we find ourselves, in company with four others, in a carriage starting for Lucerne over the Brünig Pass, the distance being forty miles. We had pleasant company, one of our number being Prof. Schmidt (a Lutheran) and son, from Eisenach, the former a teacher in the gymnasium there. The morning was all that we could desire for a pleasant ride. The road took us along the high shores of Lake Brienz. By some this is regarded the most beautiful lake in Switzerland, although its length is only seven miles, and its width about two. Its depth is from five hundred to two thousand feet. Is is certainly a charming sheet of water. Its shores are beautifully wooded with delightful groves, and mountains tower in sublime heights on every side. After an hour's ride we reached the end of the lake, where is located Meyringen, an inviting village in the beautiful vale of Hasli. On the opposite side of the lake we see the wonderful Giessbach Falls, a series of cascades leaping from a height of eleven hundred feet down into the lake. In the summer months, until September, they are illuminated with colored lights every evening—an attempt to "paint the lily," which is less ridiculous than that sort of presumption generally proves. The town of Meyringen abounds in carvers in wood, and is a favorite place for tourists. It is a centre for excursions, six Alpine routes converging here.

From this point begins the steep ascent of the mountain pass. As we rise above the valley on the zigzagging road, we are treated to the most charming scenery. We have mountains of snow and ice towering all around us;

beautiful cascades on our right and left; now passing through villages and vineyards and quiet homes amid the lonely mountains. Among the surprising things in the Alps are the fine roads. They are as solid and smooth as the finest carriage roads in our finest city parks, and this contributes very much to the pleasure of travel.

We have now reached the top of the Brünig Pass, three thousand four hundred feet above tide. From these heights we look down upon the valley of *Unter Land*, with its silvery streams threading their way in the beautiful sunlight, its dense forests, its shady groves, and rich harvest fields waving their golden grain. To ride leisurely along, through such a picturesque country with such scenery, could not fail to contribute rare pleasure and profitable enjoyment.

At Lungern we rested for dinner at the Hotel Brünig, and partook of a most refreshing repast. Our descent from this point was equally enjoyable, our surroundings being full of interest and inspiration. There is so much variety of scenery that one never wearies. We also meet with great numbers of tourists traveling in almost every conceivable way, some on foot, some in carriages, others in *diligence*, all trying to take in the glories of the great Alps.

We now come into the lake region. First we pass Lake Lungern, then comes Lake Sarnen, and then others of smaller note. These waters sleep in their quiet beauty, hemmed in by moss-covered and grassy banks, with forest groves, overshadowed with great mountain peaks of snow. Nearly all the way from Lungern to Lucerne the roadway is lined with crosses and crucifixes, thus reminding the traveler very sensibly of the faith cherished by the natives of those regions.

Towards evening we approached the shores of Lake Lucerne; and now we are in the presence of another of the many wonderful and beautiful attractions of Switzerland. At once we are impressed with the indescribable beauty of the lake. Its water is so clear; its shores adorned with attractive cottages and white villages; at different places the mountains with their broad green sides standing out of the very water's edge. In passing upon its shores we think of the tradition which tells us that it was in this lake that Pilate of the Scriptures drowned himself. If so, he could hardly have selected a more lovely spot to sleep the long last sleep.

At six in the evening we reached Lucerne, and found excellent quarters at the *Hotel des Balanges a Lucerne*, on the banks of the river Reuss, which flows immediately out of the lake. Here I had a most charming view of the city, and among other things was not least the clear running river, with its fine large fish disporting themselves in its waters immediately below the balcony of my window.

Lucerne itself is an interesting city of fifteen thousand people. It is the capital of the canton of the same name. The city is highly picturesque, and the environs are noted for the exquisite beauty and grandeur of their scenery. It is beautifully situated at the northwest extremity of Lake Lucerne, on both sides of the river Reuss. Among the principal objects of interest are its quaint bridges spanning the Reuss. The *Capelbrücke* is a bridge open on the sides, but roofed, and on the ceiling is a set of paintings representing episodes in the lives of Sts. Leger and Maurice, the patron saints of the city. The *Ancient Tower* in the middle of the river was formerly used as a light-house, whence the name of the city (Lucerne signified light-house). The *Muhlenbrücke* is another bridge, ornamented with thirty-six paintings representing the Dance of Death, celebrated in Longfellow's " Golden Legend." Of course we did not fail to visit the celebrated *Lion of Lucerne*, sculptured in 1821, in memory of the Swiss guard who fell defending the Tuilleries, August 10th, 1792. It is hewn out of the natural sandstone rock in the side of a hill. It represents a lion of colossal proportions, twenty-eight feet long by twenty high; the lion holds the lily of France in his paws, which he endeavors to protect with his last breath, his life-blood oozing from a wound made by a spear which still remains in his side. The names of twenty-six officers who fell in the same battle, are also cut in the solid rock below the lion. Above is carved: " *Helvetiorum fidei ac virtuti;* " " To the fidelity and virtue of the Helvetians."

We also visited the *Hofkirche* (built in 1506). It contains many interesting things, such as carved stalls and altars, and the famous organ, which some judges prefer to the one at Freiburg.

CHAPTER X.

LAKE LUCERNE—WILLIAM TELL—ST. GOTHARD PASS—ITS PASSAGE—OVER THE ALPS INTO ITALY.

PERHAPS the chief attraction of Lucerne is its beautiful lake. It certainly is one of the grandest in Switzerland, and is invested with special interest because of its many historical associations connected with the exploits of William Tell, the national hero of Switzerland.

It was a bright noon day when we embarked on the boat at Lucerne, bound for Fluelen, twenty-five miles distant. Before sailing far, we found ourselves perfectly entranced with the beauty and grandeur of scenery that lay all about us. The lake itself was a perfect calm, its waters pure and of light blue, mirroring the clouds in its frame of mountain glory. Its shores are dotted with many charming villages and towns, its hills green robed, its mountains abrupt, perpendicular, grand. None of them are less than three thousand feet in height, and most of them are six thousand; and, with their summits reflected in the glassy water, they present a scene in nature both grand and sublime. At several points on the lake we could see, high up on the mountain-sides, large hotels, with four or five hundred feet front, with flags waving from their steeples, and all the evidences of being occupied to their full capacity. The width of the lake is not more than a mile to a mile and a half, and its windings and turnings among the mountains are so abrupt that the eye cannot discern its course more than half a mile ahead. In the gorges of the precipitous mountains are located towns with their array of hotels. At these places the boats touch, leaving and taking passengers. After stopping at Buochs, Beckenried, and Gersau, we reached Brunnen, one of the most charming towns on the lake, and a place of much resort. Leaving Brunnen, we enter the bay of Uri, or south arm of the lake, where the banks approach each other and become more precipitous, with glimpses of snowy peaks here and there through the gorges. A short distance from Brunnen, a perpendicular rock rises from the water over one hundred feet high, called the Schillerstein.

Now we pass the Rutli, the meadow where on the night of November 7th, 1307, the Swiss patriots bound themselves by an oath to fight their oppressors, the Austrians, to the death. According to tradition, on the same spot where the conspirators took the oath to deliver their country from this tyranny, three springs of water (in honor of the three leading representatives of the three cantons) spouted up, over which a small hut has been erected.

About six miles farther on we arrive at Tell's chapel, the Mecca of all Switzerland. It is situted on a small plateau washed by the waters of the lake. It is a beautiful structure. It was erected by the canton of Uri in 1388, thirty-one years after the death of William Tell, to whose memory it was consecrated in the presence of one hundred and fourteen persons who, it is said, knew him personally. The chapel is erected on the precise spot where, according to tradition, Tell escaped on shore from the boat in which Gessler, the Austrian governor, was conveying him to prison.

The traditionary circumstances in the life of Tell are cherished in the memories of his countrymen with the fondest affection. Yet, there are those who are bold enough to assert that the whole story is a fable. We were told, however, that every Sunday after Easter a procession of boats, richly decorated, proceeds slowly to the chapel, where, after mass is celebrated, a patriotic sermon is preached to the worshiping pilgrims.

At two o'clock in the afternoon we reached Fluelen, located at the end of the lake, and at once proceeded to Altdorf, a small town two miles distant, made so famous by the exploits of William Tell. The place is pointed out where Tell shot the apple from his son's head. The spot where Tell stood is marked by a fountain surmounted by a statue, representing him standing erect with his left hand resting on his bow, and holding an arrow in his right hand pointing heavenward. About one hundred paces from this, another fountain marks the spot where Gessler hung his hat to be worshiped by the passing people, and where the son of Tell was bound with the apple on his head, preparatory to the famous shot which led to the freedom of Switzerland.

After visiting the old church and its quaint cemetery and adjacent buildings, which contain some fine paintings, and where are kept on exhibition a large number of skulls of Swiss soldiers who fell in defence of their country, and not forgetting to supply ourselves with a good Swiss dinner, we returned to Fluelen; where, at 4 p. m. we took the *diligence* (stage) for Andermatt, through the St. Gothard pass, on to Italy.

The pass of St. Gothard is one of the oldest and most frequented of routes across the Alps, but the present admirable highway dates back only some thirty years. By this path many of the barbarian hordes made their way into Italy in the old Roman days. Though the pass affords a good road, and we had a span of four excellent horses, a true son of Jehu as driver, and were, in every way, well equipped for the ride over the Alps, a distance of eighty miles, yet the dangers of the way are many and great, and the discomforts not a few. The precipices are indeed fearful, and one almost holds his breath as he sees himself drawn over the edges of perpendicular heights of two thousand feet. Were a trace to break, or the *diligence* to get as much as one foot out of its appointed way, nothing could avert a fearful catastrophe, the fall of the coach into the deep abyss below, a distance of two thousand feet. The road itself shows marvelous engineering skill in its construction.

From Fluelen to Andermatt, seven hours' ride, ascending the defile of the river Reuss, presents a road unsurpassed for desolate and magnificent scenery. The giant mountain peaks from four to six thousand feet high towering in sublime grandeur on every side, the rocky cliffs, the roaring and dashing of the Reuss through the deep, narrow defile, now to the right, then to the left of the way, the steep ascent of the zigzagging road apparently hanging by the mountain-side, along which it is walled many hundreds of feet high, the sudden descent of the great and dense clouds, rolling down from the high mountain peaks, the distant thunder of the avalanches, the solitary grandeur which marks every aspect in nature—all contribute to make the scenery indescribably desolate and picturesque.

We passed through a number of small and large towns, which nestle even in these solitary mountains. The coming of the *diligence* is quite an event to the people of these villages. Now we are overtaken with impenetrable darkness, and the rain pours down in torrents. At the next turn we pass above the clouds, the stars glitter above us, and the rain falls below us. A little way below Andermatt we cross the famous Devil's Bridge or *Teufelsbrücke*, with the old ruined bridge below, the scene of desperate fighting between the Austrians and French in 1799.

Soon after we pass through the *Urner Loch*, or hole of tin, a long tunnel hewn through the solid rock.

At 11 p. m. we reached Andermatt, the table land of the Alps (five thousand feet above the sea), weary and cold, and after some refreshments even at so late an hour, rested for the night at the hotel *Drie Könige* (Three Kings). We were not surprised to find, in so high an altitude, hotel bills proportionally *high*.

At four next morning we were called out, and at five were again on our way, in the *diligence*. A few miles on and we reached Hospenthal, where commences a new ascent on the St. Gothard, zigzagging for three hours to the summit. It is a dreary, cold, and desolate way, but the monotony is broken now and then by getting out of the *diligence* and taking it on foot, and plucking flowers which here and there lift their modest heads amid the frowning rocks. Now we enter the snow and ice fields, and at 8 a. m. the summit is reached, at a height of seven thousand feet above the sea. Here burst upon our view a panorama of mountain scenery that we never saw equaled but once, and that when standing upon the top of Pike's Peak in our own Rocky mountains.

It is cold even this July day, and the wind blows a gale. Within a circle of ten miles of this point are the sources of the Rhine, and the Rhone, and the Reuss. Near the summit is a stone on which the inscription *Suwarrow Victor*, commemorates his victory over the French in the year 1799. Here he was repulsed by the French for the first time; indignant, he caused a grave to be dug, and lying down in it declared he would die where "his children" had suffered disgrace. The appeal aroused them to a more determined attack, and the French were driven from their position at an immense sacrifice, twenty-five thousand Russians following their leader Suwarrow.

After a little warming up by the side of a warm stove, and with some hot coffee and dry bread taken inwardly —for that is all the hotel man had that day—we again repair to the *diligence* and proceed on our way, passing a number of small lakes which sleep in the crown of these mountains. And now begins the rapid descent on the Italian side as far as Airola. We go down five thousand feet in eight miles. We go swiftly, and being on the sunny side of the mountains, it is more pleasant. The construction of the road-bed is a wonder, as well as a marvel of skillful engineering. The turns and zigzags are numerous, and at times entire circles are made. At some points, as many as ten and twelve terraces of the road are visible at once, as you gaze down the dizzy mountain side. Seven miles away, down in the green valley, sleeps the first Italian town, Airola, though still in Switzerland. Here we have time for a hurried breakfast; but the bread being so hard, we leave it for others who have more time to break their jaws over it than we, and continue our journey through a hilly and mountainous country, with here and there a village, until we reach the town of Biasco, on the St. Gothard railway, where we gladly leave the *diligence* in exchange for the cars. We now quickly pass on through Bellinzona, to Locarno, where we rest and wait for the steamer that is to carry us over the beautiful lake Maggiore into Italy.

CHAPTER XI.

LALE MAGGIORE—ARONA—MILAN—ITS CATHEDRAL.

ON our way through the Gothard Pass we saw large numbers of workmen busy constructing the St. Gothard railway. This great public enterprise has now reached completion. We have just read an account of a successful trial trip that was made through its great tunnel, the St. Gothard, by a train of cars, and that the entire road is now open to traffic. This tunnel is the longest in the world, its length being nine miles and a half, and shows wonderful skill in engineering, as indeed does this entire railway. The total cost of the work of the tunnel is 56,808,620 francs, or about $11,000,000.

As these old countries catch the spirit of our free institutions and republicanism, the spirit of improvement and public enterprise is witnessed—the towns and cities grow, and thrift is everywhere manifest. The St. Gothard railway is destined to draw Italy and Germany closer together, and will exercise an important influence upon the politics and commerce, as well as religion, of those nations. Railway traffic between the German and Italian cities has heretofore been compelled to make a long detour to the east and go through the Tyrol over steep grades, or a still longer detour to the west by way of the Mt. Cenis Tunnel and France. Now it can go by a direct route under the Alps and through Switzerland.

After a few hours rest under the grateful trees on the banks of Lake Maggiore, we took ship for Arona, on the opposite side. This is the largest of the Italian lakes, being forty-five miles in length, and averaging three miles in breadth. Steamers run its whole length, touching at many points on both sides. We go zigzagging over the lake. There is much to interest and charm the tourist on this lake. The water is almost crystal. Its many islands, especially the Borromean, are most inviting. There are four of these, on one of which, Isola Bella, was built the large palace by Count Vitaleo Borromeo, about a century ago, with terraced gardens, fountains, and grottoes, all very elaborate and artificial.

Much of the surroundings of the lake is mountainous, though not abrupt, excepting at a few places. Villages, towns, and summer boarding-houses of elegant structure, abound numerously all along its shores. At one point on the lake I counted as many as twenty of these villages. Being built of white stone and marble, it was not one of the least inviting prospects to see these villages interspersed along the mountain sides among the beautiful green foliage. The charm, however, of many an exquisite bit of Italian village scenery is dispelled as soon as one gets within smelling distance of it. There are places which you enter full of romantic enthusiasm, and escape from with a shudder; instead of raising your hands in admiration, you employ them in holding your nose.

The middle of Lake Maggiore marks the dividing line between Switzerland and Italy. The day being bright and sunny, and the lake a perfect calm, our sail across was delightful. In the evening we witnessed the going down of the sun beyond the snowy peaks of the Alps in clouds glowing with splendor, painting the tips of the mountains in purple, scarlet and gold. Later in the evening we found a comfortable resting-place at the hotel *De Italia E. Post*, in Arona. Here, then, we had our first experience of Italy, and for one I have no complaints to lodge. It may be I was looking out for something to complain about, for I was told so many things about Italy in books I read, and by others, which savored of so much discomfort, that it would not be surprising if I had been filled with some fear. If so, my apprehensions were not realized. I had an excellent, clean bed, plenty to eat that did not swim in oil, polite attention, and very reasonable charges. But now for the first time I felt the need of more language. Well, no, not that exactly, for I could talk as much as ever; but it did no good; it lacked *variety*. My English and German wouldn't do. The best thing to do was to go it on faith, and as a rule I hit it pretty well.

The railway ride from Arona to Milan was made in little more than an hour. The country abounds in orchards and vineyards, and nearly all the way there is a magnificent view of the Alps.

It was on a warm July noonday that I reached Milan, passing through the beautiful Marengo Gate, especially interesting on account of the battle once fought near by, which it is designed to commemorate. Milan is one of the largest and wealthiest cities of Italy, and indeed there are few cities in any country that can excel it in appearance and attractiveness. It has some magnificent thoroughfares. It is a walled city, but the interior side of the wall is laid out with gardens and planted with trees, an arrangement which surrounds the whole city with a park. It is now a great manufacturing place, with about a quarter of a million of inhabitants. Its streets are well-paved, and cleanliness is observable everywhere. Men go about all day with small hand-carts and brooms, carefully sweeping and sprinkling to prevent dust. The people, generally, are fine-looking. They are quick in their movements, show good taste in their dress, and are extremely polite. They know how to drive a sharp bargain. They charge foreigners enormous prices for everything they purchase, if they are foolish enough to pay it. The ladies of Milan appear in simple but elegant attire, the only covering for their heads being light gossamer veils. The younger females are quite handsome, but, evidently lose their beauty at an early period, for you seldom see a handsome elderly lady in Italy. The children, with their large, dark and piercing eyes, are very fine-looking, and are full of brightness and vivacity.

There are many stores in Milan of great elegance. The "Galleria Vittorio Emanuele," forms the central point for the traffic of the city. It is an immense arcade, roofed in with glass; the roofing at the central point of the cross which it forms having an elevation of one hundred and eighty feet. The lower story is devoted to fancy and jewelry stores, of which there are fully one hundred and fifty. In the evening the building is lighted with several thousand gas-jets, and adding to these the brilliant lights within the stores, presents a dazzling brilliancy and scene of gayety. Its avenues are fifty feet wide, the flooring consisting of finely executed mosaics of different colors. This is the place of resort and promenade of the *elite* of the city, and is well worth a visit in the evening or afternoon.

I saw many fine paintings in Milan, among the finest were "The Nuptials of the Virgin," "Abraham and Hagar," and Rubens' "Last Supper."

The great centre of attraction of Milan is its famous cathedral, being next to St. Peter's at Rome. It is impossible to give the reader any adequate and intelligent description of this wonderful structure. It is a combination of elegance and beauty, of splendor and wealth, of history and genius, which it is impossible to delineate. As a monument of ornamental architecture, it will probably stand forever unrivaled. If the exterior amazes you, the elaborate interior, resting on fifty-two marble columns, charms you. Its foundations were laid five hundred years ago, and while its vast dimensions astonish you, you are lost in admiration of the exquisite perfection of the work, requiring an expenditure of labor and money almost incalculable. It is largely Gothic in its architecture. From whatever point you look at its exterior walls, you are gazed at in return by a throng of those "stone men and women," who Father Barrett protests are the main production of Italy. It presents, besides, a perfect forest of marble pinnacles, with life-sized statues peeping out from every niche in the walls. There are thousands of such statues adorning the exterior, the precise number being doubtful, and changing constantly; there is estimated to be as many as seven thousand, and there is room for many thousands more.

The building is constructed entirely of pure white marble, which, in the sunlight, shines with dazzling splendor. It is built in the form of a Latin cross, the length being four hundred and ninety feet, breadth one hundred and eighty feet, height to top of the statue three hundred and fifty-four feet, the length of the transept two hundred and eighty-four feet, and height of the nave one hundred and fifty-two feet. The wonderful tracery in beautiful white marble which surrounds the roof, the central tower and spire, surrounded by a throng of many smaller spires, each surmounted by a statue, present a combination of elegance impossible to describe. The prospect from the great spire—which I ascended—is wonderful. It commands the city and country about it, with the snowy Alps stretching through more than a semi-circle, and the Apennines filling half of the remaining horizon.

But the interior of the cathedral is even more wonderful and imposing than the exterior. The marble columns which support the roof are ninety feet in height, eight feet in diameter, and fifty-two in number. Its double aisles and clustered pillars, its lofty arches, the lustre of its walls, its numberless niches filled with noble figures, its monuments, its chapels, and its matchless windows, combine to give a grandeur and solidity to its appearance much more effective than the exterior.

To get the full effect of this wonderful cathedral, one needs to go there at vespers, and standing under the lofty nave, amid that wilderness of white columns, watch the evening sunbeams streaming through the windows of stained glass, and listen to the pealing organ as the solemn notes steal out under the lofty arches, and die away in the distant shadows.

On the morning of my departure from Milan I paid another visit to the cathedral, and spent a long time within its inviting walls, trying to be devotional as I witnessed large numbers of worshipers so devout in their service, and many receiving the early communion. With our benediction of peace upon them I departed with the silent prayer that they might eventually be saved, and we all be gathered into the greater and still more beautiful temple of our common Lord on high.

CHAPTER XII.

VENICE—THE CITY OF THE SEA—GONDOLAS AND GONDOLIERS—ITS CANALS AND BRIDGES—PRIESTS AND FEMALES—ST. MARK'S CATHEDRAL—ITS BRONZE HORSES—ST. MARK'S PLACE—DUCAL PALACE—BRIDGE OF SIGHS—THE PRISONS—RIALTO BRIDGE—THE CAMPANILE—PIGEON FEEDING—THE STREETS OF VENICE—ITS STORES—ITS BEGGARS—THE VENETIAN PEOPLE—A SAIL ON THE ADRIATIC.

IT was one of the last days in July, near sunset, approaching from Milan, that the city of Venice loomed up in the distance, looking to the eye like a city rising from the sea, with towers, steeples, domes, and turrets of white marble gleaming in the sun. We had scarcely emerged from the cars when we were confronted by the strangest of all novelties thus far. Instead of getting into an omnibus and riding to our hotel, or walking, we are invited to take one of the many gondolas which literally encircle the railway station. The gondola is the mode of conveyance. It supplies the place of coaches and carriages and horses; there are no such things as horses in Venice, excepting the bronze ones in front of St. Mark's, many of its inhabitants having never seen a horse. So, when you are in Venice, you must do as the Venetians do, get into the gondola as *the* mode of conveyance. And it is not as slow as you might think; it cuts its way so rapidly through the water that in a short time you may go over a large part of the city. They are long narrow, light vessels or boats, containing in the centre a black cabin, something like the body of a hearse, nicely fitted up with glass windows, blinds, curtains, and cushioned seats for four persons. The gondolas are invariably painted black, inside and out, the trimmings being of the same color.* The wood-work is ornamented with carvings and tracery, and the boat is in all respects tidily kept. It is decidedly the most Venetian thing in Venice —the flower of this lotus of the sea.

Byron very graphically describes it in the following lines:

> "Didst ever see a gondola? For fear
>   You should not, I'll describe it you exactly:
> 'Tis a long covered boat that's common here,
>   Carved at the prow, built lightly, but compactly,
> Rowed by two rowers, each called gondolier;
>   It glides along the water looking blackly,
> Just like a coffin clapped in a canoe,
> Where none can make out what you say or do.
>
> "And up and down the long canals they go,
>   And under the Rialto shoot along,
> By night and day, all paces, swift or slow,
>   And round the theatres, a sable throng,
> They wait in their dusk livery of woe;
>   But not to them do woful things belong,
> For sometimes they contain a deal of fun,
> Like mourning-coaches when the funeral's done."

As many as four thousand gondolas are now daily in use in Venice. When the city was in its prime, with

---

*A law of Venice prescribes this color, to prevent extravagance of decoration, as well as to secure uniformity of style.

twice its present population within the same area, the moving throngs upon its water-streets must have presented a spectacle singularly striking—almost a fairy scene. One gondolier is generally considered sufficient to a boat, though there are often two. Their dress is somewhat after the sailor style. No watermen have ever equaled them in the dextrous management of a boat, or in the graceful use of the oar. To go about the city in this way costs less than the most ordinary hack-riding in another city, and besides, you are not punished by jolting. It is smooth sailing and delightful.

Venice is certainly an odd city, but also beautiful. Its streets are water canals, and its coaches gondolas and boats. If one is not careful, he is all the while under the impression that he is in a flooded city. At first you are timid, almost to fear, in venturing out doors, especially after nightfall. Think of it, *floating* about from place to place, instead of riding or walking—your front door as well as your back door opening in the water, without a foot of earth to stand upon. If you want to go to see your neighbor, you must go by water. It is true, some parts of the city can be traversed without recourse to water; but it would require a walk many times of half a mile and more to go to your neighbor's, five doors away. There are lanes or streets four and five feet wide, from house to house, paved with slabs of stone, over which one may pass; but these foot-ways form the most incomprehensible network imaginable—a perfect labyrinth from which the stranger will find it difficult to extricate himself should he venture abroad without a guide.

Perhaps the first thought that strikes you is the singular taste which induced a polished and educated people to select so damp a site for a city. The history of Venice is briefly this: When the Roman Empire was destroyed about twelve hundred years ago by the barbarians, the inhabitants of northern Italy calling themselves Venetians, had their cities also destroyed by the same hordes. It was the inhabitants of these towns and cities who took refuge on a vast collection of small islands, separated from the main land by a narrow arm of the sea (the Adriatic), and there founded a city, calling it Venice. They formed a republic, and elected their first Doge, or President, in the seventh century. From that time, down through all the centuries to the present, this city has had a most eventful history, but has singularly and fortunately passed through all her trials, and to-day Venice numbers one hundred and thirty thousand inhabitants, and the people appear to be happy. Perfect religious freedom is enjoyed under the reign of peace.

Its earliest days were its best, its most beautiful. "The first period of nine hundred years presents the most interesting spectacle of a people struggling out of anarchy into order and power, and then governed for the most part by the wealthiest and noblest man they could find among them*—the best, the very best, *un ottimo solo*," says the Venetian historian Sansovino.

"We find a deep and constant tone of individual religion characterizing the lives of the citizens of Venice in

---

*Ruskin, "Stones of Venice."

her greatness—we find this spirit influencing them in all the familiar and immediate concerns of life, giving a peculiar dignity to the conduct even of their commercial transactions, and confessed by them with a simplicity of faith that may well put to shame the hesitation with which a man of the world at present admits (even if it be so in reality) that religious feeling has any influence over the minor branches of his conduct."*

So writes one of the most distinguished of modern authors respecting Venice; and, toning down a little his deep-voiced eulogium, we feel constrained to admit the truth of it taken as a whole. But of its decay and decline—of what is commonly designated "its fall" there can be no denial. Its naval, its commercial, its colonial, its political, and as to productive power its artistic glory, are gone. "Ichabod" is written on its walls. The place is rich in monuments, in memorials, in remains—none richer, or so rich. They proclaim past magnificence; but as to present achievements, present power, present prosperity, present nobleness, there is silence—silence like that which the stranger feels when he has reached the summit of the Campanile, which towers from its midst, and listens in vain for such sounds as arise from the streets of other cities.

The islands on which the city of Venice is built are in number one hundred and fourteen; the streams running between them, with the exception of the Grand Canal, being seldom more than fifteen feet in width. The

---

* Ruskin, "Stones of Venice."

Grand Canal, one hundred and twenty-five feet wide, which takes a serpentine course through the city, is intersected by nearly two hundred smaller canals, over which four hundred and fifty bridges are built. These are arched bridges of elegant structure, composed of white marble, and intended only for foot passengers. Out of these canals the houses all rise abruptly on both sides, their principal front and entrance always facing the canal, the water street visitors stepping from the gondola on to the door-sill. The depth of water is from three to ten feet. The number of fine private residences is quite large, mostly built on heavy piles of massive structure, and more remarkable for their gorgeous style than for comfort and convenience. The palaces, however, occupied by the upper classes, are usually magnificent structures and gems of beauty and style, being built of the finest marble, and profusely decorated with statuary, paintings, and other works of art. Our hotel, the *Victoria*, was once such a palace. So you see, we lived in a palace once for four days.

No wooden houses are seen in Venice. The prevailing color of all its houses is white, thus giving to the city a cheerful appearance. It is compactly built, about seven miles in circuit, and perfectly accessible in all its parts. Its principal buildings are of marble or of light-colored stone, and the remainder are of brick covered with mastic. Italy is so rich in marbles and other building stones that these materials were the cheapest which could be used.

There is much in the city that has the appearance of

decay, and the sea is leaving its impress indelibly upon the walls of its buildings. With all this, it has been represented as a delightful place to reside in. At first no doubt, the novelty gratifies and pleases, but it is too monotonous to be a favorite residence for any length of time. The knowledge that you are dependent upon boats to carry you about, and the want of rural beauty, make one weary of the scene. The saltness of the water and the changes of the tide make it more endurable than it otherwise would be. If the water were fresh, it would be uninhabitable. Artesian wells supply the city with water for domestic use.

But besides the novelties of a flooded city, canals, gondolas, there are many other things in Venice which interest the foreigner—indeed, so many that one pressed for time makes selections with difficulty. Its numerous Romish churches, being one hundred, in the principal part of the city, are a wonder. There are six of these immense structures within five minutes' ride. The most of them were built three centuries ago. Those we visited were all highly ornamented and embellished with paintings, and statuary, and tombs, and monuments; some of their altars rich with rare stones and sparkling gems. Expense appears to have been no consideration, and we find few churches at the present day in the construction of which there has been such lavish expenditure.

The number of priests connected with these churches exceeds one thousand, being about one for every hundred inhabitants. Would it not be a charity to relieve poor suffering Venice? We cannot help but remark upon the great freedom with which the priests mingle with the female portion of the population in Italy. We found it so in all the churches we visited, as well as on the streets of the towns and cities. A thing so common there would strike us as very *uncommon*, because we see so little of it in our country.

Among the many interesting places in Venice stands first *San Marco*, the St. Mark's Cathedral. This is the great central attraction for many tourists. The form and style of this ancient church are taken from the church of the Mother of God, in Constantinople. The present structure was built in the tenth century, and is composed of marble and ivory. It is a building difficult to describe, as it is built in a form peculiar to itself, and unlike any other existing church. In style it is at present Romanesque-Byzantine, in the form internally of a Greek cross with equal arms. A great dome rises in the centre, and four smaller ones crown the arms of the cruciform structure. In ground dimensions it is two hundred and fifteen feet front on the square, and two hundred and sixty-five feet deep. Five portals, of which the central is the largest, give admission to a portico or vestibule, which traverses the entire front of the church and a part of its two sides. The ceilings of these portals are vaulted, and covered with mosaics, representing Scriptural events. From the vestibule, which is exterior to the main walls, the interior is entered both in front and upon the sides.

The first impression of the interior of St. Mark's is

one of disappointment, and of baffled understanding. Its marble columns, of which it contains five hundred in its external and internal construction, and its marble pilasters and wall facings are dingy and soiled with time. Its almost innumerable mosaics look "faded and gaudy with tarnished gilding;" and its floors, inlaid with marble and mosaics, are uneven and sunken, as well as broken in pieces. Besides this, it is badly lighted, shedding forth a "dim religious light," and giving its heavy architecture a gloomy aspect. It requires a number of visits to overcome the impressions thus awakened; but familiarity with the interior is certain to work a change of impression, and in the end to arouse the most profound interest. "It will gradually become possible to picture it as it appeared in the full lustre of its gilded mosaics and glistening marbles, and in the pristine splendor of its profuse decorations."

Perhaps the nearest approach to a word-picture of the interior of this remarkable church is to be found in Ruskin's *Stones of Venice*, Vol. 2: "There opens before us a vast cave, hewn out into the form of a cross, and divided into shadowy aisles by many pillars. Round the domes of its roof, the light enters only through narrow apertures like large stars; and here and there a ray or two from some far-away casement wanders into the darkness, and casts a narrow phosphoric stream upon the waves of marble that heave and fall in a thousand colors along the floor. What else there is of light is from torches, or silver lamps, burning ceaselessly in the recesses of the chapels; the roof sheathed with gold, and the polished walls covered with alabaster, give back at every curve and angle some feeble gleaming to the flames; and the glories round the heads of the sculptured saints flash out upon us as we pass them, and sink again into the gloom. Under foot and over head, a continual succession of crowded imagery, one picture passing into another, as in a dream; forms beautiful and terrible mixed together; dragons and serpents, and ravening beasts of prey, and graceful birds that in the midst of them drink from running fountains and feed from vases of crystal; the passions and the pleasures of human life symbolized together, and the mystery of its redemption; for the mazes of interwoven lines and changeful pictures lead always at last to the cross, lifted and carved in every place, and upon every stone; sometimes with the serpent of eternity wrapt round it, sometimes with doves beneath its arms, and sweet herbage growing forth from its feet; but conspicuous most of all, on the great rood that crosses the church before the altar, raised in bright blazonry against the shadow of the apse."

We attended services here on Sunday morning, but it was all in an unknown tongue to us. Great crowds of people were there, and the greatest confusion; but the monks vigorously kept up their part of the service, intoning and doing the most boisterous singing. There was no sermon.

Over the central portion of St. Mark's stand the four elebrated bronze horses which once adorned the Arch of Nero at Rome. Constantine carried them from Rome to Constantinople, whence Marius Zeno brought them to

Venice in 1205; they were taken to Paris by Napoleon in 1797, but restored to this cathedral in 1815. These horses are remarkably well modeled, as well as interesting remains of ancient art. They have an eventful history, and should remain where they are.

"Before St. Mark still glow her steeds of brass,
Their gilded collars glistening in the sun."

St. Mark's Place, at one end of which stands the church just described, is the great square of the city, and is the great centre of business, and the centre no less of pleasure and amusement, as well as the grandest and loveliest in Venetian architecture. In this place gather the great crowds in the evening to hear the fine music. Here are located all the fine stores, the larger number being jewelry stores. By gaslight this presents a most brilliant and attractive scene. Round the whole square in front of the church, there is also almost a continuous line of cafés, where the idle Venetians of the middle classes lounge, and read empty journals; in its centre the Austrian bands play during the times of vespers, their martial music jarring with the organ notes—the march drowning the *miserere*, and the sullen crowd thickening around them—a crowd which, if it had its will, would stiletto every soldier that pipes to it. And in the recesses of the porches, all day long, knots of men of the lowest classes, unemployed and listless, lie basking in the sun like lizards; and unregarded children—every heavy glance of their eyes full of desperation and stony depravity, and their throats hoarse with cursing—gamble, and fight, and snarl and sleep, hour after hour, clashing their bruised centesimi upon the marble ledges of the church porch. And the images of Christ and his angels look down upon it continually.

The entire square is paved with smooth blocks of granite interspersed with iron pillars, bearing clusters of gas jets, while another line of illumination extends along the entire fronts. The buildings fronting the square are all of white marble, four stories high, and adorned with an abundance of statuary. The entire length of the square is five hundred and forty feet, and the width two hundred and sixty feet, whilst the Piazzetta leading past the Palace of the Doges and the old Library, which is really a portion of the square, is three hundred and eleven feet long by one hundred and forty-six in width, extending down to the water's edge at the mouth of the Grand Canal.

But now let us go and see the Ducal Palace (Palazzo Ducale) or the Doge's Palace, as it is also called. This is the building in which the old Senate used to meet, and is well worth a visit. This was the great work of Venice, the principal effort of her imaginaton, employing her best architects in its masonry and her best artists in its decorations for a long series of years. The late Charles Dickens in his " Pictures from Italy," thus speaks of this famous palace: " Going down upon the margin of the green sea, rolling on before the door and filling all the streets, I came upon a place of such surpassing beauty and such grandeur that all the rest was poor and faded in comparison with its absorbing loveliness. It was a great piazza, as I thought, anchored, like all the rest, in the deep ocean. On its broad bosom was a palace more majestic and magnificent in its old age than all the buildings of the earth in the high prime of fullness of their youth. Cloisters and galleries, so light that they might have been the work of fairy hands, so strong that centuries had battered them in vain, wound round and round this palace, and infolded it with a cathedral gorgeous in the wild luxuriant fancies of the East."

This building dates back to the fourteenth and fifteenth centuries. It contains many apartments of great splendor and elegance, reflecting the cultivated tastes and resources of the Venetian aristocracy. The hall of the Senate surpasses all apartments in the Palace, with perhaps one exception. It is one hundred feet long and forty-eight feet wide, with a ceiling about thirty-five feet high. Its walls and ceilings are also covered with frescoes of the highest grade. In this chamber the Venetian Senate, consisting of three hundred members, held its sessions. The many suites of rooms throughout the Palace, adorned with works of Titian, Tintoretto, Palma and Paul Veronese, are not easily to be forgotten. Here there is great wealth of finest art. The mind is bewildered by the unsparing profusion, fertility and brilliancy of imagination and skillful delineation displayed by these eminent artists of the Venetian school. The "Hall of the Grand Council," is said to be one of the finest rooms in Europe. In this chamber the entire body of the Venetian aristocracy were wont to assemble, but rather for social than governmental objects. The private apartments of the Doges are not exhibited.

This palace of palaces united in itself the two qualities of a parliament house and a ducal residence, which explains at once its magnitude and its magnificence. As the capitol of the Venetian state, it expresses the munificence and wealth of the aristocracy; and as a ducal residence, it indicates the elegant habits of the Doges, the chiefs of the aristocracy.

The Ducal Palace is connected by the Bridge of Sighs with the prisons. This bridge has been immortalized by Lord Byron in the fourth canto of Childe Harold. A bridge crosses the canal or street just below, and another just above the Doge's Palace, from which a fine view of the Bridge of Sighs can be obtained—and it is true as Byron says:

> "I stood in Venice, on the Bridge of Sighs,
>   A palace and a prison on each hand;
> I saw from out the waves the structures rise
>   As from the stroke of some enchanter's wand.
> A thousand years their cloudy wings expand
>   Around me, and a dying glory smiles
> O'er the far times when many a subject-land
>   Looked to the winged islands' marble piles
> Where Venice sat in state, throned on her hundred isles."

Howells, in his "Venetian Life," speaks of it as "that pathetic swindle, the Bridge of Sighs." The bridge itself is no work of special merit. It is of marble, and arched, springing from the second story window of the criminal court over to the prison. It stands some thirty feet above the water. It is closed at the top and sides, the light entering through open sculptured work. The interior of the bridge is divided into two passage-ways, each with its own means of ingress and egress. This bridge was the means of communication between the criminal court and the criminal prison. Through these passage-ways criminals were conveyed to hear their sentence, and thence led to their execution; and from this the bridge derives its melancholy but appropriate name. The sighing company that crossed it must have been made up of "housebreakers, cut-purse knaves, and murderers." The name was given to it " by the people, from that opulence of compassion which enables the Italians to pity even rascality in difficulties."

By special permission we passed through this famous bridge into the prisons—not, however, under sentence, nor as criminals. There are two tiers of dungeons, one above the other, consisting of ten each, with a floor between, constructed of heavy stone masonry. The apartments are for two kinds of offenders, political and criminal. This distinction is presented in the very architecture of the dungeons. Those for criminals were above, and those for political prisoners below. The dungeons are entered through a low arched opening. After passing through this opening with a torch to light the chamber, the visitor finds himself in a room inclosed by massive stone walls, twelve feet long, eight feet wide, and nine feet high, with an arched ceiling. The floors are of cement, hardened into stone, and bare of all furniture save a stone pillow set in the floor. Every dungeon repeats this cool " inhuman mockery" of a pretended regard for the necessities of the prisoner. A common paving-stone, two feet long, fifteen inches wide, and rising about four inches above the floor, was the pillow offered by the state, in the dark days of the Venetian aristocracy, to political as well as criminal offenders. "Two Doges, at least—Marino Falieri, in his eightieth year, and Antonio Foscari—were brought to the bitter experience both of the dungeons and of the stone pillow." It is doubtful whether these had dreams as pleasant and visions as celestial as the patriarch Jacob, who rested his weary head on a stony pillow in the days of his pilgrimage at Bethel. At the side of each door of these dungeons, there is a small round opening through the wall for the introduction of food. The darkness is substantially total. To be incarcerated in such a prison was at once a woe and a double sorrow. In a short hall, which is still pointed out, the prisoners were executed at midnight— the political by beheading, and the criminal by strangulation. These horrible dungeons are still used to pen in political prisoners. We experienced a pleasant sense of relief when again brought out of these dark and dismal caverns into the sunny light of day.

Among the many other attractive and interesting sights in this novel city is the celebrated Rialto Bridge over the Grand Canal. This is a wonder in itself, consisting of a single arch one hundred and eighty-seven feet long, and forty-eight feet wide. It consists of marble. Its foundations rest upon twelve thousand piles. Commenced in 1588, and finished in 1591, it was, for the period, a remarkable structure. It connects the eastern and newer part of the city with the island of Rialto, on the west side of the Grand Canal, the oldest part of the city. There seems to be a question whether Shakspeare, in the "Merchant of Venice," refers to the island or the bridge when he causes Shylock to say:

> "Signior Antonio, many a time and oft
> In the Rialto you have rated me
> About my moneys and my usances."

Shakespeare, who was born in 1564, was twenty-seven years old when the bridge was completed, and doubtless its fame as a public work had reached him with his other information of this marvelous city. "The latter opinion, that the reference was to the island and not to the bridge, seems unfounded."

On our return to our hotel we were interested in the Campanile, not the least conspicuous ornament of St. Mark's Square. It is three hundred and four feet high, forty-five feet square, and was erected in the twelfth century. Within it is an enclosed square tower, leaving a space between the outer and inner walls about five feet wide. We climbed this tower, and were amply rewarded for our toil by a magnificent view we had from its summit of the city of Venice. The ascent is comparatively easy. It is made by inclined planes. It is a singularly convenient method of mounting to the summit of a tower, well understood by the ancient Romans. Napoleon, it is said, performed the feat of riding his horse from the base to the summit.

Feeding the pigeons is certainly a novelty as well as an interesting sight in Venice. This is done every afternoon at two o'clock, in the Square of St. Mark, at the public expense. They are the pets of the people, and to injure one of them in any way would surely send the perpetrator to the guard-house. They have the freedom of the city, and the windows of the lofts of the public buildings are left open, and free access is given to them. The process of feeding is very interesting. At the moment the bronze man on the town-clock strikes the first blow announcing two o'clock, the pigeons flock in from all sides by thousands, and sweep up the square towards the window from which they are daily fed, and many hundreds of them even enter the room. They are very tame and literally swarmed over us, and partook of the food, which is corn, from our hands.

As to the meaning of this care for the pigeons, there is no settled theory. It is said by some that on one occasion during the Venetian wars, whilst Admiral Dandolo was besieging Candia, at the commencement of the thirteenth century, a carrier-pigeon brought him important information from the islands. But the old chroniclers differ as to the origin of feeding the pigeons, which has been a custom for centuries. One says that on Palm Sunday it was the custom to loose pigeons, many of which repaired for shelter to St. Mark's, and, multiplying with time, they remained about the square as the best place for obtaining food. "The practice," however, "of maintaining pigeons at public expense is very general in Russia and Persia, as well as among the Arabs, and the custom might easily have been carried thither by Venetian merchants." Other authors assert that, although the city is credited with feeding the pigeons, they are in reality fed and cared for by the liberality of an old lady who left a large amount to be expended for this purpose.

The streets of Venice are silent as compared with those of other cities. There is neither a horse nor a carriage, nor even a hand-cart, to be seen in any thoroughfare. In this respect it is a noiseless city, and is free from the din and dust of other cities. Yet there are great throngs of people in the streets, which present animated scenes like those of other cities. Business is carried on with dispatch and apparent ease. Small packages are generally carried in baskets, and anything cumbrous is placed in the gondola, and conveyed from place to place. Though the city is free from din and rattle of vehicles, let no one suppose that it is free from *all* noises. The gondoliers, as they glide along on the watery streets, give out their cries with a zeal and earnestness that are at times quite startling. Among others are men carrying demijohns of water, with lime-juice, which they sell at two centimes, or less than half a cent, a glass. Others sell candied fruits, and various articles not usually found in stores. Then come along the flower girls, offering the most beautiful flowers for sale. These girls are mostly perfect beauties themselves, rivaling the article they offer in no small degree. The cries of these street venders are of course in Italian, a language peculiarly fitted for shrill but smoothly flowing notes. From early in the morning until late at night you hear these shrill street cries, to your annoyance.

Venice has many and beautiful stores. These are mostly found on the extensive Piazza of St. Mark.

Jewelry of all kinds can be purchased at very reasonable rates. The shop-keepers are determined to sell, and they seldom allow a purchaser to leave their establishment without selling him something. You are almost overwhelmed with attention and politeness. To enter any of these stores without removing your hat would be regarded not only impolite, but really an offence. A shop-keeper, whether male or female, would not pretend to return you change with the bare hand, but placing it in an ornamented small silver waiter, gently pours it into your hand. As to the honesty and fair dealing of these people, we could not find fault, but must commend them. We purchased some views of Venice, and not wishing to carry them with us, requested the dealer to mail them to our address. We paid for the pictures, left our address, and on our return home found our goods awaiting us.

Perhaps in no city is the tourist more constantly besieged by beggars than in Venice. There are many idlers everywhere on the streets, and at a glance they know the foreigner. All sorts of tricks are resorted to, to extract a centime from your pocket. Boys turn summersaults in front of you and give you to understand that they have earned something, and that you ought to pay them. Others give you an exhibition of diving in the watery streets, and having emerged from the deeps, quickly stand before you, expecting their reward. As you approach in a gondola one of the public buildings you wish to view, you see approaching a man with a long pole in hand, at the end of which is a crook, which he is sure to fasten on your boat, and professes to be very helpful in giving you a safe landing. You are scarcely out of the gondola, when off goes the hat of your benefactor, and you can not move until the beggar is moved, which a centime will do quickly. As you are about to enter the building, be it a church or any other edifice, your ears are well nigh deafened by the rattling of tin boxes in the hands of a flock of beggars at the door. Having satisfied all these outside, you begin to think you shall enjoy quiet within. But not so; for the inside is besieged in the same manner, and even the different apartments in the building. The only way to conquer this army of beggars is to give them *something*, be it ever so little, or let them mutter their story and rattle their boxes until they weary, and pay no attention to them.

Many of the Venetians are fine-looking people, bright and entertaining. The ladies are fond of fine dress, and are mostly beautiful and handsome. The difference, however, in Italy, as well as in all European countries, between what are called the common class and better class of people, is very much greater than in our own country. This is apparent to the most casual observer. The same is true in the mode of living.

Before leaving the city we took another long and extended sail on the gondola, going out into the Adriatic, perhaps not exactly where St. Paul sailed, but still on the same sea, and must say that it was with some reluctance that we bade adieu to the Queen of the Adriatic.

CHAPTER XIII.

OVER THE APENNINES—THE CITY OF FLORENCE—PITTI PALACE—SAVONAROLA—PALACE VECCHIO—UFFIZI GALLERY—CHURCH OF SANTA CROCE—MICHAEL ANGELO'S HOUSE—A FUNERAL SCENE.

THE day we left Venice for Florence was intensely hot, and to be boxed up in a small, cushioned compartment of close, dusty cars, with nothing to eat and no water to drink, was an impressive realization of the difference between home and foreign car riding. The cars in Italy are inferior to those in many other parts of Europe. The first half of the one hundred and eighty miles of our journey was most disagreeable, for the way was dusty, the weather swelteringly hot, and the scenery not particularly attractive. Everything looked parched, with scarcely anything green. After passing beyond Bologna, the Roman Bononca, a walled city of one hundred thousand inhabitants, and approaching the Apennines from the plains of Lombardy to the valley of the Arno, the scenery of the country became much more inviting, and the weather cooler. The railway crosses the Apennines from the valley of the Arno, and is a grand piece of engineering. There are as many as forty-two tunnels, varying in length from one hundred yards to two miles. They are constructed in enduring masonry, and the equipments of the road are of a very superior character. With all this, one is utterly surprised that the internal arrangements of the cars are so bereft, not only of comforts, but necessities.

There are many beautiful views of the wild scenery of the Apennines, and further on, of the fertile plains of Tuscany, the garden of Italy. Here we passed over historic ground, every foot of which has been trodden by Roman legions, a thousand and more years ago.

At ten o'clock in the evening we passed through the city gates into Florence, whose streets were thronged with people and brilliant with gaslight. Florence has been awarded the title of "the fairest city of the earth." It certainly is a delightful city, of two hundred thousand people, situated in the rich valley of the Arno, surrounded by beauties of nature and art, immortalized by Byron and Rogers, and revered as the birth-place of Dante, Petrarch, Galileo, Michael Angelo, and many other celebrities. How the recollections of the past come trooping up in the appreciative mind, while tarrying in a place which has given birth to such noble contributors to poetry and the arts! Beautiful gardens adorned with statues, vases, fountains, and other decorations, as well as the open squares or piazzas, continually attract the eye of the visitor; and the palaces, which are very numerous, each containing rare paintings and sculptures, form the principal objects of interest in this delightful city, which is the pride of Italy. Like all European cities, Florence is solidly built. There are no wooden houses. The people seem to live all sorts of ways, and much out doors. The streets are mostly broad, and all smoothly paved with large square-cut stones half a foot thick, grooved with the chisel. It can never be muddy here, for the streets are kept so perfectly clean that even so good a housekeeper as the dear Mrs. Partington, with her finest broom, could not gather a shovelful of dirt from any square in the city. The people of Florence are evidently industrious, and impress the stranger most favorably. The persons to be dreaded are the beggars. These meet you at every turn on the street, at every church door you visit, within and without; they follow you and run after you if you happen to be riding in a carriage.

In Italy at least, Romanism makes beggary respectable. The most honored religious orders are the mendicant orders. A noble joins the order of the Jesuits. His superior places him, hat in hand, at the door of his church, to beg for his new brethren from his old associates. The Pope himself is supported by Peter-pence contributed by the faithful. We do not know whether the Apostle's precept, "If any would not work, neither should he eat," is in the Douay version or not, but the principle certainly has no place in the religion of the Romans. Under a system in which mendicancy receives religious veneration, beggary is not shameful, nor the beggar an outcast.

The stores and cafés are brilliant and most attractive by gas-light, and are visited by great multitudes. Such shining scenes would never be seen in any American city except on the eve of some national holiday. The cafés are all immense establishments, some of them old palaces, and they are thronged to the curb-stones with parties eating and drinking. So are also some of the broad avenues, where as many as a thousand persons sit down at the marble tables and sip beer and wine, and this in the most orderly manner, there being no drunkenness nor rowdyism. The people at least enjoy themselves, and show a great deal of sociability. The climate of Florence is delightful, varying but thirty degrees from summer to winter, and the city is frequented by many people from the cold and severe winter climates of Europe. Not a few Americans have taken up their permanent abode here.

The first place of special interest we visited was the *Pitti Palace*, at one time the residence of King Victor Emanuel, but its chief attraction now is the collection of paintings. Here are some of the finest paintings in Europe, and it is simply bewildering to walk amid the wealth of such art as is here displayed. Besides the matchless paintings, which the masters have here left for the world to admire, there are beautiful sculptures, vases and mosaics, of untold value. We were especially attracted by a Mosaic table, about seven feet long by four feet wide, which cost over two hundred thousand dollars, and fifteen years were occupied in completing it at the government manufactory. In the great business square of the city the place is still pointed out where Savonarola, the Italian reformer, was burned at the stake in 1498. The spot is marked by a magnificent fountain, surmounted with a bronze statue of Neptune. This good man was here put to death when Luther was but seven years old, and twenty-seven years before the famous theses were nailed on the church-door of Wittenberg, proclaiming the coming liberator of Northern Europe. This Christian hero was committed to the flames for denouncing the usurpations and detesting the wickedness of the church of Rome, and because he thought Christ better than the Pope, and love than a scarlet hat, and purity than an indulgence. The night before he suffered, he laid his head in the lap of his deeply-affected guard, and slept the calm sleep of one whose conscience was at rest, and was ready to be offered, knowing that the crown and palm of martyrdom were now laid up for him in heaven. With two comrades, one of whom had given the rash and fatal challenge, he was led to the scaffold, barefooted and bareheaded, clad only in a woolen shirt. As he passed along a temporary gangway, cruel boys were allowed to amuse themselves by pricking his feet with pins. But weeping and dim eyes were in the concourse, and in many a closed and melancholy house, that day. They clothed Savonarola in priestly robes, which a bishop immediately tore off, at the same time pronouncing the words of doom: "I separate thee from the church militant and from the church triumphant." The martyr's face, sombre hitherto and overcast, brightened with an excellent glory while he made answer: "Not from the church triumphant—that is beyond thy power." Who spoke to him those lofty words but He who is with His people always, and who said, "Fear not them who can kill the body, and after that have no more that they can do?" Serene, dauntless, humble and forgiving as becomes a pardoned Christian, with nothing abject and nothing boastful in his bearing, he saw his comrades strangled and burned; and then committed his body into the hands of the executioner, and his soul into the keeping of Christ. So they quenched the light of Italy, and flung his ashes into the Arno, and that impetuous river swept them to the sea. It was the last small insult which hate and fear could inflict in their hour of triumph. Yet what fitter tomb for the orator of many moods, threats, entreaties, defiances, hopes and fears, than the many-sounding, many-changing sea—for the freeman whose life was battle against the tyrants of the soul, than those free waves, whose children are the champions of liberty for the body and liberty for the soul.

We read that as he stood ready to be offered, the martyr fixed one long, strange glance upon the fierce democracy that he had formerly wielded at his will. We may picture the sadness and majesty of that look, but his thoughts we cannot follow. Yet if he had, as he dreamed, the gift of prophecy, then would his visions have been like these: "I see the people soon, under the scourge of pestilence, remembering and bewailing me, and driving out my enemies. I see the hateful tyrant whose snares entangled and whose minions doomed me, taken at last in a pit of his own digging, with murderous greed coiled like a serpent round his heart; and it is better to die a martyr for Christ than the victim of deeds like his. I see a mightier testimony, a more vital energy, a deeper and farther-reaching truth than my teaching expressed, shaking realms I never trod, and building into mighty empires races whose very names are strange.

"And gazing down the centuries, what is this which dimly looms to view? Florence, the fair and stately—Florence, in which I labored, and for which I die—reinforced by the patriotism of all Italy, and dear to the enlightenment of all the world, no longer the lonely and turbulent city that I knew; but now the august capital of a great, united and free empire; confronting, with often baffled but always inexorable purpose, a Rome how darkly changed! Emblems they of the new time and the old, liberty and bondage, life and death; Rome, through all changes, reeling to an inevitable fall—Florence, in fair weather and foul, erect in the energy and buoyant in the hopefulness of youth renewed."

Facing this great square, in which Savonarola was burned, stands the *Palace Vecchio*, the old capitol of the republic. It was begun in 1298, and is a striking example of the Florentine castles of the middle ages.

We spent many hours in the famous *Uffizi Gallery*, founded by the Medici, the paintings in which are reputed to be the richest and most varied in the world. The hall known as the *Tribune* is the inner sanctuary of this temple of art (the richest room in all the world, a heart that draws all hearts to it, as Hawthorne says), and contains the *Dancing Faun*, the *Appollino*, the *Wrestlers*, and other marvels of ancient sculpture; while in painting, Raphael, Michael Angelo, Titian, Correggio, and other great masters, are represented by some of their best works.

Time and space forbid to speak of more than a few of the many churches of Florence. The Cathedral (the

Duomo) holds the first place. Its dome from the paved floor is the highest in the world. The exterior of the building is coated with white marble, and is five hundred feet long. The interior is grand and impressive, and contains many fine monuments.

The church of *Santa Croce* is the Pantheon of Tuscany, and contains the tomb of Michael Angelo, who is buried here. It also contains the monuments of Dante and Galileo. On the tomb of the latter we read the following inscription in Latin: "The great restorer of geometry, astronomy, and philosophy; none of his age is to be compared to him; here may he sleep well."

Of course we would not miss Michael Angelo's house. This contains a collection of pictures and rare antiquities, and is kept as a perpetual exhibition. We rested a little while in the distinguished man's private room, and occupied his chair at a small table. Here on the wall are exhibited his sword and two walking-sticks. This is the man who being asked why he did not marry, answered, "Painting is my wife, and my works are my children."

The second evening we spent in Florence we witnessed two very strange funeral scenes. The procession, bearers and all, did not number over a dozen people, all males. They all wore black frocks, broad-brimmed hats, masked faces, leaving only two openings for the eyes; each one carrying a flaming torch, and presenting a most ghostly appearance. The hand-barrow was covered with a black canopy, beneath which rested the corpse. The procession walked with a rush, but the people raised their hats as it passed by. We learned that there is a religious order in Florence which took its rise during the prevalence of the cholera some years ago. It undertook to superintend the funeral rites and burial of all persons who had neither friends nor money and died in the city. These societies are composed of the order of friars, whose pious work includes also the nursing and attending of the sick poor—a merciful provision.

We met a great many Americans in Florence, and the ceremony of introduction was anything but formal. We all seemed to know each other, and at once became quite sociable. Seeing the Stars and Stripes floating from the staff of the American Consul's house was beautiful, as well as inspiring. Before leaving the city, we took a carriage and rode out to Basoa, situated on the high range of hills, where we had a magnificent view of the whole city, the Arno and valley, and were treated to a glorious sunset. Would that we could go again to Florence, the fairest of cities!

CHAPTER XIV.

ROME—THE PALACE OF THE CÆSARS—ARCH OF TITUS—THE COLISEUM—THE CATHEDRAL OF ST. PAUL.

AT last we find ourselves in the Imperial City, the centre of history, glory and shame. We left Florence at 10 p. m., and, therefore, can not speak from personal observation in regard to the country through which we passed for two hundred and thirty miles. As the morning dawned we approached the Holy City; and as her towers and domes loomed up in the distance and her ancient walls came in sight, we were thoroughly aroused from our slumbers and were not a little stirred in mind and heart. While we did not, like Luther, on his visit to Rome, fall on our knees, exclaiming, "Holy Rome, I salute thee!" yet we could adopt the language of another,

"A thousand busy thoughts
Rushed on my mind a thousand images."

And as we passed within the walls I could scarcely realize that we were entering

"The city that so long
Reigned absolute, the mistress of the world."

As in subsequent days we wandered amid her tombs and fragments of temples, broken columns and crumbling monuments, attesting the grandeur of the Imperial City, I would sometimes say,

> "And am I here?
> Ah! little thought I, when in school I sat,
> A school-boy on his bench at early dawn
> Glowing with Roman story, I should live
> To tread the Appian, once an avenue
> Of monuments most glorious, palaces,
> Their doors sealed up and silent as the night,
> The dwellings of the illustrious dead—to turn
> Toward Tiber, and beyond the city gate,
> Pour out my unpretending verse,
> Where, on his mule, I might have met so oft
> Horace himself."

It would be unsatisfactory to attempt to give in a few chapters the many events in the history of Rome; yet it might be proper to say that the founding of Rome is attributed to Romulus, 753 years B. C. (before Christ.) Rome is famous both in ancient and modern history, formerly for being the most powerful nation of antiquity, and afterwards the ecclesiastical capital of Christendom and the residence of the Pope. The ancient portion of the city, under the emperors, was much more extensive than the modern. Nearly all the seven hills upon which ancient Rome is said to have been built are merely eminences, being of but slight ascent, with the exception of the Capitoline and Palatine Hills. The situation of the city is generally low, and is divided into two very unequal portions by the river Tiber. Ten of its sixteen gates have been walled up.

There are many signs of improvement in the city. In the neighborhood of the railroad depot, which is one of the most magnificent in Europe, there are many fine new streets of elegant buildings, both public and private, of which our hotel, *The Continental*, is one. In the central part of the city we found entire rows of superior new residences going up on every side, old palaces being renovated and almost reconstructed, and new ones being built. The streets of Rome are kept clean. Whilst many of them are narrow, yet others, especially in the new part, are wide. Every paving-stone in the city is carefully swept during the night, and the dust carted off before breakfast. The streets are also watered, and in the early morning it would be difficult to find any city, except Paris, cleaner than the Rome of the present day. This all grows out of the fact that Rome is the capital of Italy, and that the Pope has lost his temporal power. There is no mistaking the fact that all Rome, except the Pope and cardinals, and the priesthood, is happy and hopeful. It does one good, especially an American, to see the Italian flag flying from the castle of St. Angelo, which was for so many years the prison-house of all liberal Italians who had the courage to entertain and express sentiments favorable to human liberty.

We were surprised to find such good water in Rome in the month of August, and plenty of excellent ice, for which there were no extra charges. As to hotel accommodations and attendance, and their *table d'hote*, both in quality and character of cooking, we found them to be better than in London.

We had some hesitancy in going to Rome in August, fearing sickness. We found the weather very hot, especially in the middle part of the day; but the nights were delightfully cool, and after learning the true state of things, we felt as safe as in any other city in regard to sickness. We avoided being outdoors much after nightfall.

To see Rome to advantage, guides are necessary. These can be had at reasonable prices, and by a little care reliable persons may be secured. It is not possible to give in detail, in a few chapters, what one sees in Rome in a single week. I shall, therefore, select some of the most interesting portions which came under our observation, hoping that all my readers may some day go to Rome and see for themselves.

The first place we visited was the *Palace of the Cæsars*, on the Palatine Hill. The entrance is through an immense archway, and from the Forum opposite the Basilica of Constantine. Nothing now remains of these extensive buildings but a mass of ruins; these, however, still show many signs of former magnificence, such as the beautiful floors of mosaic, parts of the throne of the Cæsars, and the fine porphyry and serpentine stone. Judging from the immense bath-rooms, the old emperors must have been great sticklers for cleanliness. We noticed also such modern conveniences as lead and steam pipes in the walls of the Palace. The arches, crushed columns, chocked-up vaults, heaped hillocks, cypress and ivy-grown walls, crumbled temples, all matted and massed together, mark the Imperial Mount. 'Tis thus the mighty fall. In our stroll through these ruins, our guide was careful to point out the precise spot, close down by the Tiber, under a clump of small trees, where the mythical Romulus and Remus were suckled by the she-wolf, and subsequently proceeded to build the walls of Rome.

Leaving the Palace of the Cæsars, we pass under the Arch of Titus, which is close by, and was erected in honor of that distinguished general on his return to Rome after his conquest of Jerusalem (A. D. 70). It is an arch of much magnificence, and well preserved. The Jews never pass under it, always going around it.

We dare not detain the reader by giving an account of the many other ruins we visited the first day, such as the Temples of Vesta, Venus, Roma, Juno, Hope, Piety, and the Column of Trajan, the latter being regarded a perfect triumph of art.

We now go to the *Coliseum*, begun by Vespasian in A. D. 72. This is the most familiar of all the ancient Roman monuments, and is by far the largest amphitheatre in the world, as well as the most august ruin. It covers five acres of ground, is nearly one-third of a mile in circumference, and was capable of containing eighty-seven thousand persons. On the occasion of its dedication by Titus, five thousand wild beasts were slain in the arena, the games lasting for nearly one hundred days. Of course it has been much damaged by the influence of time, yet parts of it are in a good state of preservation. The dens are still distinct where the wild beasts were kept, and the passage-ways open through which they were conducted into the arena to kill and devour the Christians. Close to the outer walls stands a small circular ruin, to which, by an underground passage-way the gladiators retired to wash off their bloody bodies. The only dome of the Coliseum is the sky; and the spectacle, when the seats, rising in circular rows one above another for four stories, were filled with people, must have been an imposing sight beyond description. As you stand in the vast arena, and look upon these ruined seats, and remember that where you stand, stood and fought and died gladiators, " butchered to make a Roman holiday," the imagination is overwhelmed at the strange and mighty past that rises before you. From the vast concourse Roman applause was thundered down to the spot your feet press, as the blood spurted from the poor wretch's heart.

To see this ruin crumbling away ; its walls and arches overgrown with green; its corridors open to the day ; the long grass growing in its porches, young trees springing up on its ragged parapets ; to see the peaceful cross planted in the centre of its pit of fight ; to climb into its upper halls, and look down on ruin, ruin, ruin, all about it ; the triumphal arches of Constantine, Septimius Severus, and Titus ; the Roman Forum, the Palace of the Cæsars, where long since the barbarian has stabled his steed ; the temples of the old religion fallen down and gone ; to see all this, is to see the ghost of old Rome, the wicked, wonderful old city, haunting the very ground on which its people trod. It is the most impressive, the most stately, the most solemn, mournful sight conceivable. The Christian can never view this, the most imposing ruin in the world, without a heavy feeling in his heart for the good, the beautiful and the holy, who here offered up their lives a willing sacrifice for the faith they bore.

We now pass out of the city through the Ostian gate, and on our way drive past the small chapel which tradition says marks the spot where St. Paul and St. Peter met and embraced each other before their martyrdom. The scene is sculptured in marble above the door of the chapel.

And now we are a mile and a quarter outside the city walls, in the magnificent cathedral of St. Paul. Nothing can exceed the richness of this whole edifice. Its altars and pillars exceed those of St. Peter. It abounds in alabaster, malachite, black and yellow marble, green basalt and porphyry. Its floor shines like a mirror, while its ceilings are white and gilt stucco, and its walls are filled with matchless paintings and likenesses in mosaic of some two hundred saints. The effect of the four ranges of granite columns, eighty in number, of the Corinthian order, is unparalleled. The high altar stands under a splendid canopy, supported by four columns of white alabaster. Under this altar is the tomb, which the tradition of the Roman church points out as the burial place of St. Paul, whose body, on the same authority, is inclosed in an urn, on which is engraved the name of the apostle. Like the tomb of St. Peter in St. Peter's cathedral, one hundred lamps are kept burning around it night and day. One of the priests took us into the sacristy, where he exhibited the chain which it is said tied the hands of St. Paul when he was executed. The chain is kept in a beautiful cushioned case, and is regarded so sacred that the priest would not touch it with his hands, but with a silk cloth. "Help our unbelief."

Near this church the spot is still pointed out where St. Paul suffered martyrdom.

On our return to our hotel we passed the house of

Pilate, the Temple of Janus, the theatre of Marcellus (founded by Julius Cæsar, 30 B. C.); through the Jew quarter, parts of which beggar description; thence by the Palace of King Humbert, near by which we saw some of the original Roman walls.

CHAPTER XV.

MORE ABOUT ROME—ST. PETER'S—REMAINS OF POPE PIUS IX.—
THE POPE'S UNPOPULARITY—THE TICKET AGENT—THE VATICAN—THE APPIAN WAY—IN THE CATACOMBS.

OF the three hundred churches in Rome, besides its numerous cathedrals, we had time to see but few; but among this number, of course St. Peter's came in for a good share. In order to gain a true conception of this, the great pride and glory of modern Rome, a mere pen picture is entirely inadequate. Many minute descriptions have been given of this magnificent structure, but its dimensions and splendor very far exceed the most elaborate that can be written. It is as the poet has said:

> "But thou, of temples old or altars new,
> Standest alone—with nothing like to thee,
>   What could be
> Of earthly structure in His honor piled
> Of sublimest aspect? Majesty,
> Power, Glory, Strength, and Beauty, all are aisled
> In this eternal ark of worship."

St. Peter's stands on the site of the Circus of Nero, where many Christians suffered martyrdom, and where St. Peter is said to have been buried after his crucifixion. An oratory was founded here as early as A. D. 90; and in A. D. 306 a basilica was begun by Constantine the Great. The present edifice was commenced by Julius II. in 1506. The expense of the work was so heavy—that of the main building being estimated at fifty millions—that Julius II. and Leo. X. resorted to the sale of indulgences to raise money, and this led to the Reformation. And here let me say by way of parenthesis that, as I wandered in the midst of popedom, even in its faded glory and enfeebled strength, I thought what faith and courage the brave Luther must have had, to stand out against Rome when in her pristine glory and power, and rebuke her iniquities! —

The front of St. Peter's is four hundred feet long, and one hundred and forty-eight feet high. It is six hundred feet in depth. The height of the dome is four hundred and eighty feet. There are five doors in the front opening into the vestibule, which is itself much longer and wider than a large church. The diameter of the dome is one hundred and fifty feet. On the roof of the cathedral is built quite a village of small houses, occupied by custodians and workmen.

To describe minutely the interior of this structure would in itself make a good-sized volume. It is a familiar fact that it does not at first sight seem so vast as it really is. The statues and ornaments, which one naturally takes as standards of measurement, are themselves of unusual proportions—"the angels in the baptistry are enormous giants: the doves colossal birds of prey." It is only by observing the living, moving figures, which look like large insects creeping over the marble floor and are almost lost in the vastness of the encircling space, that one begins to get an idea of the immensity and grandeur of the edifice. Byron refers to this in his description of the church in Childe Harold—

> "Enter: its grandeur overwhelms thee not;
> And why? It is not lessened: but thy mind,
> Experienced by the genius of the spot,
> Has grown colossal, and can only find
> A fit abode wherein appear enshrined
> Thy hopes of immortality."

Gradually it expands until it fills the full measure of your anticipations, and far exceeds them. Its walls, railings, columns, corridors, arches, piers, and numberless altars, glitter with gold. The tombs and monuments of nearly all the popes, and of many kings, are here. As you approach the bronze canopy and gaze up into the solemn dome of mosaics circling away four hundred feet into the heavens, you exclaim, "It is enough." The high altar, directly under the dome and over the tomb of St. Peter, is too magnificent for us to attempt a description. This alone is estimated to have cost nine millions of dollars. Service goes on perpetually, both night and day. The moment it ceases in one part it immediately begins in another. Hundreds of people are constantly kneeling at the many altars while mass is in progress. Near the high altar, seated on a magnificent high chair of fine marble, is St. Peter in silver and bronze. Hither all good papists resort daily in great numbers, even to small children, to kiss the saint's toe. To such an extent is this kissing done, that three-fourths of the saint's big toe has been kissed away. In the side wall of the edifice was pointed out to us the place whence the remains of Pope Pius IX. had recently been taken, and interred outside the city walls for their final resting-place. As his remains were conveyed through the streets of Rome, large crowds of Italians followed, mocking and shouting words of derision, demanding that his body be thrown into the Tiber. This sacrilege greatly grieved the present Pope, and to show his grief he issued a most mournful proclamation, and totally secluded himself from the outside world for the space of three months. So it happened that we did not see the Pope; but neither did he see us. A liberal government has made the Pope very unhappy, and his residence uncertain. The ardent love which the Roman people once had for the head of their church has so far abated that even the silver coin bearing his image is utterly worthless, and will buy nothing. The moment they see it they cry, "*Non papa!*" Straws tell which way the wind blows. The Roman is very quick in detecting the foreigner, and in one instance at least, was not too scrupulous to attempt an advantage over us. We had purchased a ticket for Naples, and among the change the ticket agent returned to us was a piece of Roman silver worth about forty cents in American money. This coin bore the image of Pope Pius IX. We at once recognized the imposition, and immediately returned to the agent's office, saying, "*Non papa!*" He paid no attention to us at first, but we then more nearly imitated the earnest Italian manner, repeating, "*Non papa!* NON PAPA!!" He handed us the right change, saying at the same time, with a smile on his face, "*Non papa!*" Language failed us, our vocabulary in the Latin being too limited; or that ticket agent would have received a severe lecture for having attempted to swindle us.

One of the many strange features which catch the American eye in Rome, and little accord with the American idea, is the presence in the church of a foreign soldiery. The Swiss guards (not composed exclusively of Swiss soldiers, but of those of various nationalities—the term being technical and not geographical), especially during great pageants, stand sentinel at the basilica and the Vatican. You meet them at every step. And as you see those bright uniforms and burnished swords, you inwardly contrast this papal kingdom with that of the Master, and find yourself murmuring, "My kingdom is not of this world." The Pope's body-guard (*Guarda Nobile*) consists to a great extent of native Romans—members of old aristocratic families.

Let us now go and see the Vatican. We ascend by long corridors and staircases. The name is derived from that of the hill on which the papal palace has been built, which is itself perhaps derived from a deity, Vaticanus, the presiding god of the first rudiments of speech—though upon this linguists, we believe, are not agreed.

It is, however, decidedly the most celebrated of all the papal palaces, and is composed of a mass of buildings which cover a space of twelve hundred feet in length by one thousand feet in breadth, with over eleven thousand apartments. It owes its origin to the Bishop of Rome, who, in the early part of the sixth century, erected an humble residence on its site. Additions have been made

7*

by all the different Popes from that time to the present. This is the winter residence of the Pope, and is contiguous to St. Peter's. It is without doubt the richest depository of antiquities, statues and pictures in the world. When it is known that there have been exhumed more than seventy thousand statues from the mined temples and palaces of Rome, the reader can form some idea of the riches of the Vatican. The Vatican will ever be held in veneration by the student, the artist, and the scholar. Raphael and Michael Angelo are enthroned here, and their throne will be as durable as the love of beauty and genius in the hearts of their worshipers. There are almost inumerable halls and galleries, with paintings and statuary of the highest order. In the Sistine (Sistina) chapel are to be seen the celebrated paintings of Michael Angelo. Among the number is his "*Last Judgment*," which occupied him seven years. In another part we looked, with transports of delight, upon "*The Transfiguration*," the masterpiece of Raphael. With more pity than delight we noticed the painting (by Podesti) in "Commemoration of the promulgation of the dogma of the Immaculate Conception of the Virgin Mary, Pope Pius IX., 8th December, 1854."

The Museum of Sculpture is equally extensive. There is so much of it that to ferret out even what is world-renowned becomes not a little irksome; one must wade among miles of stone men and women, many of them nameless, moveless, noiseless, *senseless*. Among the famous antiques is the *Laocoön*, pronounced by many as exceeding all that the arts of painting and sculpture have ever produced. Among so much merit in painting and sculpture, there is, of course, some mere trash and rubbish.

But we now go to take a ride on the Appian Way (*Via Appia*), leading from Rome through what were known as the Pontine Marshes, to Capua. Horace describes these. When Paul was taken to Italy, he undoubtedly entered Rome by this " Way." The Roman Christians, we know, when they were apprised of his coming, journeyed to meet him at " Appii Forum and the Three Taverns." The former is only forty-three miles from Rome on this " Way," and the latter ten miles nearer, also on the great road (*Via Appia*). We pass the tombs of Scipio, Caius Cestius, and Mæcenas. At the famous tomb of Cecilia Metella, the beauties of the *Via Appia* really begin. On every hand appear the remnants of departed glory. A short distance further on we emerge from the city walls, and enjoy uninterrupted views over the extended Latin plain, strewed with ruined castles and villages, and the long line of aqueducts, to the Sabine and Alban mountains, blue in the distance, and some of them hoary with the sunny snow. The tombs and monuments which line both sides of the Appian were once rich in marble and precious stones, but have been much dismantled and robbed of their beauty and wealth by the late Pope Pius IX., and the treasures converted into relics, and sold as revenues for the Romish Church.

Whether in ancient times better roads and pavements were built than at present, or whether only the best ones remain, is uncertain; but it is certain that some of the remains of such structures found in Rome evince engineering skill and perfection of work in a high degree. These were laid out carefully, excavated to solid ground, or in swampy places made solid by piles. Then the lowest course was of small sized, broken stones, none larger than three or four inches in diameter; over these was a course, nine inches thick, of rubble or broken stone cemented with lime, well rammed; over this a course, six inches thick, of broken bricks and pottery, also cemented with lime; upon this was laid the *pavimentum*, or pavement, composed of slabs of the hardest stone, joined and fitted together as closely as possible. This was costly—the Appian Way, about one hundred and thirty miles in length, having almost exhausted the Roman treasury—but it was as enduring as Nature's own work. In Peru and Central America similar remains, fifteen hundred to two thousand miles long, were found by the Spaniards, which, as Prescott says, were built of heavy flags of freestone, and in some parts, at least, covered with a bituminous cement which time has made harder than the stone itself. The roads of modern times lack most of the elements of durability which these possessed, and consequently wear out in a very few years.

Having gone out on the Appian as far as to the neighborhood of some of the catacombs, we stop to visit some of these. The St. Calixtus being represented as the best specimen and the most interesting, we prepared to see it. Every man with his overcoat on, a lighted taper in hand, and a special guide for all, we descended a long, narrow flight of steps into the dark depths below, and were soon on our way through the many subterranean galleries. The passage-ways are sometimes regular for a considerable distance, but the multiplication of cross alleys and branches at last forms a labyrinth into which it would be rash to venture without a guide. These galleries and corridors are of various lengths and heights, generally seven to eight feet high and three to five feet wide. The tombs are excavations in the side walls, and remind one of the large shelvings in a store room. The roof is supported by that part of the tufa which is left between the passage-ways, and in these walls the tombs are excavated. The tombs that are in a good state of preservation are closed up, either with a slab of marble or with a large thin brick. Inscriptions and emblems are found sculptured or painted on many of the slabs, and in some cases a small vase, supposed to have held blood, is attached to the end of the tomb. There are also large sepulchral chambers of various shapes—square, triangular, and semicircular. These were doubtlessly family vaults, the walls of them being full of separate tombs.

The origin of the Catacombs is involved in considerable mystery. It is likely that most of them were originally quarries, which afterwards came to be used as places of burial for the dead or as hiding-places for the living. It certainly appears settled that many, if not most of the existing Catacombs, were excavated by the Christians of the first three centuries, and were used as places of refuge in the times of the earliest persecutions, for example, that of Nero. They have served three distinct purposes:

as places of burial, places of worship in times of persecution and trouble, and places of refuge for the early Christians.

We saw but few remains of the dead, and, upon the whole, were disappointed with these great under-ground receptacles. We were glad to leave the foul air and polluted odor down amongst the skeletons of past generations, and breathe the better air in the light of day.

CHAPTER XVI.

OUR LAST DAY IN ROME—CHURCHES AND FESTIVALS—PILATE'S STAIRCASE—INDULGENCES—THE PANTHEON—VICTOR EMMANUEL'S TOMB—THE MAMERTINE PRISON—PAUL AND PETER—THE INDIGNANT GUIDE—THE CAPITOL—EMANCIPATED ROME.

ON our return from the Catacombs over the Appian, passing the church Santa Maria Maggiore, and seeing so many people passing in and out its doors, we were inclined to enter and see for ourselves. We soon learned that the festival in honor of the Immaculate Conception of the Virgin Mary was being celebrated. The crowds were great, the service carried on with astonishing zeal, the confusion bewildering, and for boisterousness, amounting even to bawling, the singing exceeded anything of the kind we ever heard. The service was held in one of the chapels of the church, the Borghese, and during all this time small white flowers were showered from the dome of the chapel down to the front of the altar, imitating the miraculous fall of snow in August. This fall of snow dates to the fourth century, which also dates the erection of this church by Pope Liberius and John, a Roman Patrician, on the highest summit of the Esquiline, in commemoration of this miraculous event. The church covers the exact space on which this snow fell, and is an edifice of wonderful magnificence. One would hardly think it possible that people can be so enthusiastically wedded to such superstition and folly, and pities rather than despises the benighted people. Coming away from that festival, I thanked the Lord that I was not born in Rome.

The next day after visiting the People's Square, which contains a number of fine obelisks, prominent among which is the one brought to Rome by Augustus Cæsar from Egypt, we spent chiefly in seeing churches of historic note. Among these are the churches of St. Augustine and Santa Maria Minerva. In the former was going on the ceremony of kissing the saint's feet; in the latter, we were delighted with Michael Angelo's "Christ" and "John the Baptist." Where this church now stands, originally stood the temple of Minerva.

We also looked into the church of the Jesuits, of which sect St. Ignatio Loyola is the founder. This saint's tomb is under the altar of this church, and a magnificent life-sized statue of silver stands above the altar.

The S. Pietro in Vincoli (St. Peter in chains) is an immense church, and was founded in A. D. 442, for the reception of the chains that had bound St. Peter in prison. We happened to be present at the annual festival which is celebrated in memory of this event. We saw this chain, and judging from its massiveness, concluded that the captors of St. Peter must have regarded him a giant in strength, for it is heavy enough to hold securely an elephant. No wonder if poor Peter could not make his escape. The priests were busy with this chain, standing inside the altar, and pressing it to the lips and foreheads of the multitude as they passed by bowing to them. Our guide being one of the faithful, went through the same performance. This privilege is enjoyed only once a year. Of the monuments in this church the most remarkable are, Julius II., and Michael Angelo's famous statue of Moses. This is a grand and sublimely beautiful piece of workmanship.

From this church we passed into another not far distant, known as the Sanctus Sanctorum, the edifice which contains the famous Pilate's Staircase. These stairs consist of a flight of twenty-eight white marble steps, ten feet wide. The steps having become so greatly worn by the crowds of Christian worshipers, who sought the opportunity of going over them on their knees, it was deemed advisable to cover them with heavy boards, in which condition they now are, presenting the appearance of a wooden staircase, excepting the face of the original steps, which is still visible. These stairs are said to be the identical ones over which Christ passed in going to and from the trial chamber in Pilate's house at Jerusalem. There is some reason to believe that they are genuine, and they are said to have been brought to Rome by Helena, the mother of Constantine, in the beginning of the fourth century. On the fourth step ascending, a stain, said to be a blood-mark of our divine Lord, is carefully encased with heavy glass. No one is allowed to ascend this stairway except on his knees, and he must utter a prayer on every step. *We* didn't ascend, but saw many passing up muttering their prayers. On the Lord's day thousands of peasants crawl over these stairs and apply for indulgences, which a notice over the door announces would be granted for "the living or the dead," price, five francs apiece—($1). It was in 1510, when Luther visited Rome, and after having tried all the mummeries and ceremonies of Popery to obtain the expiation of his sins, that one day he undertook to crawl upon his knees over this staircase, to secure a certain indulgence promised by the Pope. While in the midst of his toilsome way up, repeating his prayer at each step, he heard the voice in his soul saying to him, "The just shall live by faith." He at once started up from his knees, heartily ashamed of the degradation to which his superstition had led him. This text had a mysterious influence on the life of Luther. It was by the means of those words that God then said, "Let there be light, and there was light." This was the decisive epoch in the inward life of Luther. Seven years after this he nailed to the church door at Wittenberg the ninety-five theses which inaugurated the glorious Reformation.

Near the Sanctus Sanctorum church stands the St. John Lateran, which takes the precedence even of St. Peter's in ecclesiastical rank, being, as the inscription on its facade presumptuously sets forth in Latin, "the mother and head of the state, and of all the ecclesiastical world." It is the church of the Pope, as bishop of Rome, and here his coronation takes place. It was in this church that the General Council, called the Vatican, assembled in 1869-70. It is an edifice of much magnificence; its doors are from the original Roman Forum. During our presence there was high mass, several cardinals participating. The vocal music exceeded anything of the kind we ever heard, the famous tenor singer of Rome, who is not allowed to sing anywhere except in this church, being among the choir. In the crypt of this church is a piece of sculpture by Bernini, called Piety, representing Jesus reclining in the lap of Mary. For delicacy in tracery and natural representation, it is the most perfect piece of statuary in Rome: art exhausted itself. The cross, the crown, the profile of Mary, the dying Saviour, all is the perfect workmanship of a master of skill.

But we must pass unnoticed a number of interesting places, and say a word about the Pantheon. This is the most perfect of the ancient relics of Rome; being erected twenty-seven years before the birth of Christ as a temple to the heathen gods by M. Agrippa. The original bronze doors still remain. In A. D. 608 it was consecrated as a Christian church, and is used as such now. The interior of this temple is a rotunda one hundred and forty-three feet in diameter, lighted only by a circular opening (twenty-eight feet in diameter) in the center of the dome. This is the only light the temple receives. The walls are twenty feet thick. It has become the burial place of painters, Raphael and Caracci being among the number. Victor Emmanuel is also buried here. Beautifully and well has the poet said of this old temple:

> "Simple, erect, severe, austere, sublime—
> Shrine of all saints, and temple of all gods
> From Jove to Jesus—spared and blessed by time,
> Shalt thou not last? Time's scythe and tyrant's rod
> Shiver upon thee—sanctuary and home
> Of art and piety—Pantheon, pride of Rome!"

The next place of special interest we visited was the Mamertine prison, where tradition says Peter and Paul were confined by Nero. It is considered the oldest relic of Rome, and attributed to Ancus Martius, its fourth king; the lower cell to Servius Tullius. The prison is under a small church, behind the arch of Severus, on the declivity of the Capitoline Hill. The lower cell is six and a half feet high, nineteen feet long, and nine feet wide, of Cyclopean architecture, the large stones being strongly united by iron clamps. The cell above is twenty-seven feet by nineteen feet, and fourteen feet high, hewn from the solid rock. It was in the lower cell that Paul was imprisoned. The circular aperture at the top shows where the prisoners were thrust down. As we were descending by the circular stairway into this place, our guide was careful to call our attention to a dent in the stone wall where, *he* said, "Peter struck his head in passing down, causing this mark in the wall." To believe this, one deserves to be congratulated on the robustness of his faith.

We annoyed not a little our guide, who was a true son of the Roman faith, by remarking that if the "head making the dent in that rocky wall had been Martin Luther's when in Rome instead of St. Peter's, we would not be so much surprised, for you know Luther had a very hard head!" This was sacrilegious language, and was received with the utmost disrelish by the guide, for he *believed* the story of St. Peter.

Below is the heavy stone pillar to which Paul, with the soldiers, was chained. Near by is the well which miraculously sprang there for the comfort of Paul. The thing to do is to drink of its water; of course we did not fail to do so. We put the Church of Rome against the world for the invention of myths and plausible nonsense. Second Timothy contains several allusions to Paul's second and *severe* imprisonment, and it may be that it was here, in this imprisonment he wrote 2 Timothy, justly called his "last testament." He was taken thence bound and in fetters to the Salvian waters, about three miles from Rome, where, on the 29th of June, A. D. 66, and in the sixty-eighth year of his age, he closed his life of persecution and trial by being beheaded, about the same time that St. Peter was crucified.

It was late in the afternoon that we visited the Capitol. On our way thither we passed the triumphal arch of Constantine, erected after his victory over Maxentius near Rome, A. D. 311. It is the best preserved and the most beautiful of Roman arches, but a singular testimony of the meanest vanity. The Capitol stands one hundred feet above the Tiber. On our approach to it we passed under the arch of Titus which stands at the summit of the Via Sacra (Sacred Way) so well remembered by the classical student as the favorite promenade of Horace, and as the route by which triumphal processions passed to the temple of Jupiter. The ancient pavement of the Sacred Way, composed of lava, still remains.

The Capitol is approached by a magnificent stairway. The open space in front of the building marks the place where Brutus harangued the people after the murder of Cæsar. The Senate chamber sleeps somber under the shadows of departed glory. The Capitoline museum contains a vast collection of sculptures, less extensive than that of the Vatican, but including some of the most famous antiques, such as the Dying Gladiator, the Venus of the Capitol, and the Faun of Praxiteles. Of course the picture gallery is also there, and has many rare paintings.

But we must leave the Capitol, with many things unsaid, and also get ready to leave the Holy City. We might indulge in many reflections; one or two must do. As we wandered amid the ruins of Rome, attesting its ancient splendor, we were constantly reminded of the power of Christianity in the overthrow of the numerous heathen temples, broken columns, and crumbling palaces. While the Roman religion is still dominant (and much superstition yet remains), yet the people are free, no longer the miserable vassals of the Pope, and the Rome of the present is a cradle of liberty compared with what it was before Victor Emmanuel's army marched into the city. Light is breaking more and more, and the people fear not to proclaim their independence. We believe that the mayor of Rome represented the true sentiment of his constituents when he said, at a recent banquet, that they "would rather see the city laid in ashes than given over again to papal domination." Hopefully we say, "Adieu to Rome."

CHAPTER XVII.

FROM ROME TO NAPLES—THE CITY OF NAPLES—ITS PEOPLE—POMPEII—THE BURIED CITY—THE WORK OF EXCAVATION—OLD COLLEGE FRIENDS—THE TESTIMONY TO THE WRITINGS OF ST. PAUL.

THERE is nothing specially interesting in scenery between Rome and Naples. The country generally is low and flat, and in August much of it parched and dry. We noticed an Eastern threshing scene, however, which greatly interested us. There was the elevated threshing-floor and the oxen making their rounds, drawing the threshing machine, formed of a heavy square frame with rollers, each of which was encircled by iron rings or wheels serrated like the teeth of a saw. In this way the grain was separated from the straw and chaff on the threshing-floor. Near by was the man with a large shovel, winnowing the grain by throwing it up in the air, the wind driving away the chaff, and the grain remaining in a heap before him.

It was near midnight when we reached Naples, but the city presented the appearance of a gay holiday. Everybody seemed outdoors, and every variety of business and trade conceivable was carried on in the streets. A regular moving panorama was witnessed in every direction. Carriages and vehicles were running all night; and the merry peals of laughter and cracking of whips during the small hours, showed that their occupants were seeking pleasure and enjoyment.

After a long ride through the city we reached our hotel, *The Metropole*, situated on the beautiful bay. My chamber window looked out over the Mediterranean, and the silvery way of the bright moon upon its waters produced a marvel of beauty.

The next day we spent in looking about in Naples, and arranged for an excursion to Pompeii. "See Naples and die," may do to say, but if this saying means that to see Naples is to have seen all that is worth seeing, we should judge the man very foolish to die, if he had the controlling of that serious event. Especially would we prefer not to die just *then* and in *Naples*. Naples is very ancient, but not the perfection of beauty, and certainly not of glory. The city was founded by the people of Cumae, a colony of Greece, who gradually spread themselves around the Bay of Naples, and was called from this circumstances *Neapolis*, or "New City." It has a population of five hundred thousand people. The country around it is rich in beautiful scenery. It is principally in respect to situation that this city surpasses most others, being partly built on a spacious bay in crescent shape, on the shores of which are magnificent villas and gardens. Most of the streets are well paved with square blocks of lava laid in mortar, and said to resemble old Roman roads. Naples carries on immense business operations, the throng on the streets being very great, the rush and noise almost bewildering. Owing to the mildness of the climate, much of the business is carried on in the open streets, and you can purchase almost anything you wish without entering a building.

There is a greater combination of street scenes in Naples than any other city we have ever seen. Elegance and squalid poverty move side by side. Men and beasts of all kinds huddle together, and seem to understand each other wonderfully well. The little donkey intrudes himself upon your view on any way you may chose to walk. Every household has its donkey, and almost every direction you take you see women perched high upon top of the loaded animal, carrying a perfect variety store, the donkey braying as loud as an elephant at every donkey acquaintance that may pass him, and the women screaming at the top of their voices in efforts to sell their wares. What harmonious sounds swell the air! Coming suddenly into an Italian community, where all the active pursuits of life are in full progress, you imagine from the violent gesticulations and loud emphatic language, that a general quarrel is in progress. But nothing could be further from the truth, for Naples is an orderly city, though it is noisy. It is the nature of the Italian to be noisy. The Neapolitans are happy. They look happy, talk happy, and are a jovial people in all grades of life, from the lazzaroni to the prince. Goldsmith's picture of Itallian manners and morals is more applicable here than in any other portion of Italy we know of:

> "But small the bliss that sense alone bestows.
> And sensual bliss is all the nation knows.
> In florid beauty groves and fields appear,
> Man seems the only growth that dwindles here.

> Contrasted faults through all his manners reign;
> Though poor, luxurious; though submissive, vain;
> Though grave, yet trifling; zealous, yet untrue;
> And, even in penance, planning sins anew."

The nobility are fond of great show and splendor. The females are proud, even when very poor. They seldom go out unless to ride, and bestow great pains and time upon their personal charms to fascinate the opposite sex. The principal promenade of the ladies is upon their own roofs, which are generally adorned with shrubs and flowers.

Naples is of course not without its many churches, some being very remarkable for their architecture and works of art. It also has its fine museum. Here we saw the collection of ancient frescoes found at Herculaneum and Pompeii. Some of the subjects are beautifully portrayed; others are abiding testimonials of the shameful and disgusting state of morals that prevailed in those buried cities of the past.

But we must leave Naples, and pass on to Pompeii. We proceeded by rail to Annunziata, a small town fifteen miles distant, and thence four miles further by carriage to the gates of Pompeii. With our loquacious guide, who puts many languages into one, we pass in, taking our course through the cemetery where we inspected the cremation furnace—for the Romans burnt their dead—and soon we were walking in the streets of Pompeii, that most weird and wonderful of all cities. It is well known to my readers that this city was overwhelmed in the year 79 by the terrific eruption of Mt. Vesuvius, at whose foot the city stood, and continued to be buried under the ashes and other volcanic matter for seventeen centuries. For many centuries its very site was unknown. At length, in 1689, some ruins were noticed, but it was not until 1755, when the peasants were employed in cutting a ditch, that ruins of the city were discovered, since which time the Neapolitan government has continued the work of excavation almost constantly to the present.

The remains found are in a remarkably good state of preservation, owing to the fact that the city was not destroyed by lava, but by showers of sand, ashes, and cinders, forming a light covering, which found its way into every nook, and, as it were, hermetically sealed up the town. It would appear that in some parts at least the matter was deposited in a liquid state, and so flowed into the remotest cellars of the doomed habitations. The immense volumes of water which poured down mixed with the ashes that had already fallen and with those that were still suspended in the air, and formed a kind of liquid mud. This is proved by the discovery of quite a number of skeletons in cellars, of men and women, enclosed in moulds of volcanic paste, which received and have retained perfect impressions of their forms. The houses were plain, closely built, and low, being seldom more than two stories high, and had all their good apartments on the ground floor. The city is about two miles in circumference, and is surrounded by a wall. The streets are extremely narrow, and it is evident that not more than one vehicle could pass at one time in any but the principal thoroughfares. They are well paved, and bordered by a narrow pavement and curb-stone, elevated about a foot above the carriage way. You see the wheel-worn streets, the ruts in the stones cut there by the gay chariots when Christ was walking by the sea of Galilee two thousand years ago, and also where were baths and dressing-rooms and dining-rooms and work-shops, where the living multitude had moved and luxuriated and toiled. There are the beer-shops, with the marks of the tumblers still fresh on the marble counter, with the brothel and theatre and dancing-hall near by. There too stands a tavern, with the rings yet entire to which the horses were hitched, and where the bones of a mother and three children were found locked in each other's arms, decked with gold ornaments elaborately worked, and enriched with pendant pearls of great value. The public bake-house is still there. It has four mills in it. The oven is precisely after the fashion of the ovens of bakers of the present day. There, too, in a marble niche, by the gate which looked toward the burning mountain, is the place where stood the faithful sentinel on that fatal day when Vesuvius burst out into an eruption, and, amid the noise of a hundred thunders, buried the fated city. After seventeen centuries they found the skeleton of the sentinel standing erect at his post, clad in his rusty armor, the helmet on his empty skull, and his bony fingers still closed upon his spear. He was "faithful unto death."

We were also in the houses of Sallust, one of the largest in the city, and of great elegance, and of the tragic poet, called the House of Homer. These dear old friends of our college days, how could we pass by their homes, having come so far? It is true, they often gave us much trouble and subjected us to hard work, early and late; but having learned the benefit of such toil, as well as reaped its good fruits, we generously forgave the ancient worthies all.

And now we pass into the houses of the nobility and the learned writers of those early days. The first one is the villa of *Diomede*. On the night of the eruption, the owner of this once splendid mansion appears to have lost the love of kindred in the eagerness to save life; for his skeleton was found, with that of an attendant, near the garden gate, the one still holding in his bony grasp the key to the villa, the other carrying a purse containing one hundred gold and silver coins, and some silver vases. While he was thus endeavoring to escape to the sea-shore, the members of his family, whom he had abandoned to their fate, took refuge in the wine-cellar, where seventeen of their skeletons were found near the door.

From the golden bracelets on the necks and arms of nearly all these skeletons, it would appear that they were nearly all females. Two were the skeletons of children, whose skulls still retained some portions of beautiful blonde hair. "After they had perished, probably from suffocation, the floor of the cellar was inundated with a fine alluvium, which hardened on the bodies and took casts, not only of their forms, but even of the most delicate texture of the linen they wore, and of the jewels which adorned their persons." One cast of a young girl, part of which we saw in the museum, was a perfect model of female beauty.

The Forum is a spacious and imposing spot, surrounded by the temple of Jupiter, the temple of Venus, and the Senate chamber. In a vault under the stairway of the latter, which was used as a prison during the progress of trials, were found two skeletons with their ankles menacled. Among the inscriptions under the portico of the Senate chamber were some verses from Ovid's Art of Love.

Besides these public places, we also noticed many buildings with their utensils of trade in them, wine shops, oil factories with their jars of stone, and restaurants. Others had signs denoting the trade that was carried on in them. Thus, a goat indicated a milk-shop or dairy; two men carrying a large jug indicated a wine-shop; two men fighting indicated a gladiatorial school; a man whipping a boy hoisted on another's back indicated a school-master. Some of the houses of bad repute remain marked to the present day by indelicate figures carved above the door.

If we had nothing more to prove the authenticity, as well as credibility of Paul's epistle to the Romans, than the paintings and indelicately carved figures still extant within and on the outside of many houses in Pompeii, these alone would be sufficient. Here remains, self-proved, in paintings and sculpture, the very dreadful state of immorality which St. Paul so graphically describes especially in the first chapter to the Romans; and this epistle was written by the apostle about twenty years before the destruction of Pompeii.

In the museum of Pompeii one sees a variety of things

taken from its ruins. Here are bodies of the dead in petrified stone, the bones yet complete, rings on the fingers; one man lying on his right side (resting his head on his hand), asleep when the city was overwhelmed. Among the household effects we saw such as loaves of bread, a nest of eggs, prunes, lamps, locks, ropes, dogs and cats.

The melancholy destitution of such a city, as one walks in its deserted streets and open houses, cannot fail to awaken feelings of awe and sympathy. The stillness that reigns falls like a shadow on the spirit. As another says:

"How sadly echoing the stranger's tread,
Those walls respond, like voices from the dead."

Everything is there that belonged to a great and opulent city, but the inhabitants. As you pass out you look back upon the disentombed city, and beyond it on Vesuvius, standing solemn, grand and lonely, sending up its steady column of fire and smoke, a perpetual tombstone for the dead at its feet. You can see the track of the lava in its wild and fiery march for the sea, and imagine just how the cloud of ashes rose from the summit and came flying toward the terror-stricken city, covering it twenty feet above the tops of the houses—and the gay, pleasure-loving and licentious city lay buried as century after century rolled by, till nearly seventeen hundred years had passed away before the first opening was made into the hill that covered it.

CHAPTER XVIII.

MOUNT VESUVIUS—ITS ASCENT BY MOONLIGHT—THE CARRIAGE WAY—THE ROPE RAILROAD—THE INCIDENT AT THE BATTLE OF GETTYSBURG—ON FOOT—THE ENCOUNTER WITH PROFESSIONAL GUIDES—ACROSS THE SULPHUR BEDS—THE BURNING MOUNTAIN—THE FINAL ASCENT—LOOKING INTO THE CRATER—THE SUBTERRANEAN THUNDERS—OUR RETREAT—THE BEAUTIFUL PROSPECT OF LAND AND SEA—WHAT VOLCANOES CAN DO.

After having spent a day in examining Pompeii, we proceeded by rail in the evening to Portici, situated at the foot of Mt. Vesuvius, and ten miles distant from Pompeii. In order to escape the heat of the day, and also to see Vesuvius to its best advantage, it was determined to make its ascent by night. It is safe to say that one who has never ascended this mountain can form no idea of its many and strange wonders. Looking at it from Naples as it rolls its column of white smoke perpetually into the sky, or reading all the numerous descriptions that have been given of it, or viewing it in engravings and paintings, can give but a very faint idea of what it is in reality. Viewing it from a distance, or at its base, and scanning its mighty proportions, one becomes possessed with a desire that amounts almost to intensity, to ascend this wonderful mountain. To have been up and back again is quite a feat, but, as a rule, one does not care to repeat it.

In company with three others, we took our seat in a carriage drawn by three excellent horses hitched abreast, and started from the railway station at nine o'clock in the evening, passing through the town of Portici. We passed through this place also on our return, when we had a view of true Italian life among the poorer class of people. The sights were "stunning." To see children of both sexes, from two to ten years old, running about the streets by day and night in a perfectly nude state; cattle and people herded together, making one family; the streets reeking with filth, the air loaded with stifling odors, the absence of all modesty and delicacy among the people—all this forcibly and sadly impressed us with the great need of the refining and elevating influences of our holy Christianity. These people have no idea of proper family life and home training. Their teachers have possibly never taught them better, for generally Rome succeeds best where it can keep its people in the greatest darkness, and in utter ignorance of all that would advance them in civilization, and make them capable of self-government. In this town, as in others in Italy, we saw, with few exceptions, no clean and tidy children, nor any of those evidences of rural comforts and happiness which are so common in the towns and rural districts of our own country. With the Italians the rule is filth and stench, beggars and fleas.

But now we pass out of Portici. It was a mild, clear night; the moon was in her prime, and the stars shone out like gems of crystallized light, without a single cloud to obscure their glorious radiance. We ascend gradually among cultivated fields and vineyards, occasionally traversing streams of old lava, black, rough and sterile.

As we ascend higher we now and then get glimpses of the burning mountain in front of us, while to our right lies the beautiful city of Naples, in crescent form, on the shore of its delightful bay. And now, as if to compete with the wonderful fireworks on top of the mountain, suddenly the city below bursts into a great glow of brightness by the ten thousand sky-rockets that shoot into the air with their colored lights, and the people rejoice in one of their numerous festivities. The scene was kept up for several hours, and was one of its own, for we cannot describe it.

Now we pass the fine mansion of an Italian nobleman who delights to call this his summer residence. To build so stately a mansion on so uncertain a foundation as the side of a burning mountain is not a little surprising, but may not be so inconsistent after all when we remember the extreme fondness the European noblemen have for "building castles in the air."

After a most delightful ride of three hours we reached the end of the carriage-way, and "put up" in a small house that passes for a hotel, hung on the side of the mountain. Here we remained from midnight till three o'clock in the morning. Sleep did not come to us readily in such a place and amid such surroundings. At three a. m. we took our places in the single car at the station of the *Ferrovia Funicalore di Vesovo*, or Vesuvian Rope Railway. The station is nothing more than a wooden shanty, sufficiently enduring until the next eruption has brushed both station and railway off the side of the mountain. This railroad is one mile and a half long, and of very peculiar construction. It goes straight up the mountain, a grade of thirty-five degrees. The line is a double one; but the carriages, of which there are two—one ascending while the other descends—run each on a single rail raised about a foot from the bed of the road on the massive sleeper. The wheels are placed beneath the carriage in a line along the centre of its floor, and on these wheels the carriage is balanced in what seems a very uncanny fashion astride the high rail. An endless wire rope working over large pulleys at the upper and lower stations is fixed to each carriage; and the rope being set in motion by a stationary engine below, one carriage mounts while the other descends the steep gradient of more than thirty degrees. Considering the exorbitant fares charged, it would not seem to be an unusual stretch of the imagination to believe that the president of this railroad soliloquized something like this: "Let us cut down our expenses to the lowest cent, and squeeze as much money as we can to-day from tourists and students of nature, for to-morrow the mountain may be on the rampage, and all our money-making machines disappear."

But now off we go up the inclined railway. A feeling akin to helplessness takes hold of one just then. The electric lights along the way, the gliding through the air, the brightness of the moon, the burning, moaning and thundering mountain, the great lava-beds stretching far away on every side, with the strong fumes of sulphur loading the air—all this formed a weird sight, and produced next to an indescribable sensation. We dared hardly think of the imminent peril we were in, or of the sudden destruction that might come upon us from the fiery mouth of the mountain above.

Being in such a place and amid such surroundings, in order to divert the attention as well as the *tension* of the minds and nerves of our traveling companions *chiefly*, we thought it good to tell the incident of the man at the battle of Gettysburg. This soldier, becoming greatly excited, and no doubt thinking of his family, in the thickest of the fight exclaimed: "Poys, dis is no place for a man mid a wife and five childs at home!"

But after ten minutes' ride we were at the terminus of the railroad, and leaving the car we were off on a long heavy tramp over a rugged and steep path, deep at places with ashes, and flanked by walls of rough scoriæ. We had scarcely proceeded on our way when four stalwart men confronted us, declaring themselves professional guides—that intolerable nuisance—and insisting upon it that each of us must pay them fifteen francs ($3) before we could go on our way, and then they would act as guides. Of course we objected, telling them that we had arranged and paid for a round trip from Naples to the top of the mountain and return, and that we would accept of no guides. This set them to yelling and screaming and to vehement gesticulating in true Italian style, and at the same time declaring that they were responsible for the lives of all tourists who ascended the mountain, and that we could not go a step forward without their permission. We at once took in the situation, and suiting our actions to our words we began to move off and upward, utterly ignoring their threats and prohibitions. On and up we made our way, slowly, laboriously; the top of the mountain, hidden until now by the slope of the cone, came suddenly into view, a dense cloud of white smoke issuing from the crater, brilliantly illuminated by immense flames of fire, accompanied by intermittent discharges of burning cinders and ashes, shot high into the air. A few paces more, quickened by the inspiration of the scene before us, and, passing over a low brow at the summit of the great cone, we found ourselves in front of a small hut of roughly thrown together lava blocks, and we have gained the top of the great cone. Here we rested and enjoyed the awful prospect. Yonder stands the burning cone, belching forth immense volumes of fire and smoke, the mountain heaving and laboring, roaring and moaning, under its weary toil.

At the first dawn of day we started to cross over the sulphur-beds, of fifty yards width, which lay between us and the fiery crater. This plateau is covered with a rough crest of sulphur, serpentine shape, whose brilliant tints of yellow and orange and green were beautiful with reptilian beauty. At its farther edge rises the final cone of Vesuvius; a steep mound of black clinkers several hundred feet high, like the cinder heaps around a great iron-works. From its mouth rose a thick column of light-colored smoke, and at intervals of a few seconds a deep, soft roar was heard, like the rushing of distant waters, and a gush of ashes and flames and fiery lumps of cinder shot up hundreds of feet into the air, with a speed gradually decreasing till they reached their culminating point, where they hovered for a moment before they went swooping downward into the crater again. *Such* fireworks are only seen on Vesuvius by night. The guides again beset us, but we fought them off, and picked our way over the treacherous floor of reeking sulphur. Our party consisting of three clergymen and one lawyer, we had both the law and gospel on our side, and of course gained a victory over the would-be guides. Walking over the furrowed and fissured field of crisp sulphur was enough to create a strange sensation. We soon found ourselves on extremely hot places—it was hot everywhere —intolerable to the hand, and standing still fatal to the soles of our shoes. All about us teemed hot vapors of sulphur, almost taking away our breath, causing us to halt and cough spasmodically every half dozen steps we made. Smoke issued from numerous crevices, at the the entrance of which a piece of paper or a stick took fire almost instantly. Stooping low, we could hear the noise like that of a liquid boiling. But now we have passed over the basin and reached the base of the final cone, up which we must crawl to have a look into the fiery crater. This last ten minutes' work up this steep slope of moving cinders was more fatiguing than all that had gone before. The sulphurous fumes curling up between every crevice grew stronger, and the heat under our feet even greater.

After an earnest struggle for victory, we were at the top and on the edge of the crater, and walking on, amid fumes of sulphur and heated air, for about fifty paces, we gained a position where we looked down into the deep, yawning chasm—a sea of rolling, sweeping flames threatening to swallow up and consume the entire mountain. One side of the crater is smooth and horizontal as if built of solid masonry. We could hear terrific reports of the subterranean thunder. Now and then vast sheets of flame and red-hot cinders would shoot hundreds of feet over our heads, and set us dodging here and there, or absurdly ducking our heads and shrugging our shoulders. Our situation was not a pleasant one; the mountain quaked, the heat was intense, the sulphur fumes almost stifling; and it did not take us long to be ready and willing to retrace our steps.

We soon turned our back on the fiery lake in that mountain crown of untold depths, and retired in rather disorderly fashion, coughing and sliding, stumbling and tumbling down the scorching hot cinder cone, until we reached the lava rampart which bounds the solid sulphur bed below. Here, breathing freely once more, we sat down that early morning and enjoyed the spacious prospect of land and sea. Four thousand feet below us lay Naples, with its beautiful sea-line; beyond the bay, with Capri and Ischia, slumbering in the blue waters. In another direction we see the ships standing afar off in the great wide sea, the fleecy clouds encircling them as with robes of white light, while inland rose Vesuvius with its everlasting plume of smoke and fire swaying in the wind, the bright blue Italian sky arching over us—all presenting a view that can never fade from our memory. Weary and jaded we reached Naples awhile before noon, wiser for having been on Mount Vesuvius—but content not to go again.

It is not often that tourists venture to ascend the last cone of Mt. Vesuvius, from which point alone one can see down into the crater. It is, to say the least, venturesome and decidedly dangerous, from the fact that at any moment an eruption may take place. Only a few days after our ascent the great mountain was fiercely shaken by volcanic action, the fiery rockets flying in all directions and the lava flowing freely in fiery streams. All the inhabitants about the mountain, and even the people of Naples, fourteen miles distant, are much exercised whenever the mountain becomes more than ordinarily restless. Neither is this surprising when we remember what volcanoes can do.

Cotopaxi, in 1838, threw its fiery rockets three thousand feet above its crater, while in 1854 the blazing mass, struggling for an outlet, roared so that its awful voice was heard at a distance of more than six hundred miles. In 1797 the crater of Tuangurangua, one of the great peaks of the Andes, flung out torrents of mud, which dammed up the rivers, opened new lakes, and in valleys a thousand feet wide made deposits six hundred feet deep. The stream from Vesuvius, which, in 1337, passed through Torre del Greco, contained thirty-two thousand cubic feet of solid matter, and, in 1703, when Torre del Greco was destroyed a second time, the mass of lava amounted to 45,000,000 cubic feet.

In 1760 Aetna poured forth a flood which covered

eighty-four square miles of surface, and measured nearly 1,000,000,000 cubic feet. On this occasion the sand and scoria formed the Monte Rosini, near Nicholosa, a cone of two miles in circumference and four thousand feet high. The stream thrown out by Aetna in 1816 was in motion, at the rate of a yard a day, for nine months after the eruption; and it is on record that the lava of the same mountain, after a terrible eruption, was not thoroughly cool and consolidated for ten years after the event. In the eruption of Vesuvius, A. D. 79, the scoria and ashes which belched forth far exceeded the entire bulk of the mountain; while, in 1860, Aetna disgorged twenty times its own mass. Vesuvius has sent its ashes as far as Constantinople, Syria, and Egypt; it hurled stones eight pounds in weight to Pompeii, a distance of ten miles, while similar masses were tossed up two thousand feet above the summit. Cotopaxi has projected a block of one hundred cubic yards in volume, a distance of nine miles; and Sumbawa, in 1815, during the most terrible eruption on record, sent its ashes as far as Java, a distance of three hundred miles.

Such being the power of volcanoes, it is not a matter of surprise in the least that people living in their vicinity should become anxious and nervous whenever these fiery mountains are given to more than ordinary eruptions.

CHAPTER XIX.

FROM ITALY INTO SWITZERLAND—SOME REFLECTIONS—PISA—
GENOA—TURIN—OVER THE ALPS—MONT CENIS TUNNEL—
GENEVA—JOHN CALVIN'S HOUSE—MONT BLANC.

HAVING reached the farthest point of our journey, we retraced our steps from Naples and returned to Rome, where we spent the night and part of the next day resting. Taking it all together, we were pleased and certainly profited by our visit to Italy, but still were not sorry when our tour was completeted. There is no country in Europe more replete with interest and instruction to the tourist, but the Italians are not, to our taste, the most desirable people to live among. There is no doubt much refinement and great elegance, but misery and wretchedness, consequent upon squalid poverty, largely preponderate. Sidney Smith summed up his experience in Italy by asserting that whilst the old Italians were all Jupiters, the present race were all Jew-Peters. Adepts as they still are in taking advantage of tourists, it is believed that they are greatly improved for the better of late years. They, no doubt, are as well advanced in morals and intelligence as other people, considering the training they have received, and the oppressive ecclesiastical hierarchy under which they have lived so long. As a rule, people do not grow in advance of their teachers. But under present rule in Italy, both the country and its people are improving. On the day that Victor Emmanuel marched with his army into Rome, regeneratian commenced in Italy, and the present King, Humbert, is carrying on the good work with energy and success. The only drawbacks seem to be the soldiers and the priests. Perhaps the former, under existing circumstances, are a necessity ; but the latter certainly are not. About every twentieth man you meet is a priest or a friar, but for all this great excess of ecclesiastics, the people do not evince any excess of piety. Judging from appearance, and the great dislike, which even amounts to hatred, that the people cherish for this class of idlers, it is evident that most of them would do better for themselves, and be of more profit to Italy, if they would work in the vineyards on the hills than in the vineyard of the Lord.

But for all this, the darkness of ignorance and superstition are giving way under the light of a better dispensation. Blind faith is being supplanted by enlightened trust in Him who alone can forgive sins. The religion which destroyed humanity is losing its hold, for that which saves and emancipates and redeems. Truly, "the entrance of Thy word giveth light."

But we now take our final leave of Rome, and are on our way to Pisa. Our way lay along the shores of the beautiful Mediterranean, and afforded us many delightful views from our car window. The day being bright and cool, we greatly enjoyed the ride and the rest. Excepting the numerous walled towns through which we passed, and the many castles perched on the tops of hills and mountains, there was nothing of special interest in the country which we traversed. It was late at night when we reached Pisa, and sleep came unbidden, and much refreshed us for our next day's work.

Pisa is a beautiful city, situated on the north bank of the Arno. It was formerly the capital of one of Italy's most celebrated republics. In its palmiest days it had a population of one hundred and fifty thousand; at present it numbers but thirty thousand. It is celebrated for its profusion of fine marble. Its principal attractions are the Cathedral, the Baptistery, the Leaning Tower, and Campo Santo. The cathedral is a magnificent structure, and contains many fine paintings, and the famed twelve altars designed by Michael Angelo. At the end of the nave is suspended the large and beautiful bronze lamp, the swinging of which first suggested to Galileo the theory of the pendulum. He was then but eighteen years of age.

The Leaning Tower is a world-wide curiosity. Every school-boy looks at its picture in his geography, wondering and puzzled. It is extraordinary, not for its beauty so much as for its inclination from the perpendicular. It is one hundred and ninety feet in height, consisting of eight stories, with outside galleries projecting seven feet. It contains a peal of six large bells, the heaviest weighing six tons. The topmost story overhangs the base on one side about fifteen feet. Looking at it, you wonder that it does not fall, but it has stood leaning in this way for seven hundred years. Some have thought the inclination was intentional, but it is pretty certain that it was caused by an unequal settling of the foundation. When it is remembered that the ground in the neighborhood is porous and almost marshy, this seems a probable, as well as a reasonable solution of the Tower's leaning.

The Campo Santo or burial ground is a curious spot, and greatly interests the stranger. It is surrounded by a stone wall forty-three feet high, and roofed toward the centre. Archbishop Waldo, in 1188, after the loss of the Holy Land, had conveyed hither fifty ship-loads of earth from Mount Calvary, in order that the dead might repose in holy ground.

But it is train time, and we are again on our way, flying along the blue Mediterranean, refreshed with its cool breezes and interested in the whales we see here and there, disporting themselves in the beautiful sea. The railroad, all the way from Pisa to Genoa, is a wonder in itself, being tunneled for many miles through solid rock projecting out into the sea. We were sorry that our time did not allow us to remain at Genoa, the birth-place of Columbus, longer than simply to take lunch, and see the great walls that surround this interesting city.

The evening brought us to Turin, where we spent the night and part of a day. This we found to be a city of marked beauty and great attractiveness. Its cleanliness is a marvel. Its public squares and gardens, adorned with fountains and flowers artistically arranged, are unsurpassed anywhere. The city is bright, and presents every appearance of thrift and wealth. At night it is brilliant with gaslight, and puts on the appearance of a great holiday. Nightly there are numerous open concerts given in the large squares, an abundance of fine music, as well as of wine and beer; but with all, the best order prevails. There are those who say that Turin is the finest city in Italy. Whilst there is so much to commend, yet it was here that we fell into the hands of a hotel man who proved himself a first-class rogue; but we will always have the satisfaction of knowing that he did not succeed in his roguery upon us. When you go to Turin, avoid the *Hotel Trombetta*.

But the hour arrived for our final departure from Italy over the Alps to Geneva. This time we go by rail, not by *diligence*. After leaving Turin we had many indications of getting into a better country. For many miles we had the river Po on our right, and the far-off snowy peaks of the Alps to our left. Near midday we found ourselves in the midst of the sublimest mountain scenery, and much refreshed by a cooler atmosphere. A little farther on, and we passed through many tunnels; but now we reached the mouth of the famous Mont Cenis tunnel. It is five miles in length, and required twenty-eight minutes to pass through it. It has a double track, and is well lighted by means of large lamps hung at close intervals. Its masonry is a wonder for beauty and strength. Twelve years ago this railroad and the completion of this tunnel were celebrated as the great uniting link between Italy and Switzerland.

And now we are in Switzerland, at Modena, where we had lunch, and our luggage examined. A short ride brought us into the Savoy country of the Alps, the most elevated tract in Europe. Here we saw signs of thrift and industry. The people seemed happy as they gathered their wheat and other various grains from the mountain sides, and their abundant crop of hay from the beautiful, dark-green meadows. An air of repose and quiet reigns amid these beautiful mountains and green valleys. The scenery is truly sublime. Here and there nestle the quiet villages, and always conspicuous amid the humble homes is the little church with its white steeple pointing heavenward. The people are honest, intelligent, religious, and enthusiastically patriotic. To our left we passed the great mountain range which buried at its feet a large number of villages some years ago. There stands the long range of bare rocks, a perpetual monument to the many hundreds of poor Savoyards who sleep beneath its earth and rocks. Toward the close of the day we reached the charming lake Bourged, a sheet of water unsurpassed in beauty, sleeping quietly in the bosom of the great mountains. This lake is seven miles in length and from one to two in breadth. We almost made a complete circuit of it. Next we reached the valley of the Rhine, and passing over large tracts of meadow land, we crossed the Rhone just after sunset. Soon the darkness of the night overtook us, and at 11 p. m. we arrived in Geneva, and soon were quartered at the *Hotel and Pension Flaegel.*

After the rapid and constant traveling of the last fifteen days, Geneva proved a most delightful resting-place for three days. It is a beautiful city of fifty thousand inhabitants, and much admired by strangers. It is mostly well built, and parts of it remind one somewhat of Paris. Its population is lively and gay. While amusements were made the order of the day by many on Sunday, yet many people attended religious worship. We spent the quietest and most home-like Lord's day in Geneva of all such days on the Continent. We attended the American English church, where we heard a good practical sermon, and much enjoyed the service. This is a church erected and kept up by the Episcopal Church of our own country.

Geneva is the great emporium of European watches and jewelry manufacture. Five thousand people are employed in this business, and as many as one hundred thousand watches are turned out yearly. Its lake is unsurpassed in beauty, and is the largest in Switzerland. The river Rhone passes out of the lake directly through the city, and rushes with wonderful speed. Both sides of the stream are adorned with fine quays and houses, the hills forming a beautiful background. The water, like that of the lake, is remarkably clear, the smallest pebbles being visible at a depth of fifteen feet, whilst great quantities of fish dart about in the rapid current.

The confluence of the rivers Rhone and Arve, a short distance below the city, is a very remarkable sight. The Rhone, rushing with arrowy speed from the blue lake, is joined by the Arve, a turbid stream from the Chamouny glaciers. At the point of junction it is possible to dip one hand in the warm water of the Rhone, and the other in the Arve, as cold as ice. The two rivers run together in the same bed for many miles without mingling—an emblem of the good and the evil, the clean and the unclean.

We did not forget to see the house where John Calvin lived. In his day, no doubt, it was a mansion of considerable note; at present it is a very humble, out-of-the-way place.

We could see Mont Blanc in the distance lifting his sublime heights covered with snow, but had not time to approach it.

In closing this chapter we wish to say that of all the cities we visited in Europe, of few have we more pleasant recollections than of Geneva.

CHAPTER XX.

FROM SWITZERLAND INTO GERMANY—THE LAND OF LUTHER—DARMSTADT—A MISFORTUNE — FRANKFORT-ON-THE-MAIN — EISENACH—URSULA COTTA—THE LUTHER HOUSE—GERMAN HOSPITALITY—THE WARTBURG—THE LUTHER ROOM—THE FAMOUS INKSTAND STORY.

IT was with some reluctance that we bade adieu to Geneva, one of the loveliest places in the old world; but knowing that we were going amongst a people and scenes still more interesting to us, we were soon reconciled to the change, and started alone on a tour of twelve hundred miles, which would embrace a number of Luther places we had not visited when in Germany a few months previous.

We left Geneva at noon for Frankfort, and greatly enjoyed our journey. A mere pen picture, however well drawn, could give but a very faint idea of the lovely scenery which lies along the lake of Geneva. For many miles the railway skirts the high shores of the lake with its waters in full view. Charmed and delighted, the eye feasts on beautiful green hills and clustering vineyards, white villas and blooming gardens. Nothing that we have seen in Europe equalled this in loveliness. Leaving the shores of the lake, we passed through a rich grazing country, its hills and meadows robed in the deepest green. Quiet and perfect content marked every cottage and hamlet, and we concluded again that the Swiss must be a happy people.

It was late in the evening when we reached Bâle, a border city of Switzerland, but our time would not permit us to stop, and we continued our journey all night, reaching Darmstadt (Germany) early the next morning. Here we met with what seemed a misfortune. The train stopping for five minutes, we stepped out on the platform, but the train moving slowly, we attempted to re-enter our car. The train despatcher, standing close by, remarked to us that " der zūg "—the train—would return again in a few moments. Having waited as we thought long enough, and not seeing our train return, we followed two Frenchmen to another part of the depot, hoping to find our car there. We failed, however, in finding it, and by the time we returned to our former place our train had backed in, and we were just in time to see it go out at the other end of the depot, carrying with it all our baggage. The gaze after that train was surely earnest, but useless. At the same time our friend, the train despatcher, who no doubt greatly pitied us, came running in full speed, and in a very excited manner exclaimed, " My dear Sir, I thought you understood what I told you!" We replied; " Yes, Sir, we did, but we became uneasy and followed two French gentlemen over to the other side of the depot, and by that missed our car." " What a pity! What a pity!" he said, " One should *never* follow a *Frenchman*, only to stick him in the back with a bayonet." Our friend was very kind, and began to comfort us by assuring us that our baggage was not lost. He sent the necessary telegram on to Frankfort, and when we reached there, a few hours later, we found our effects all " safe and sound."

Being delayed at Darmstadt for two hours, we had the pleasure of witnessing a soldiers' parade. There were several regiments of infantry and one of cavalry. For soldierly appearance, fine uniforms, and general good equipments, we never saw anything to surpass these men and officers. We thought, no wonder they were too much for the French. An hour's ride brought us to Frankfort. With this city we were greatly pleased. It numbers nearly one hundred thousand inhabitants, and is distinguished for its wealth and industries. Here we have the old and the new of Germany. The business sections of the city are very fine, the streets being broad and clean, abounding in stores of superior elegance. There are a number of private streets on which are located magnificent villas and mansions, surrounded by gardens and the finest floral displays. Then, on the other hand, there are narrow, winding streets with curious gabled buildings of the olden times. The people are bright, of refined and intellectual appearance.

Like all European cities, Frankfort has its full share of monuments and places of historic interest. We have space only to name the famous monument of Gutenberg, the inventor of printing. It is very elaborate and finely executed. Near this, in the Gœthe Platz, is Schwanthaler's monument of Gœthe, this being the city in which he was born. The house, which bears an inscription recording the birth of the poet on the 28th of August, 1794, is still pointed out. We also noticed the memorial on the wall of the house from one of whose windows Luther preached to the people whilst remaining here over night on his way to the Diet at Worms. It consists of a finely-executed bust of Luther, encircled by the text from which he preached.

After paying a hurried visit to the annual exposition and the wonderful Panorama painting, by Prof. Brown, of the siege and battle of Sedan, all our time was consumed, and we took the train amid rain and storm, bound for Eisenach. The country between Frankfort and Eisenach is rich in agricultural resources, and much of it very beautiful. There is no waste land, every spot being utilized by the thrifty German.

Having some time before dark, after our arrival at Eisenach, we improved it by seeing something of this noted town. Of course Luther and Luther's work are uppermost in a Lutheran's mind in coming to this place. Accordingly we started from our hotel, Rinker, for the *Luther House*, in which Ursula Cotta gave the sweet-voiced Luther a home when a student in the cloister school of Eisenach (1498–1501). The House is quaint and leaning, as if burdened with great age, which it certainly is, for it is said to have been erected in 1200. It is built of stone with smoothly plastered walls, three and a half stories high, and has a cone-shaped roof, with two dormer windows. The house stands on one of the corners of the market square. After considerable rapping, we were kindly admitted into the house by a very aged couple who took great delight in showing us the apartments on the second floor of the house, occupied by Luther during his student life at the cloister school. We patiently listened to the well known stories in Luther's life which were narrated, chief among which was the one about his singing for bread on the streets of Eisenach.

We were taken into two rooms, both small, one occupied by the boy-student as a study, the other as a bed room. The furniture, some of which the custodian declared to be the identical articles of Luther's time, consists of several three-legged, straight-backed chairs, a study table, a wooden water jug, a candlestick which is a knot of wood with a hole bored in; a water-mug, shaped like a bear sitting on his haunches; also a Bible dated 1522, and some autograph letters. Adjoining this is Luther's bed-room, which contains nothing but a small bedstead, very plain. If this is the furniture used by Luther it was certainly very humble, and our college boys would murmur if they had no better, though some of them may not turn out to be as great men as Luther was.

In accordance with a previous invitation, we called to see Prof. Schmidt, a teacher in the gymnasium of Eisenach. He had been a traveling companion from Interlaken to Lucerne, and had cordially invited us to come and see him when we visited Eisenach. We embraced the opportunity, and were most heartily welcomed. The Professor introduced us to his entire family, and we spent a most delightful evening. Of course the hospitalities of German life were extended, and we were sumptuously entertained. We soon felt at home. Many questions were asked about our wonderful America. The cordial welcome, the sincere politeness, the confidence reposed in us as a perfect stranger, deeply impressed us with the honest, noble, and generous character of the Germans. When the time for retiring to our hotel arrived, the Professor would not permit us to go by ourself but took us by the arm and accompained us. We shall always have pleasant recollections of our visit to Prof. Schmidt at Eisenach.

The next morning, August 17th, was ushered in amid heavy rain, but it was the day set for an excursion to the Wartburg, and we faltered not in our purpose, and 7 a. m. found us on the way on foot, the distance being one and a half miles. The road is excellent, leading most of the way through a dense forest. After reaching the outskirts of the town, we passed some beautiful villas, while high hills and delightful valleys greeted us on every side. The road becomes very steep, until the first level is reached; passing over this, there is another and still steeper ascent, on the highest point of which stands the castle—the famous Wartburg, "beautiful for situation," and certainly a joy to every Lutheran. The castle was built in 1067, and stands six hundred feet above Eisenach and thirteen hundred above the sea. It will be remembered that on the 4th of May, 1521, as Luther, in company with Amsdorf and his brother James, was returning to his home from the Diet at Worms, he was captured by a body of armed knights in the Thuringian Forest, Luther alone being made prisoner, and was conducted to the Castle of Wartburg. Here he discovered the whole affair to have been managed by the order of his friend, the Elector of Saxony, who was present at the Diet when Luther left. Although the Emperor Charles V. had given Luther assurance of safe conduct, a decree for his arrest was instantly sent after him, and his sentence of death decided on. The Elector's band reached him before the warrant of arrest, and he was carried in secret to the Wartburg, where he remained for ten months, and was known by the name of Knight George. The solitude which he here enjoyed truly proved

"An isle of calm amid the sea of life,
 A Patmos, where the harbored soul retired
 From earth's loud shock, to feel the hush of heaven."

Arriving at the ramparts of the castle, we were directed by the soldier sentry who guards the entrance, to the Ritterhoff, where we procured a ticket of admission, and then passed in over the heavy drawbridge, in company with three others and a guide, through the gate into the court-yard. It was through this passage that the captured monk was taken by the friendly hands which protected him.

Our guide took us first into the chapel, where it is said Luther preached during his captivity. (Our friend Prof. Schmidt says it is not so.) Then we passed into the large Music Hall, where the celebrated Sanger contests were held as early as 1207; thence into a still larger room, the great Festal Hall, of most beautiful construction, having been rebuilt in 1862. We were also taken into the museum, which contains many relics of the Thirty Years' war, and the armor worn by Luther's friendly captors, and that of the Electors Frederick and John. The last but not least in interest was the *Lutherstube* (the Luther Room). This is about fifteen feet square, and about as homeless and bare as can be well imagined. It contains what is said to be some of Luther's furniture; the bedstead panelled over the entire top, the edges of the posts and rails being bound with zinc to prevent vandalism; his chair, a most uncomfortable one, a small book-case on his table, which contains some autograph letters by Luther, dated 1533-1539. Also his stove, pyramid shaped, his iron traveling chest, his parents' chest of wood, his foot rest, the coat of mail he is said to have worn, some pictures of himself, his parents, and Melanchthon. Of course the place on the wall marked by the famous inkstand is very conspicious. Luther having defeated his foes with *pen* and ink, thought he would try the ink *alone* on the devil, and, seizing the inkstand, he hurled it violently at the head of his Satanic Majesty, hitting his — imagination and the wall, making a greater impression on the latter than Satan did on the former. The spot is quite large, much of the plaster having been picked from the wall by relic-seekers. It is now protected against such vandalism.

We feel reluctant to break the illusion of beautiful fancies that have been woven about this old and almost classic story, but fidelity to history compels us to do it. Luther himself never said anything about this reputed inkstand battle, and no one else could know what took place in the privacy of his lonely night study. "In the absence of any allusion by Luther himself to this marvellous vision and conflict, we are obliged to reject the story itself as fictitious, and the various theories and speculations about it as the idle dream of fancy." Doubtless the story arose from the fact that in the activity of his imagination Luther attributed everything unfavorable in temporal or spiritual affairs to the direct personal agency of the devil, just as he blamed the envious Satan for revealing the secret of his presence at the Wartburg.

While there prevails considerable doubt as to the genuineness of the furniture and relics here, yet after all, the room and the window with its many little panes of glass in lead, and its small opening, *are* genuine. The window opens in the middle, like a double door, and looks out upon the Thuringian forest. Here, in this little room on the highest story of the castle, amid lonely solitude, Luther watched and prayed, wrought and contended. Here he was led by the mind of the Spirit to understand and fathom the mysteries of the divine word, which enabled him to give to the world that matchless translation of the New Testament into the German language.

Besides the translation of the entire New Testament, he translated some of the Psalms into German, and wrote a number of important works, all in ten months' time. What a vast amount of literary labor this was for one man to accomplish in so short a time! Were it not so well authenticated by history, one would not be inclined to believe it possible.

Here, in his meditations, he watched the stars, the sun and the moon in their silent marches. The blue mountains that surround the Wartburg, with occasional breaks in the range, opening up the beautiful plains of Thuringia, that golden vale, which the Count of Mansfeld preferred to the Promised Land; the fresh and balmy air about the lofty eminences; the singing of the birds; his lonely isolation from social diversions; all seemed to lift Luther above the world, and to bring him into nearer communion with heaven and Him who inhabiteth eternity. Luther was accustomed to call the Wartburg his Patmos, from its silence and solitude, and because he was there "for the word of God, and the testimony of Jesus Christ." And thus the castle of Wartburg stands immortalized, in history and Christian memory, as Luther's Patmos.

> "Die Stätte diè ein güter Mensch betratt
> Ist eingeweiht; nach hundert Yahren klingt,
> Sein wort und seine That dem Enkel Wieder."

> "The place once trodden by a righteous man
> Is sacred; centuries may revolve,
> And still the echo of his voice and deeds
> Is heard."

It was with reluctance that we withdrew from that humble chamber, once the abode of the greatest man since the days of the Apostle Paul. With lingering steps and frequent halts, looking up at the ancient fortress, and the man in our thoughts who has forever made it memorable, we continued our way down through the lovely Marienthal, happy and thankful that we were permitted to visit this place, so full of sweet and blessed memories of Luther. Truly this was a red-letter day in our journey through Germany.

CHAPTER XXI.

THE LAND OF LUTHER—MORE ABOUT EISENACH—WITTENBERG—LUTHER'S HOME—THE CASTLE CHURCH—LUTHER'S GRAVE AND MELANCHTHON'S—BRONZE STATUES—MELANCHTHON'S HOUSE—THE SLEEPING DEAD ABOUT THE STADT KIRCHE (CITY CHURCH)—BURNING OF THE PAPAL BULL—THE WITTENBERG SEMINARY IN THE AUGUSTEUM—DR. SCHMIEDER—PEN-PICTURE OF LUTHER.

BEFORE taking final leave of Eisenach, we called on the Rev. Dr. John Marbach, Oberpfarrer and Superintendent of the city. We were met at the door by a bright young "dame" who conducted us up stairs to the Doctor's study, where we found him busily at work over some manuscript, writing at his table, and at the same time drawing inspiration from a long-stemmed pipe. Immediately upon our entrance the Doctor, rising from his chair, earnestly but politely said, "Wer stehet vor mir?" (Who stands before me?) Well, we mustered our best German, apologizing for it at the same time, and told him. We were kindly invited to be seated, and soon felt as if we had met an old acquaintance, the Doctor being so cordial and friendly. He asked a great many questions about the Lutheran church in America, and was deeply interested in all we had to say on the subject. He informed us that he had a church in his district where a Lutheran clergyman by the name of Wilson preached

English. This was as surprising as new to us, but at the same time gratifying. The Doctor is yet a young man, possibly forty-five years old, of splendid presence, in manner reminding us much of our worthy Rev. Dr. Mann, of Philadelphia. When about to take our departure, the Doctor took us heartily by the hand, and sincerely thanked us for our call. It was here as in every other instance where we called on German pastors, we received a cordial welcome and had a most delightful interview.

With many pleasant impressions we took our departure from Eisenach that afternoon, and were soon on our way to Wittenberg, passing through Gotha, Erfurt, Weimar, and Halle. Having been informed by our German friends that the Luther relics at Erfurt were but few, we continued our journey, deeply interested in the country through which we were passing. On our right and left were many eminences, crowned with ruined castles, abiding monuments to the high-born individuals who, long ago, lorded it over the common people. But those days have passed away, and the people live in quietness and peace in their humble villages, till their fields, and reap their harvests in cheerful trust.

It would be difficult to describe our feelings, as late in the afternoon the train approached Wittenberg. Yonder to our left we see the towers and steeples so often pictured in our mind even from childhood, and soon the city we desired above all others to see, because immortalized by the greatest man since the days of Paul, stretched out before us. It was seven o'clock in the evening when the train stopped at the station, a short distance outside the city gate. The heavy rains had ceased, and the bright sun bathed in golden light the tops of the houses as we rode through the street in the one-horse omnibus, jogging slowly toward the little inn, *Hotel Adler.*

After "abendessen" (supper), we took a stroll through the town, and everywhere were signs of great age. At present, Wittenberg has a population of twelve thousand, which includes the regiment of soldiers stationed there. It was once a walled town, but these are now being removed, new streets laid out, and new buildings are going up. Many of the old streets are narrow, but well paved.

We retired weary and jaded to our room, but thankful and glad to sleep in Wittenberg; though by reason of the rapid current of new ideas and fresh images of the past, sleep was borne away, and much of the night passed in wakefulness.

The first place visited the next day was the Augusteum, the former Augustinian monastery—where Luther resided in his unmarried state—and part of which was given to him by the Elector for a residence when he became a married man. The building has a wide front on the street, and you enter through an arched gateway into an open court, around the four sides of which the building extends. Passing through the courtyard, which contains some trees and a garden, you reach the portion of the building which Luther occupied. The occupants of the old home, knowing my wishes—for daily visitors come to see the place—at once conducted me up a narrow winding stairway of stone to the second floor where Luther lived. The first is something of an ante-room, which contains some oil paintings of Luther and Frederick the Wise. From this I was taken into a large room possibly thirty feet square. Here Luther spent most of his life whilst Professor in Wittenberg from 1508 to 1546. It contains some of the original family furniture and a few relics. In one corner, in its old place, stands the tall stove, elaborately ornamented with reliefs of the evangelists. Around it the household drew together in the long harsh winters of Saxony. In another part stands the table at which he sat and wrote. On the wall hangs Luther's seal, of his own design, under glass cover, and is formed as follows: black cross, red heart, white rose, blue field, encircled with gold, and the following couplet connected with it:

"Das Christen Herz auf Rosen gehet
 Wenn's mitten under'm Kreuzen stehet."

One of the most unique relics in this room is the autograph of Peter the Great, in chalk, encased in glass, over the door-frame. Two windows look out into the courtyard. The glass is circular, about the size of the bottom of a common tin-cup, and set in lead. At one of the windows are two raised seats facing each other, where Doctor Martin and Frau Kathe often sat looking out into the open yard, where Melanchthon, and Bugenhagen, and Jonas, and Luther himself, had many a stroll and chat together. What wonderful work that busy pen did, in that now cheerless and solitary chamber! What conversations were held there! What scenes of domestic joy and sorrow were witnessed by these walls!

In another room we were shown some fine needle-work, wrought by the industrious and skillful hands of the good wife Katherina. Here are also her beads in a glass case, which she faithfully counted when yet a Roman Catholic. In a small cupboard are the fragments of Luther's drinking goblet, which Peter the Great, not being allowed to carry away (in 1712), dashed on the floor and broke. In another place is also a beautiful cup, of laurel wood, which Frederick the Wise gave Luther.

Next we passed into Luther's lecture room, where he taught thousands the pure word of God, and by his sound doctrine infused new life and hope into the church. This is a large room, seventy-five feet in length and forty in width. There remains the original platform, with lecture-stand and book-rack. In the rear on the wall hangs the best painting known of Luther, by Lucas Cranach; also portraits of his wife and parents.

After we had enjoyed with supreme satisfaction the quiet old home, and procured a number of portraits of the place, we re-crossed the court-yard, and entered another department of the Augusteum, which is used as a theological seminary. We were politely admitted into the lecture-room on the first floor by the grandson of the senior professor, where a "forlesung" (lecture) was going on. One of the students read a thesis on Materialism, and Prof. Dorner, a son of the distinguished theologian, afterwards lectured on the same subject.

Leaving the old University building, we walked down the "College strasse" (college street) to the Schlosskirche (castle church). It stands at the end of the street, close against the infantry barracks. Upon the original doors of this church, Luther nailed the ninety-five theses, October 31, 1517, which startled the world; but during a bombardment of Wittenberg by the Austrians in 1760, the doors were burned. King Frederick William re-placed them with bronze doors, bearing the original Latin text of the theses.

Standing by this church, we seemed to see the burly Reformer, as he came to the spot three hundred and sixty-five years ago, with the immortal theses in one hand and his hammer in the other. He does not dream himself what results are to come from that simple deed. With sturdy strokes he sends home the nails, until the ring of that hammer begins to startle Germany out of the slumber of the Dark Ages, and its sound is still ringing round and round the world, until every kindred and tongue shall confess and rejoice in the God of our salvation. We enter the church, of which once Luther was the pastor, the bright and modest Saxon girl, daughter of the sacristan, being our guide. It is a very plain building, with an unfinished appearance. Its walls are bare, with double galleries, and an arched ceiling. It is now the garrison church, and services are held here each Lord's day. We now move in silence a few steps further on, and our guide, takes, at the floor, an iron ring in her finger, lifts a wooden cover, and the brief inscription, in raised letters on a metal plate, tells us that all that remains on earth of the mortal part of Luther lies at our feet. Here we stand and gaze and reverently meditate. Here sleeps the mighty dead. Here repose the mortal remains of the mightiest man since Paul of Tarsus. "The eyes that shone in the fire of purpose, the lips whose utterances were bolts of lightning, the heart which beat in strength of courage and tenderness of love, the foot which planted itself in the outward expression of immutable resolve, the hands which were so often raised to God in omnipotent prayer, and put forth toward man in pleading for Christ, and in blessings to the needy—all that is left of these is here—a little ashes." But the true Luther, of whom all these were but organs, lives forever. The true Luther is buried nowhere, but is immortal in the pure faith, and in its graces world-wide.

A few steps to the other side, and another wooden cover discloses the plate that rests over the remains of Philip Melanchthon. Here he sleeps under the same central pavement of the church. The partnership was never broken. Loving in their life, in death they were not divided. United in life, and united in glory, their bodies sleep near each other, waiting for the resurrection. There may they sleep in peace, until the angel trumpet shall sound the day of resurrection and of the endless liberty of the children of God.

"The year after Luther's death, Wittenberg was filled with the troops of Charles V., many of whom were full of intense hate to the great Reformer. One of the soldiers gave Luther's effigies in this church two stabs with his dagger. The Spaniards earnestly solicited their Emperor to destroy the tomb and dig up and burn the remains of Luther, as this second Huss could not now be burned alive. To this diabolical proposition the Emperor sternly replied: 'My work with Luther is done; he has another Judge, whose sphere I may not invade. I war with the living, not with the dead.' And when he found that the effort was not dropped to bring about this sacrilegious deed, he gave orders that any violation of Luther's tomb should be followed by the death of the offender." (*Krauth's Conservative Reformation, p.* 44.)

Next we proceed to the altar, and there are two large brass plates inserted in the floor which cover the mortal remains of two of earth's greatest princes, and worthy champions of the Reformation—the Electors Frederick the Wise and John the Constant. Before leaving the church we ascended the pulpit and stood for a moment in the place where the great Luther so often stood and preached the everlasting gospel. Time is precious, and now we are in the market square of the town, where stand two statues of bronze, probably forty feet high, and about a hundred feet apart. One of them, erected sixteen years ago, represents a slender figure, robed in a gown, with a countenance almost emaciated, and wearing a saintly expression. Upon the pedestal is inscribed, "Endeavoring to keep the unity of the spirit in the bond of peace." On the other side is written, "I will speak of thy testimonies also before kings, and will not be ashamed." That slender, seraphic figure is Philip Melanchthon, who was the gentle and beloved *Jonathan* to the burly Psalmist and warrior who stands on the twin pedestal not far away. A genuine Teuton is that robust character, planted firmly in his bronze shoes, and holding his finger to the open page of God's Word. The short, taurine neck and heavy jaw mark the holy obstinacy of the man. The inscriptions on the pedestal are exceedingly happy. Underneath the open Bible is inscribed (as if Luther himself were just speaking it from his bronze lips): "Glaubet an das Evangelium" (believe the gospel). The east side of the monument bears Luther's famous words: "If this be God's work it will endure; if it be man's it will perish." On the west side is carved the immortal motto: "*Ein feste Burg ist unser Gott.*"

The partnership of the two great leaders of the Reformation, which is marked by the similarity of their monuments, holds good all through the town.

Proceeding up the "College strasse," we came upon a three-story house of rather modern appearance outside, bearing the inscription in German, "In this house Philip Melanchthon lived and labored and died." We entered the house, and were conducted up stairs into the room where Melanchthon died. The only furniture left is a large chest, in the wall a small cupboard, near which hangs a likeness of him, dated 1526. Thence we walked out into the garden, and sat under some trees where Melanchthon often walked and rested and meditated.

"Into the narrow hallway of this house the jolly face of Luther must have been thrust many a time, when some new idea was to be discussed with brother Philip, or when some very racy scandal about Tetzel or Eck had come to brother Martin's ears. With many a boisterous laugh that house has rung. No doubt of it, for there was infinite fun underneath Luther's well-lined ribs. There must have been almost hourly intercourse between the two men, for their homes were only a few steps apart.

But now we proceed to the end of this street, and a little beyond the Elster gate, where it had been the custom to burn articles infected with the plague, and see the place, where, in sight of the university buildings, Luther burned the Papal bull, on the 10th of December, 1520. The blaze of the burning "bull" was pretty distinctly visible from the Vatican. A large oak tree marks the spot, surrounded by a beautiful grass-plat and a few flowers, all inclosed by a neat iron fence.

In the *Rath's House* we saw what is said to be Luther's original clock, and a number of interesting relics. From the tower of the *Stadt Kirche*, we had a fine view of the scenery about Wittenberg, and it reminded us somewhat of the view one gets from the cupola of the seminary at Gettysburg.

We now retrace our steps and go and walk about the old *Stadt Kirche*, in which Luther often preached, close to the market square. Here we seemed to be in the presence of Luther's old neighbors, for many of his intimate friends and brother professors lie buried under this church or close to its walls. All around the outer wall of the building stand their moss-grown tablets, with epitaphs barely legible. Some of these worthies of the sixteenth century are represented in queer effigies of stone, either clad in armor or in scholastic robes. Here is a head broken off, there an arm is missing. Time has dealt roughly with these stout old protesters; but to us, that morning, they seemed to be living yet, and their spirits still haunt the ancient church in which they once crowded to hear brother Martin denounce the "man of sin." Nay, Luther himself seems to abide there still. All Wittenberg is full of his spiritual presence, and as we looked out of our window that bright September morning, we thought we could see him, walking with lumbering gait down yonder College Strasse, with a roll of his MS. German Bible under his arm. He walks across the market-place, stops to salute Brother Philip with a *Guten Tag*, and then vanishes out of sight.

Before leaving Wittenberg we again visited the Augusteum, upon invitation of Dr. Schmieder, Oberkonsistorialrath, the senior professor of the theological faculty in the seminary here. The venerable Doctor received us most cordially, and welcomed us to Wittenberg and his study. He is now seventy-eight years of age, of small stature, and in manner and courtesy reminded us much of our sainted Dr. C. F. Schaeffer. Father Schmieder said it gave him the greatest pleasure to meet with Lutheran clergymen from America. He said he had heard of Dr. Krauth's visit to Wittenberg the summer previous, but was sorry he did not get to see him. He made many inquiries about the Lutheran church in this country, and was deeply interested in what we had to say. He presented us with several pamphlets giving a full history of the present theological department of the seminary in the Augusteum. It was with reluctance that we took our departure from so delightful and saintly a man as Dr. Schmieder.

And now we must leave Wittenberg, having for more than a day walked in Luther's accustomed paths. We go with joy and love, sweet memories and inspiring hopes. We go, thankful that in the good providence of God we were permitted to see the place where the mighty Luther lived, loved and labored, and whence have radiated the forces which have changed our whole modern world, and have built up a spiritual empire before whose moral glory all the pomp of war and of state fades away.

We cannot more appropriately close this chapter than quote part of the sainted Dr. Krauth's pen-picture of Luther, in the Conservative Reformation (pp. 86–87). "The greatness of some men only makes us feel that though they did well, others in their place might have done just as they did; Luther had that exceptional greatness, which convinces the world that he alone could have done the work." * * * "He was not a mere mountain-top, catching a little earlier the beams which, by their own course, would soon have found the valleys; but rather, by the divine ordination under which he rose, like the sun itself, without which the light on mountain and valley would have been but a starlight or moonlight." * * * Luther "has monuments in marble and bronze, medals in silver and gold; but his noblest monument is the best love of the best hearts, and the highest, purest impression of his image has been left in the souls of regenerated nations. He was the best teacher of freedom and of loyalty. He has made the righteous throne stronger, and the innocent cottage happier." * * * "He was tried by deep sorrow and brilliant fortune ; but whether lured by the subtlest flattery or assailed by the powers of hell, tempted with the mitre or threatened with the stake, he came off more than conqueror of all." * * * "He tore up the mightiest evils by the root, but shielded with his own life the tenderest bud of good." * * * "Faith-inspired, he was faith-inspiring. Great in acts as he was great in thought, proving himself fire with fire, inferior eyes grew great by his example, and put on the dauntless spirit of resolution." * * *

"Living under thousands of jealous and hating eyes, in the broadest light of day, the testimony of enemies but fixes the result; that his faults were those of a nature of the most consummate grandeur and fullness, faults more precious than the virtues of the common great. Four potentates ruled the mind of Europe in the Reformation: the Emperor, Erasmus, the Pope, and Luther. The pope wanes, Erasmus is little, the emperor is nothing, but Luther abides as a power for all time. His image casts itself upon the current of ages, as the mountain mirrors itself in the river that winds at its foot—the mighty fixing itself immutably upon the changing."

CHAPTER XXII.

BERLIN—THE CAPITAL OF PRUSSIA—"UNTER DEN LINDEN"—
THE PALACES—THIERGARTEN—FREDERICK WILLIAM AND
QUEEN LOUISA—OPPRESSIVE MILITARY SYSTEM—GERMAN
UNIVERSITY—BEER AND WINE DRINKING—THE GERMAN PEO-
PLE—AN INCIDENT—PRUSSIAN-FRANCO LOVE.

LESS than two hours' car riding from Wittenberg brought us to Berlin—the great capital of Prussia. The district of country between these two cities is a perfect garden in point of cultivation; the abundant harvest that was being gathered being proof of a rich and productive soil. We arrived in Berlin in the evening after dark, but had some time for an extended stroll, by gaslight. We were at once impressed with the quiet and perfect order that prevailed on the streets. In all respects this is a fine city, and has many attractions. It is solidly built, and it is said to be the determination of the present Emperor to make Berlin rival Paris as the most attractive city of Europe. It will, however, take King William longer to accomplish such an undertaking than it did to rival Paris in the late war, and humble that city before his siege guns. But judging from the many improvements that are going on in many parts of the city, it is evident that it will be still a more elegant and attractive metropolis than it is at present. It has many broad and delightful streets, with many handsome and imposing dwellings. Its streets are well paved and kept very clean. The houses, as in Paris, are largely built of light colored stone, or of brick covered with plaster to resemble it. The city contains many fine business streets, full of elegant shops and stores.

The most prominent objects of attraction to the stranger are the splendid palaces and other buildings located on both sides of the principal street, called "*Unter den Linden*." We must confess to some disappointment as regards the *lindens* of this street, they being few in number and small in size. Other parts hardly came up to our expectations. We know the street is considered one of the finest in Europe. It is one mile long, extending from the Royal Palace to the Brandenburg Gate. There are four rows of trees, two on each side of the central avenue, while the roadway is on either side. We took a morning walk over the entire length of the central avenue of this street. There is no grass on it, but it is a sandy waste kept moist by sprinkling with water. The trees are composed of chestnut, linden, plantain, acacia, and aspen, whose various foliage contrasts beautifully with the elegant palaces and public buildings that line each side of the street. The palaces face this street, the Emperor's and that of the Prince Royal. Here are also the Academy of Fine Arts, the Opera House, the Arsenal, the Seminaries of the Artillery and Engineers, and some fine hotels. Here the fashionable and wealthy exhibit themselves and their splendid equipage. It is the favorite street of the Emperor, who delights in an early morning walk "*Unter den Linden*." The tree is still pointed out, and remains well protected, under which the

King was resting when the fiendish would-be assasssin fired upon him with buckshot a few years ago, and came well nigh accomplishing his murderous end.

On the Linden street, opposite the palace of the Crown Prince, stands the colossal equestrian statue of Frederick the Great, pronounced to be one of the most magnificent monuments in Europe. Its pedestal is of granite, divided into three sections. The two upper sections are of bronze. At the corner of the upper are figures representing Justice, Fortitude, Prudence, and Temperance. Between these are bas-reliefs representing different periods in the life of Frederick—the Muse teaching him history; Mercury presenting him with a sword; and one representing him walking in the garden of his palace, surrounded by his favorite companions, the greyhounds, playing his flute. The central section contains bronze groups, life size, of all the leading generals and statesmen during the seven years' war, amounting in all to thirty-one persons. The lower section contains names of other prominent men, especially soldiers of the time of Frederick. The equestrian statue of Frederick the Great surmounting the top is seventeen feet high, and perfect in all its proportions; a mantle hangs from the monarch's shoulders, his stick hanging from his wrist, all natural and true to life. It is the production of Rauch, and certainly is a magnificent work of art. The monuments in Berlin are not so numerous, but are of a superior character. The *Victory Column*, in honor of the victory over the French in the late Franco-Prussian war, is among the foremost for beauty and attraction.

At one end of the broad avenue of lindens is the Palace

Bridge, with its eight groups of statuary, and at the other the portal of the Brandenburg Gate, surmounted by its colossal chariot of victory. Immediately outside of this gate is the *Thiergarten*, a magnificent park. This is a perfect picture of beauty. It contains the finest combination of natural forest scenery, and artificial park beauty that we have ever seen anywhere. It is two miles in length, and half a mile in breadth. All along, on both sides of this park, there is an array of the most lovely palatial residences, the extensive gardens around which are adorned with statuary and fountains, and brilliant with flowers and ornamental trees.

The monuments of Frederick William III. and Queen Louisa stand in the Thiergarten, and are very beautiful, being made of the finest white granite. They stand in sight of each other, facing. The spot near by the beautiful stream, where it is said these two royalists were accustomed to meet in their youthful days as lovers, is carefully noted. It occurred to us this would form the basis for a first-class story in romance.

The military display in Berlin is a perfect wonder to a foreigner. So numerous are the soldiers and military parades, that one thinks that King William must be engaged in actual warfare. The fact that Prussia is a military government and Berlin its head-quarters is every where apparent. Almost everything is military. All the railroads and telegraphs are in the hands of the government, and all these officials are in military dress; so are all the police, and all who do guard duty around the public buildings. Every able-bodied man in Germany is a soldier in some period of his life; and so well are they drilled, and constantly ready for the field, that every man, though belonging to the landwehr (militia), knows his number and place in rank, and where to report in case of an emergency. An officer told us that in twenty-four hours the entire military force of the United Empire could be on the move to do service in any part of its realm. Thus it was that there were no raw recruits in the immense army brought so suddenly into the field to resist and drive back Napoleon in the late war. King William is always ready for the fray. It is, however, a very expensive readiness. It oppresses the people with enormous taxation; and this is one of the reasons why so many thousands of Germans annually throng the steamers for America. But the state of things in Europe is such that military power, almost amounting to despotism, has become a necessity as a means of self-preservation.

Berlin is undoubtedly the capital, too, of taste in the fine arts, and of intellectual culture. We saw more intelligent and intellectual-looking people in Berlin than in either Paris or London. Its university, with one hundred and fifty professors and two thousand students, is composed of the most distinguished men of science who can be collected in Germany, or in any one of the European countries. It is the centre of instruction and intellectual development in Northern Germany. Its libraries are immense and numerous, and its educational facilities of the very highest order. Its museum stands unrivaled in Europe. Its picture gallery may be surpassed by the Uffizi Gallery or Pitti Palace at Florence.

Berlin is not a gay city like Paris, except on the occasion of some commemoration of victories in war, or in honor of the Kaiser and "Our Fritz;" then the German shows what he can do. Ordinarily, however, the people are quiet even over their beer and Schweitzer cheese, and there are no noisy, jolly, frolicking gatherings of an evening, such as you find in gardens and saloons of our own larger towns and cities.

As to drinking, we are free to say, there is much of it —that is, *everybody* drinks *wine* and *beer* in Germany— but as for *drunkenness*, we saw none. We were in many beer gardens, and in other places of social and public resort, where we saw as many as five thousand people assembled, seated with their families at the small marble tables, sipping beer and wine. The best of order prevailed; no boisterousness, and no drunkenness could anywhere be noticed. The German does not gulp down half a dozen glasses of beer in an hour's time, but spends an entire evening over one or two glasses in pleasant conversation, and at ten o'clock goes to his home. You bring together five thousand, or even five hundred Americans, or possibly Germans *in* America, and give them all the wine and beer they want to drink, and see what a frolic you would have! Then, too, the Germans drink no whisky over there, and their wine and beer are pure and unadulterated. The government regulates their manufacture, and no inferior make is allowed to be sold. Adulteration of their beverages is severely punished, and there is no attempt at it now. We saw no bloated drunkards in Germany. No one need tell us that the Germans are the great drinking and drunken race of the world, as they are generally represented to be. Our experience in Germany emphatically disproves this.

We did not see a single intoxicated person in all our travels in Germany; and with one exception—and he was an American—only one drunken man in all our journeyings on the Continent. We saw more drunkenness, however, in London than we ever saw anywhere in our own country. It seemed to us that the Germans in this particular, in the great cities of the Fatherland, are an entirely different class of people from some of their own race in America. We do not hesitate to say that the more we saw of the Germans, the better we thought of them. For disinterested kindness, genuine politeness, honesty, good behavior, general industry, and thrift, we unhesitatingly give the palm to the Germans. They stand head and shoulders above all the Europeans.

But with all the attractions of the great city of Berlin, we must leave it, and in the evening we are on board the train bound for Cassel, where we remain but a few hours; thence are off for Hogan. This section abounds in many beautiful towns. We passed through *Aaronsburg*, but not our native town by that name, in Centre Co., Pa. After passing through Elberfeld and Deitz, we reached Coln (Cologne) on the Rhine. Having spent some time in this city before, we tarried only part of a day, and then bidding adieu to *Vaterland*, we started for Paris, passing through much delightful country scenery, and many large towns and fine cities, such as Vervier and

Brussels in Belgium, and the next morning at six o'clock we reached Paris in a rain storm.

On our way to the Rhine from Hesse Cassel we had one of a number of exhibitions of *Prussian Franco love.* The greater part of the forenoon we had occupied a compartment on a car by ourselves; but at Elberfeld, a gentleman and lady, both attractive in appearance, entered the car and became our traveling companions for the entire day. Having been in the cars all night previous, we were not in a talking mood. Finally, however, we broke the silence by giving expression, in the German language, to our delight at the beautiful country we were traversing.

"My dear sir, you greatly surprise me," replied the gentleman, "I took you to be a Frenchman, and a Frenchman would have nothing good to say of Germany." In a vein of humor we remarked, "My friend, may that be the reason why you refrained from speaking to me, your silence growing out of fear or dislike for the French?" He quickly answered, and with the greatest animation, "No, sir, my dear friend, Germans *never* fear the French, and the next time they attempt to cross the Rhine, we will *annihilate* (vernichten) them." This is about the feeling of the Germans toward the French, and so *vice verse*. We found this gentleman and his daughter most delightful traveling companions.

CHAPTER XXIII.

IN FRANCE—THE CITY OF PARIS—ITS CLEANLINESS—ITS STORES—THE BOULEVARDS—THE INWARD AND OUTWARD—ITS GREAT PUBLIC SQUARE—PLACE OF CONCORD—THE CHAMPS ELYSÉES.

TO speak of all the interesting things one sees in Paris, even in a two weeks' visit there, would require a volume itself. The most minute description, however, can give but a faint idea of this remarkable city. It is full of charms, and grows into a perpetual wonder as one tarries to see its beauties and admire its attractions. The first thing that impresses the stranger in Paris is its wonderful cleanliness and brightness. The streets are nearly all paved with asphaltum, hence the carriages and omnibusses make little noise as they glide along on the smooth pavements. The sweeping machines are busy during the night, making the streets as clean as they could be swept with a corn broom by hand, and afterwards are carefully sprinkled, so that the dust may be completely washed out of all the crevices.

The peculiar light-yellow stone (almost white) of which the houses are constructed, gives the city a remarkable brightness, especially in sunny weather. The houses are generally four or five stories, and support the beautiful mansard roof. There are miles of these palatial structures, with magnificently built arcades, which afford perfect protection to the foot-man against the heat and rain. The houses have no steps or stoops in front, the entrance being by an arched gateway into a courtyard, from which you pass into the interior dwelling. This adds an additional width to the streets, which without this arrangement are wider than in most large cities. It gives a very wide pavement, and affords plenty of space for promenading room in front of restaurants and cafés, where large numbers of the people gather from morning until late at night, sipping their favorite beverage and taking their meals.

Paris by gaslight is a brilliant scene. The boulevards extending for miles through almost all sections of the city present a gay appearance at night. The large number of cafés, brilliant with gas-jets and electric lights, have their tables out on the broad pavements, and from eight to ten o'clock in the evening it is difficult to obtain a seat at any of them. Here the Parisians luxuriate, spending their summer evenings in promenading the boulevards, and frequently stopping for a cup of their favorite drink. The best of order prevails, and no drunkenness is visible. Everybody seems to be happy and bent on enjoyment. The broad streets are also filled with carriages and omnibusses of every description, of burnished brightness. Every vehicle being obliged to carry from two to four lighted lamps, the vast numbers swiftly gliding over the smooth pavements present the appearance of immense torch-light processions. The vehicles having the right of way, there is little respect shown to pedestrians; and should you happen to be run over, the law punishes you for having put yourself in the way. It often seemed to us as if the drivers were intent on driving over somebody, so furiously did they urge their steeds. In London it is far otherwise.

The stores of Paris are a perfect wonder of beauty and attractiveness. They are not only brilliantly lighted, but nearly all of them have rows of gas-lights on the outside, above the doors and windows, making the streets almost as light as day. The artistic display of goods, the dispostion of the lights, and the reflection in the side-glasses with which the shop windows are always provided, presents a continuous spectacle of surpassing beauty. The almost innumerable number of jewelers' windows, sparkling with diamonds and precious stones, present an array of brilliant beauty that constantly attracts the admiring attention of the throngs of promenaders. Everybody seems to be out-doors in Paris at night, and intent on being gay and happy. There are no streets in any other city like the boulevards—wide thoroughfares, running in every direction, all teeming at night with life and animation. There are sixty of these thoroughfares, which are from house to house one hundred and sixty feet wide, ninety feet being given to the carriage-way, and thirty-five feet on each side for the pavements. Fine rows of trees line the curb-stone. The houses lining both sides of the streets are nearly all of uniform construction, none less than five stories high, and many of them towering up to six and seven, including the mansard-roofs. On these thoroughfares the people mass, and it presents an ever-moving, dazzling panorama of humanity, baffling all description, and equaled in no other city.

In every direction you go, there is one continuous charm of attractive beauty. The Parisian does not worship the "dust of ages," or take pride in smoked and begrimed walls, as the Lond oner does. If the former has anything that is handsome, he tries to make it handsomer. Antiquity has no worshipers, and is made to yield to the spirit of improvement. Paris is not beautiful in spots, but every portion of it abounds in attractions.

It is needless to say that the dressing is fine in this, the city of the world's fashions. There is much taste and great elegance displayed in this particular. A ragged, filthy child or adult, if seen on the streets or found anywhere in the home, must be able to give an account of himself, and is required by a law, strictly enforced, to be clean and tidy. The Parisians, whatever else may be said about them, certainly set a good example in this particular, worthy of all imitation. "Wash, and be clean." Let the cleansing be inward as well as outward.

The inhabitants of Paris have long considered themselves at the head of European civilization, and if such an eminence can be gained by mere external polish, they perhaps deserve it. In matters of dress and fashion, the lead is conceded to them by a kind of common consent. None succeed better, not only in practicing the agreeable arts of life, but even in observing the outward decencies of society. But "not all is gold that glitters," and beneath this pleasing surface runs a strong and polluted current, and perhaps there are few places in the world where the more substantial virtues are more rare, and where so much dissoluteness exists within such narrow limits.

The means of conveyance in Paris are much the same as in other European cities. The cab system makes it very convenient for sight-seeing, as one can be obtained anywhere. The omnibus and horse-car arrangement, two stories high, with seats on top, if their conductors were more polite, like they are in London, would greatly add to the stranger's comfort. The best way to get a good view of the city is to climb to the top of one of these huge omnibusses and ride all over the town. To one who has been in Paris, it is no wonder that people who delight in pleasure, gayety, festivity, and endless amusements, love to linger so long in such an attractive and almost bewitching city.

There is perhaps no city in the world that can boast of more fine gardens, open squares, pleasure grounds, and places of public resort, than Paris.

The *Place de la Concorde* (The Place of Concord) is the most beautiful and extensive square in the city, and one of the finest in the world. It covers an area of four hundred yards in length by two hundred and fifty yards in width, and is located in the heart of the city. Though called the Place of Concord, it is nevertheless the place where human blood has been spilt, and more scenes of horror and confusion have been enacted, than upon any similar space of ground in the world. Here it was, in 1770, that during the celebration of the nuptials of Louis XVI. and Marie Antoinette, in the midst of a panic caused by the discharge of fireworks, the carriages were driven among the people, and over twelve hundred persons were trampled to death, besides the thousands wounded. Here also took place the collision between the people and the soldiers, which was the signal for the destruction of the Bastile. It was here, in 1793, that the guillotine began its bloody work with the execution of Louis XVI., and so soon afterwards of the ill-fated queen, Marie Antoinette. Soon followed the bloody death of Charlotte Corday, Danton, Robespierre; and in a little more than a year and a half over twenty-eight hundred people were executed by the guillotine in this square. It was well said by one who opposed the erection of the large fountain on the spot where the scaffold stood, that all the water in the world would not suffice to remove the blood-stains which sullied the " Place." It was here that the first disturbance in the revolution of 1848 took place. It was here also that the Prussian soldiers bivouacked in March, 1871, and where, in the following May, the desperate struggle between the troops of Versailles and the Communists took place, during which the earth was soaked with blood. A more appropriate name for this " Place " would be the " Place de la Discorde."

But for all this, it is a majestic square, and its adornments are very grand. In the centre stands the famous Obelisk of Luxor, a monolith that was presented to the French government by Mohammed Ali, Pasha of Egypt, whence it was brought by Napoleon I. It formerly stood in front of the temple of Thebes, and had been erected by the great Sesostris, fifteen hundred years before Christ. Every side is covered with hieroglyphics. Near the Obelisk, and in the spot where once was erected the guillotine, stands a magnificent fountain. Its basin is fifty feet in diameter, colossal figures surrounding it, separated by spouting dolphins, held in the arms of winged children. Around the square are eight colossal statues representing the principal cities of France.

This square forms a beautiful link between the Tuileries gardens and the *Champs Elysées*. Toward the north, at the terminus of the Rue Royale, stands the Madeleine, or the church of St. Mary Magdelene; on the south, over the Pont de la Concorde, you see the Legislative Palace, nearly behind which looms up the gilded dome of the Invalides. Under this dome is the matchless tomb of Napoleon I.

Continuing westward, we enter the Champs Elysées, which is a continuation of the walk from the gardens of the Tuileries. No pen-picture can do justice to this magnificent avenue and pleasure-ground of splendor and beauty. Its length is one mile and a quarter, its width two hundred and fifty yards, terminating at the Arc de l'Etoile (the triumphal arch). The avenue has foot pavements twelve feet wide, laid in bitumen. All its smaller avenues are planted with magnificent trees and bordered by delightful walks. Thousands of gas and electric lights produce an effect that is charming at night. During fine weather the Champs Elysées is the favorite spot for all classes; continually from morning till late at night are circulating a multitude of sumptuous equipages, going and coming from the *Bois de Boulogne;* while on every side we see beautiful groves, surrounded by banked flower gardens, open concert-rooms, handsome coffee-houses, restaurants, elegant fountains, encircled by flower-beds; and, when all is lighted up by the ten thousand gas and electric lights, the scene is truly brilliant and entrancing. But on "fete" or holy days, when an illumination takes place, the scene is beyond description. When every building is transformed into a palace of fire and every tree into a pyramid of colored lights, when the brilliancy of coloring disputes with the elegance of decoration, it is enchanting indeed.

CHAPTER XXIV.

MORE ABOUT PARIS—THE TRIUMPHAL ARCH—BOIS, OR PARK OF BOULOGNE—LOUVRE—THE GREAT ART GALLERY—HOTEL DES INVALIDES—THE TOMB OF NAPOLEON I.—TOMB OF JEROME BONAPARTE—LUXEMBOURG PALACE—HOTEL DE VILLE, OR CITY HALL.

AS you approach the eastern terminus of the magnificent avenue, the Champs Elysées, you arrive at the *Triumphal Arch*, one of Paris' attractions. This is the largest structure of the kind in existence, and is visible from almost every part of the environs of the city. It was begun by Napoleon I. in 1806, and was completed by Louis Philippe in 1836. It was erected to celebrate the victories of the French under the Republic and Empire. It consists of a vast arch sixty-seven feet in height and forty-six feet in width. The whole structure is one hundred and sixty feet high, one hundred and forty-six feet in width and seventy-two feet in depth. Each front has a group of statuary. One represents Napoleon I. standing in a dignified attitude, whilst Victory places the crown upon his brow. The cost of the structure was over two millions of dollars. It was under this arch that the German army marched after the capitulation of Paris to King William, in 1871. Whilst the great arch contains a number of tablets in memory of victories achieved over the Germans, yet the German army made a terrific *score* against the French that day, which needs no sculpturing in stone or brass. After mounting two hundred and sixty-one steps we reached the top of the arch, from which we had one of the finest views of Paris on one side, and the *Bois or Park of Boulogne* on the other.

This is the principal park of Paris. It is approached from the city by the Avenue of the Champs Elysées. There is nothing in Europe that can compare with it. Here art and taste have conspired to charm the eye with the most picturesque scenery. Everything that wealth and art combined could do has been done, to add to the natural beauties of the place. Its beautiful lakes and the rich turf which clothes their banks down to the water's edge; its white pebbled walks lined with mossy green; its charming flower-beds, elaborate fountains, and extensive array of fine statuary; its stately and natural forest trees; its many winding paths emerging from the cool fir groves; its snug little Swiss cottages seen peering here and there from behind the trees; and added to this, the rich equipages enlivening the carriage-roads which wind around the lakes, the crowds of people enjoying the cool shade under the stately trees or sauntering along the gravel walks, children flocking about in the height of merriment and glee, the boats flying to and fro with their white canvas awnings shining in the sun; all this presented an enchanting view and a maze of bustle and animation on that fine summer afternoon as we drove through the park, that was most pleasing to the eye and most exhilarating to our spirits. But it is vain to attempt even a pen-picture of this thoroughly charming and delightful park. It was a most refreshing place for King William's soldiers to rest after the fall of Paris in 1871.

But we must leave, for a while, the out-door attractions of Paris, and look at some of its in-door places. These are almost numberless, but let us mention the *Louvre*, the most important public building in the city, both architecturally and on account of its treasures of art. It is Paris' great art gallery and museum, in the Tuileries, which cover a space of forty acres. We need not say that it is of unequalled proportions. It requires fully three hours to walk through its rooms and halls at a regular pace and glancing at objects as you pass. The French armies returning to Paris from their victorious campaigns in Italy, the Netherlands, and Germany, laden with treasures of art of every description, made the Louvre collection not merely the most important of the kind in France, but some think, *par excellence*, the museum of Europe. To see even all that is possessed of striking beauty and artistic skill, to the most trained eye in this department of human accomplishment, would require months of time, and then any attempt to *describe* what one has seen and admired, could only prove unsatisfactory and very insipid. In the great forest of paintings you see every school of art in the world represented by its masters, and representatives of almost all ages. No gallery in Europe is so well supplied with works of Raphael as the Louvre. Besides, the master hands of such as Murillo, Titian, Corregio, Rubens and Michael Angelo, and men of less fame, are here enthroned in their great splendor. Here you see how these masters embodied their grand conceptions, and you are filled with wonder and admiration at the skill of human genius. The presence of so much beauty and splendor becomes oppressive as you revel in it day after day. We walked through miles upon miles of paintings, seeing the works of all the old and new masters, and for days tasted of this overflowing cup of knowledge and beauty.

Besides the art collections, the Louvre contains an ethnographical museum, a marine museum, and untold numbers of other objects of interest. The museum of Egyptian antiquities is the most important collection in Europe, and so far as is possible without the appropriate architectural surroundings, affords an almost complete survey of the religion, the customs and the art-life of the most ancient of peoples. The Assyrian museum is also very large and full, and so are the antiquities of Asia Minor. The wonders of all ages and all lands are here brought together, and are the treasures of the student and scholar.

The collections of ancient and modern sculpture, though inferior to the great Italian collections, boast of many works of the highest rank. We cannot speak of any particular piece of sculpture excepting the world renowned *Venus of Milo*. This has a hall to itself. At once you see the superior workmanship over all the rest. Although armless, the figure is perfect, the attitude the most natural and graceful, while there is a calm purity, modesty and resoluteness about the sweet and lovely face.

But we may as well dismiss the Louvre, for an attempt

to give you a description of it is entirely unsatisfactory to us, and fails to convey to you anything like a proper conception of what it is, in its wealth of beauty and treasure.

We now go and see the *Hotel des Invalides* and the *Tomb of Napoleon I.* The former is an immense granite building for soldiers disabled by wounds, and those who have served for thirty years in the French army. This soldier's home has its church, and contains all the banners taken by the French in their wars with other nations, arranged along both sides of the nave. The remains of Napoleon were temporarily placed in this building after being brought from St. Helena (in 1840). But there was a second church built which joins the *Hotel des Invalides*, and is one of the most magnificent and impressive buildings in Paris. It is built of the finest marble and precious stone, and a most appropriate burial place for one of the most remarkable men the world ever saw. The church is a square pile, one hundred and ninety-eight feet in breadth, surmounted by a circular tower with twelve windows, and a lofty dome, three hundred and forty-four feet in height. The dome is eighty-six feet in diameter, gilded with gold. Situated beneath this wide and lofty dome, twenty feet below the main marble floor, is an open circular crypt, around which is formed a marble balustrade or wall. As you lean and look over this marble parapet into the circular space which it encloses, your eyes rest on the massive sarcophagus which holds the remains of the Emperor. Around the walls of the crypt, which are composed of polished slabs of granite, stand ten noble angelic forms in spotless white marble, bearing emblems of victory, while each sad and beautiful countenance turns to the centre, guarding and mourning the mighty conqueror who was overcome by death. On the mosaic pavement, which represents a wreath of laurels, rises the sarcophagus, thirteen feet long, six feet and a half wide, and fourteen feet high, consisting of a single huge block of reddish-brown granite, brought from Finland at a cost of $30,000. Above the crypt, at a height of one hundred and sixty feet, rises the lofty dome in two sections. The first of these is divided into twelve compartments, painted with figures of the Apostles. The upper section is adorned with a large composition—St. Louis offering Christ the sword with which he had vanquished the foes of Christianity. The faint, bluish light admitted from above, and the sombre appearance of the crypt and its surroundings, greatly enhance the solemn grandeur of the scene. The whole expense of the tomb was $2,000,000. The entrance to the crypt (always closed) is at the rear of the high altar. Over the entrance-way is a quotation from the Emperor's will: "I desire that my ashes may repose on the banks of the Seine, in the midst of the French people whom I have ever loved."

It is a sight to see the great crowds going into this building and gazing upon the tomb of one of the world's most wonderful men. It is very evident that the spirit of Napoleon still lives in Paris, and that he is still ardently loved by the French people. Thousands of them go to Napoleon's tomb as they go to a shrine to worship, and still love to speak his name and works in devout love and lavish praise. Though his glory has been tarnished by the revelations of his utter selfishness and cruel ambition, yet multitudes of the French people feel the magic of his name, and glory in his extraordinary ahievements.

The church contains the tomb of *Jerome Bonaparte*, who died in 1860, once King of Westphalia, a small sarcophagus with the remains of his eldest son, and another containing the heart of his wife. In another part of the building rest the remains of *Joseph Bonaparte*, who died in 1844, and was once King of Spain. Taken altogether, the tomb of Napoleon ranks among the finest things one sees in all the marvels of a European tour.

We cannot omit to mention the *Luxembourg Palace*. It is a building of great beauty and of many historic associations. Part of the palace is occupied by the *Musée de Luxembourg*, which contains a collection of works of living artists, consisting of paintings, sculptures, drawings, engravings and lithographs. The works of the most distinguished masters are generally transferred from here to the Louvre, ten years after their death. Especially fine are the specimens of sculpture in this museum. The gardens which surround the palace are of great beauty and charm. The flower beds are embellished with the most beautiful fountains. The terraces are adorned with many statues in marble. It is the only remaining Renaissance garden in Paris, and with its balustrades and steps and many other artistic beauties, reminds one of the famous Boboli gardens at Florence. It is a lovely spot to visit and rest in, and at the same time enjoy the sweet strains of music by the excellent band.

We have only space to mention the *Hotel de Ville*, or town-hall of Paris. This magnificent edifice was burned by the Communists on the 24th of May, 1871. Many ruins are still visible. It is being rebuilt, and promises to be restored to its original beauty and magnitude. The fire however destroyed much that can never be restored, including the library of one hundred thousand volumes, numerous works of art, and a great many important public documents. May our land ever be preserved against the cruel hands of Communism!

CHAPTER XXV.

PARIS CONTINUED—A PARISIAN SUNDAY—A PLEASANT SURPRISE—THE CHURCHES—THE NOTRE DAME—HYACINTHE LOYSEN—THE MADELEINE—SAINTE CHAPELLE—ST. BARTHOLOMEW—THE PRISONS—VERSAILLES—MARIE ANTOINETTE—AN ACCIDENT—SYMPATHY FOR THE PRESIDENT.

IF we had time and space, we would be glad to give you a description of the beautiful *Colonne Vendome* and the *Palais Royal*. The former is an imitation of Trajan's Column at Rome, and was erected by order of Napoleon I., to commemorate his victories over the Russians and Austrians. It is surmounted by a life-size statue of the Emperor. This magnificent column was pulled down by the Communists in 1871, but has been rebuilt out of the old fragments. The *Palais Royal* is a building of great beauty, and covers a whole square. The ground floors are occupied by shops, which exhibit a tempting display of jewelry in quantities sufficient to supply all Paris. This palace was also the object of the Communists' wrath, and was set on fire chiefly with a view to destroy the departments of Prince Napoleon.

We spent two Sundays in Paris, and like a true son of the church, looked for a Lutheran church; and though we have fourteen places of worship, yet we were prevented from attending service in either one. The next best thing we could do the first Lord's day, was to attend service at the Wesleyan chapel, where we heard an excellent sermon from Bishop Simpson. It was a great pleasure to hear a preacher of our own country and in our own tongue in a foreign land. The congregation was largely composed of Americans, and all seemed to know each other. Rev. W. H. Steck, of our church, sat down almost by our side before he was aware of our presence. Think of our mutual surprise as well as pleasure thus to meet! The second Sunday morning we attended service at the Scotch chapel of the Presbyterian church, and heard an excellent sermon by Rev. Ewing, of Edinburgh. The attendance was small, but so was the chapel.

Being anxious to know how the Lord's day is kept in Paris in a general way, we confess to having made a pedestrian investigation one Sunday afternoon. Contrasted with our own, this is the Parisian's great pleasure day. We made our way to the Champs Elysées. As we approached this great avenue we seemed to be coming into the midst of a grand mass meeting of all the children of Paris, who were congregated here by many thousands, all in the higest glee and gayety. All manner of contrivances for amusement were in progress, the most popular of which appeared to be Punch and Judy shows. Great numbers of these little theatres were in progress, around each of which were crowds of spectators, mostly children, who occupied the seats at ten *centimes* (about two cents) each. Under the groves were toy and gingerbread stalls, and every variety of attractions for the young and old. A great number of revolving horse-machines of the most brilliant adornings, with children astride wooden ponies, were doing a successful business. There were also various concert gardens, and cafés scattered among the trees on either side, where open-air concerts were in progress attended by large audiences, and every variety of drink was furnished. At the same time the avenue on this thoroughfare, for driving and promenading, was thronged with the grandest vehicles Paris can afford, whilst the gay and lively spectacle was enjoyed by thousands of persons seated on the iron chairs with which the side-walks are lined. At night all the cafés and concert places were brilliantly illuminated, and bands of music swelled the air with their sweet strains. The numerous circus buildings were also illuminated, and the doors thrown open for a grand equestrian performance.

You may imagine, but you cannot *realize*, how strangely and sadly all this panoramic scene of gayety and pleasure on the Lord's day, contrasted with our own at home. It seems to us that it was sowing to the wind, from which will be reaped the whirlwind. This the French have often experienced. It is true, most of the business places in Paris are closed on the Lord's day, but all Paris seems to be given up to pleasure and frolic on this sacred day, and a very small proportion of its people go to church.

As to church edifices, there are many in the city, and not a few of wondrous beauty and magnitude. The *Notre Dame* is among this number. The interior of this church, with its lofty arches and massive pillars, makes a most imposing appearance. Notre Dame certainly is great, and so was Father Hyacinthe in the days when he was the most popular preacher in Paris. The church in which he now preaches is a very unpretentious edifice in comparison with this, where he delighted thousands with his eloquence. Romanists and infidels have no good will for Hyacinthe Loysen. In the *treasury* of this church we were shown fragments of the "crown of thorns" and the "true cross," a nail of the "true cross," and many other relics and ecclesiastical vestments.

The *Madeleine* is perhaps the most chaste and magnificent of all the modern churches of Europe. During the reign of the Commune in 1871, three hundred insurgents, driven from their barricade in the streets, sought refuge in this sacred edifice; but the troops having soon forced an entrance, not one of the unhappy miscreants escaped alive.

For exquisite beauty, richness of windows and architectural finish, we pronounced the *Sainte Chapelle* a *celestial* chapel. Not far from this beautiful edifice stands the church from whose small tower sounded the preconcerted signal for the massacre of St. Bartholomew, and during the whole of that fearful night the bell unremittingly tolled its funeral peal. As we stood looking at this tower and began to fill up with thoughts of the horrid scenes of that bloody time, we were tempted to believe it would be a good thing to pull down that tower, and concluded that *that* church was only a cumberer of the ground.

While in this neighborhood, we failed not to see the prison so famous in the annals of France. It is underneath the *Palace of Justice*, adjoining the Seine. Most of the political prisoners of the first Revolution were confined here before their execution. Profound interest attaches to the small chamber of the cell in which Marie Antoinette was imprisoned. The crucifix and arm-chair belonging to the ill fated queen, used by her during the sixty days she spent here, are still there. An altar has since been added, and the cell has been embellished with paintings representing the queen taking leave of her family, and her last communion. Adjoining this chamber, and now connected with it by an archway, is the cell in which Robespierre was afterward confined. The place, an excavation in the immense stone wall, where the beheading was done, is still pointed out. The only flourish on execution days in those times, was the ax in the hands of the executioner.

But we must leave unsaid many things that would be interesting to you, as they were to us, in the gay and wonderful city of Paris.

After telling you someting about a trip to *Versailles*, with its wonderful palace, we will get ready to leave France. In company with twenty-seven other Americans, all in one immense tourist wagon, we started for Versailles. It was a beautiful morning, and we were happy with bright anticipations. We passed through some of the most delightful parts of Paris, out through the Triumphal Arch. As we reached the outskirts of the city, we observed many extensive fortifications of the memorable siege. We also passed the residence of Marshal Bazaine, and a few miles farther on we stopped, and for an hour strolled through the Mongso Park, which is loveliness itself. The flowers, the green turf, and the avenues under the arched trees, presented a picture in nature, unsurpassed for beauty and loveliness. We then passed on to St. Cloud. Here is the Palace, once the home of Marie Antoinette, and in later times the favorite residence of Napoleon. It is at present a mass of ruins, having been burnt by the French themselves during the late siege. The palace gardens, the park, the fountains and flowers, are still greatly attractive.

As a town, *Versailles* contains little to interest the tourist. The house which was the scene of the negotiations between Prince Bismarck and Jules Favre in 1871, and resulted in terms for the capitulation of Paris, is still to be seen. The great attractions of the place, however, are the palace and its picture gallery. These are rich in historic interest, and of great extent. The palace was the headquarters of the King of Prussia during the late siege, and a great part of the edifice was then used as a military hospital; the King showing his appreciation of the fine arts by having all the pictures carefully covered to protect them against injury. In the *Grande Gallerie*, a superbly decorated hall, the impressive scene of proclaiming King William of Prussia Emperor of Germany, was enacted on the 18th day of January, 1871. Here is hall upon hall filled with the richest paintings by distinguished artists. It is a palace decidedly Napoleonic. Every battle in which the great soldier was victorious is elaborately put on canvas here. Napoleon's clock, with its exquisite vase of golden flowers, is to be seen here, and is a gem of rich beauty. The apartments of Marie

Antoinette are still very beautiful. Most of the original furniture has disappeared. The waiting room of the maids of honor—the richly furnished red and blue libraries, filled with the choicest books—the bath rooms and saloon of the Queen, are all preserved in their original state.

"The world has never seen and never can see a sadder and more pathetic biography than that of Marie Antoinette. As Andromache and Hecuba moved by their accumulated and mysterious sorrow the sympathy and tears of the ancient world, so has the story of Marie Antoinette moved those of the modern." Now, even after the lapse of so many years since her sad death, to walk in her accustomed paths and move freely about in her departments, tends to rekindle and freshly stir one's sympathy on her behalf. "It will in a few years more be a century since the French Revolution broke out, and it was ninety years ago, on the 16th of October, since her noble and afflicted life was ended by the guillotine. Yet her figure is as prominent and distinct in its personality to-day as when she died; and when a child, still in its teens, is asked to give instances of beautiful women distinguished for their misfortunes and heroism, the first that occurs to it, in answer, is nearly always Marie Antoinette. The hapless queen is still an object of sympathy as well as a sense of national shame to all intelligent and honest Frenchmen." "And not only in France, but in England and America, and in every country of the Old World and the New where there are minds to study history and hearts to feel for the unutterable woes and cruel sufferings of a woman, the grave of Marie Antoinette is kept green and flower-strewn and tear-watered in the memory." *

In the *Grand Trianon* we were taken into the sleeping apartments of Napoleon. These are still possessed of great richness and beauty. Near these is the bed room and bed where Queen Victoria slept when on a visit to Paris in 1846. Everything displays great elegance. The *Petit Trianon*, the favorite resort of Antoinette, contains beautiful trees and a charming artificial lake, and was well worth a visit.

We also paid a visit to the building which contains the collection of state carriages. These are marvels of splendor. They contain all such conveyances from the time of the first Empire to the baptism of the Prince Imperial in 1856. Josephine's is among the number. Nothing like this collection of royal carriages exists anywhere. If these royalists could *always* have luxuriated in such vehicles in all the rides they took, they would have been happier than they were. Millions of money are stowed away in these golden, gilded carriages.

The gardens in the rear of the palace are specimens of wonderful artificial style, and so are the small park and ornamental lakes. Such landscape gardening you can only see here. The gardener's chief object seems to have been to subject nature to the laws of symmetry, and to practice geometry, architecture, and sculpture upon lawns, trees, and ponds.

---

* "The Mothers of Great Men and Women."—Laura C. Holloway.

After spending a whole day in and about this palace, so richly adorned with all that wealth and art could afford, we are on our return to the city, considerably subdued in tone, and still worse frightened before we reach our hotel. As we were approaching the Seine at a good rate of speed, there was a sudden collapse of our huge wagon, and twenty-eight people were quickly brought to the ground and deposited on the broad street. The writer was the only one who received any injury, which at the time threatened to be of a serious nature. This was not a little provoking, as *we* had several times reminded the rest of the happy company of the defective wheels of our huge wagon. The spill-out and sprawl in the street was an amusing spectacle to the Parisians, but not quite so to us. With some assistance we limped away, saying to our friends, "*Didn't I tell you so?*" Ever after that, they looked upon us as something of a prophet; if not that, then as one who knows something about wagons.

After a short inspection of the great porcelain manufactory, which was near by where we made the sudden halt, we made our way to the Seine, where we took a boat and had a pleasant ride up into the city on this historic river. The evening was one to remain indoors, for we were greatly fatigued, but much delighted with our trip to Versailles.

Though much more remains to be said about Paris and the French people, yet we must close with this. While we saw many things we could not like among the French, there were many that we could not help but admire. One cannot but be astonished at the *vitality* of the

French nation. Possibly no other people could have undergone all that has befallen them in the last twelve years without being thrown back half a century at least. Their trials and losses and political disquietude and turmoil seem to have done them a world of good. To an American it was most gratifying to see the deep and unabated interest shown by the French, as by the Germans, in President Garfield, who was lying at the point of death. They read with ourselves the daily bulletins, showing much sympathy for the suffering President. The heart of the French people has generally been warm and true to us in every trouble and affliction.

CHAPTER XXVI.

FROM FRANCE INTO ENGLAND—ROUEN—JOAN OF ARC—A STATE OF TRIBULATION—ON THE BRITISH CHANNEL—BRIGHTON—REV. F. W. ROBERTSON—LONDON — THE SOMBRE CITY—ITS STREETS—THE GREAT COMMERCIAL CENTRE—THE MARCH OF IMPROVEMENT.

RELUCTANTLY we took our departure from so attractive and beautiful a city as Paris. It was a rainy morning when we left our comfortable family home, the *Hotel De Dijon*, 29 *Rue Caumartin*, and soon were on our way to Rouen. There is nothing specially interesting in country scenery on the way to this city. There remain not a few historic towns and castles of the olden times. We passed through Poissy, a town of five thousand inhabitants, where, in 1561, a conference was assembled by order of the States-General with a view to adjust the differences between the Roman Catholic and Protestant parties. Their deliberations, however, led to no result, owing to the strong condemnation of the Calvinists by the Sorbonne, the celebrated theological faculty of Paris.

At Rouen, the Roman *Rotomagus*, formerly the capital of Normandy, we spent part of a day. It is a city of over one hundred thousand people, and parts of it very beautiful. Besides its extensive cotton manufactures, it is a city of much historic interest. Its cathedral is a beautiful structure and well worth seeing, but *St. Ouen* is one of the most beautiful Gothic churches in existence, and far surpasses the cathedral, both in extent and excellence of style. We much enjoyed the extensive and beautiful garden in the rear of this church. Near by is a relic of a citadel where *Joan of Arc* was once imprisoned. Another place of interest in Rouen is the spot where this same woman was burned at the stake in 1431. About twenty-four years later she was declared innocent of the crime of witchcraft by a papal bull, and the French, who it is well known had been her betrayers, being now masters of Rouen, erected a cross to her memory on the spot where she had suffered. The place is now occupied by a paltry figure over a fountain. The Europeans, it would seem, have wonderful faith in the efficacy of water as washing out the stains of foul crime; for at almost every place where deeds of horror have been committed, they have erected flowing fountains.

Leaving Rouen at 5 p. m., after two hours' ride, we reached Dieppe, situated on the British channel. We had intended to cross over during the evening; but owing to the tide being out, we were obliged to spend the night here, and sailed at five the next morning. Scarcely had the steamer passed over the bar, when we made haste to meet our destiny. Horrid qualms were upon us, and the time of tribulation commenced. The groaning and the moaning became universal; basins were handed around in profusion. In all our experience we never witnessed a more rapid transformation. If we had all taken emetics the effect could not have been more simultaneous. Before "going abroad," we were told by the *knowing* ones, that when these things came on we must resist them. We honestly tried it, and quickly made our way up on deck; but if ever the resisting forces were completely taken out of any one, they were out of us. The night previous had been stormy and the channel was very rough, and the short, chopping waves sent our boat bobbing up and down—and there we were, hanging over the bulwarks of the vessel, holding by a rope, and leaning against a post, and at short intervals lifted to our tip-toes by reason of the violent *upward* tendency within. We could neither live nor die. We were flanked on our right and left with persons in the same state of tribulation. A more subdued, forlorn, cast *down*, and yet casting *up*, set of passengers no vessel ever carried. At one time we thought the end of all things had certainly come, but it was only in order to begin afresh; and now we were reminded of Mark Twain's experience, and thought that next "our immortal spirit would come up." It was our first experience in sea-sickness, but not our last, though the most violent. We never want five hours more of such experience as we had on the British channel. We never will know what the Frenchman said, though we heard him say it, to whom we attempted to speak in his troubles by our side; but from the expression on his face, we would not wish to be guilty of saying what we *think* he said. It is best not to speak to a man when he is *sea-sick*. With the sight of the English coast came deliverance, and we were soon in the harbor of New Haven, and were almost as suddenly well as we had become suddenly sick.

After an hour's delay we were in the cars on our way to Brighton. This is a beautiful city of one hundred thousand people, with an annual influx of over fifty thousand tourists and visitors, it being now by far the most frequented sea-side resort in the British Islands. It afforded us much pleasure to see the church of the late great and distinguished preacher, the Rev. F. W. Robertson. It is an unpretentious brick building of medium size. The preacher, however, was one of the greatest. He delighted as well as profited the multitudes that went to hear him. The wide diffusion of his published sermons in England, as well as in our own country, has given him a deservedly great reputation.

Brighton is noted for its colleges and superior schools for both sexes. The chief attractions of the place for many consist in its clear and bracing air, the fine expanse of sea bordered by white chalk cliffs, its bathing facilities, and its gay crowds of visitors. The extension and admirably appointed *Aquarium* is well worthy a visit. Externally it makes no great show, being built on a site below the level of the street. The forty large tanks in the interior facing the halls are made of glass, and contain great numbers of fish, some of which, *e. g.* like the octopus, are exceedingly curious and interesting. There are here seal and sea-lion ponds, alligators, and stuffed specimens of fish and reptiles. The flat roof is laid out in beautiful flower beds, and is used as a promenade.

In the after part of the day we were on our way to London, where we arrived at six, in a London rain. We had scarcely emerged from the train when we were greeted by a Jehu, not like in our country, however, with howlings of an unearthly nature, but with the polite salutation, "Will yer 'onor 'ave a coach, sir?" To hear English traveling companions giving directions for the careful "'andling of their 'at boxes" was truly amusing. Every Englishman travels with a ponderous sole-leather hat-box, which is the object of his supreme attention. You may smash his trunk, tread upon his favorite corn with impunity, provided you only "'andle his '*at-box*'" carefully.

Well, we were glad to get back to old England again. We felt somewhat at home, and it was refreshing to hear one's own language spoken once more. The *Armfield Hotel, South Place*, near the Bank of England, proved this time, as formerly, a delightful home place to us.

Having visited both Paris and London, one is apt to think of these two great cities by way of contrast. Coming directly from the former bright and sunny city to the latter cloudy and so smoky, is enough to bring on a gloomy sensation. The brightest and most ornamental, as well as most cleanly and attractive portion of Paris is its business centre, but the very contrary is the case in London. The majority of the buildings are nearly coal black, or streaked and stained, whilst the mud and dirt on the streets partake largely of soot, and make a terrible mixture for pedestrians; but they do one good thing too—they prevent ladies from indulging in the luxury of trailing skirts. The mud part in London is easily explained, on account of the great humidity of the atmosphere. The streets are constantly damp from this source, and sprinkling is unnecessary, and dust a novelty. There are few straight and wide streets in London. It seems to have been built in a sort of hap-hazard way, without plan; and, of course such a thing as *change* being against the creed of an Englishman, nothing *is* changed, hence the streets in London remain crooked and narrow. The architecture of the city is heavy and gloomy. The streets are generally well paved, many of them with asphaltum. Like all large cities, London is not without its public parks of great attraction. Among these are St. James, the Green Park, Hyde Park, and the Kensington gardens. These lie so close to each other that one may walk from Charing Cross, the very heart of the city, to Bayswater, a distance of three miles, without taking one's feet off the sod. These parks alone embrace six hundred acres, and are very rich and lovely.

The stores of London, with few exceptions, are small. The merchants display wonderful skill in showing goods to an advantage in their windows, but when you go inside you are often not a little disappointed in the size of the room and the comparative emptiness of the shelves, the window seeming to be the chief receptacle of their meagre stocks. But then, there are so many such stores in every part of the city, that you can readily and easily get what you want. The dealers are the very pink of politeness, obliging and accommodating as any people in the world. To an American the prices of goods are astonishingly low, so that one feels like buying large quantities of all kinds of merchandise. Of course they know a man from the States as quickly as they see him, and

they like to sell him goods, for they take it for granted
that every man that crosses the ocean has *oceans* of money.
As a rule the American spends his money more freely
than any other tourist.

London has every variety of conveyances for the accommodation of its vast multitudes. There are a great
many passenger railways above ground, and a good many
underground. There is an immense amount of business
carried on below the city, lumber, coal yards, and as
many as two or three railway tracks cross and recross
directly under each other. So densely crowded is everything that this is now a necessity. But with all this, the
omnibus, of which there are two thousand in the city, is
the great vehicle for travel. And the best way to get a
good idea of the city, is to mount to the top of a double-decker, and take a seat alongside the driver, and you will
get from him a great deal of useful information. These
men, as well as the conductors of the omnibus lines in
London, are among the most polite and accommodating
people in the world. The naming of the streets of this
great metropolis is a system most perplexing. The name
of a street is frequently changed every few squares.
There are within the city limits thirty-seven King streets,
thirty-five Charles streets, and twenty-nine John streets.

London is a great, grand old city, full of wonders and
of untold interest. It is the great business centre of the
world; being essentially devoted to commerce, everything
goes on a rush. It is almost a bewildering sight to witness the constant stream of rushing population. Some
idea of its traffic may be gathered from the fact that in

a single day, between 8 o'clock a. m. and noon, three thousand four hundred and fifteen vehicles, and eighteen thousand seven hundred and seventy-two pedestrians, passed the Mansion house on an average, *every hour*. Twenty-five thousand people cross the London bridge every hour. The population of the city is nearly four millions, inhabiting nearly half a million houses. Nine thousand new houses, it is said, are built in the great capital every year, and twenty-eight miles of new streets are thus added to it. Eastward and westward the city is extending rapidly, while northward it is stretching its arms toward Hempstead, Highgate, and even tranquil and blooming Finchley. Truly the spirit of this age is in strong contrast with that of the time of Henry VIII., when (1580), to prevent the increasing size of London, all new buildings were forbidden to be erected "where no former hath been known to have been." The march of improvement nowadays carries everything before it; even British conservatism is at some points giving way ; and the London of Dryden and Pope, of Addison, Sheridan and Byron, will, as time passes, find more and more difficulty both in tracing the footsteps of fame and in finding that sympathetic, reverent spirit which hallows the relics of genius and renown.

CHAPTER XXVII.

LONDON—ST. PAUL'S CATHEDRAL—THE WHISPERING GALLERY—WESTMINSTER ABBEY—THE TEMPLE OF FAME—THE HOUSE OF PARLIAMENT—THE HOUSE OF COMMONS—THE LONDON TOWER—CONSECRATED PLACES—THE JEWEL TOWER—THE CROWN JEWELS—THE UNFADING CROWN.

LONDON is a city of so many attractions that one is puzzled to know what to select when writing about it. Among the many churches, *St. Paul's* cathedral is the most worthy of note. The church resembles somewhat St. Peter's of Rôme, though much smaller, and is built in the form of a Latin cross. It is so hemmed in by streets and houses that it is difficult to find a point of view whence the colossal proportions of the building can be properly realized. It is the third largest church in Christendom, being surpassed only by St. Peter's at Rome and the cathedral at Milan. It was the hour for morning prayer when we entered, and a large congregation was present. The singing was specially inspiring, and we much enjoyed the impressive service with our English cousins.

After looking at some of the numerous monuments erected in the church by the nation in honor of distinguished men in civil and military life, we ascended the dome, stopping in the whispering gallery, which is an acoustic wonder, and another wonder is that it happens to be such not from intention, but merest accident. A slight whisper uttered by the wall on one side of the gallery is distinctly audible to an ear near the wall on the other side, a distance of one hundred and eight feet in a direct line, or one hundred and sixty feet round the semicircle. From this point there is also obtained a fine view of the interior of the church below. We proceeded still higher to the *Stone gallery*, which runs round the foot of the great dome. Here we had an admirable view of the city, it being an unusually bright morning for London. Though so enticing, we did not go to the *Golden gallery*, feeling that it would not be just to waste all our strength in climbing still higher. We retraced our steps and went to the opposite extreme, descending to the crypt. Here we were conducted by a polite gentleman into a chamber lighted by four large candelabra of polished granite, in the centre of which stands the Sarcophagus of the Duke of Wellington, and farther on, exactly under the centre of the dome, that of Lord Nelson, the two great representatives of the army and navy, of which Englishmen are particularly proud. The massive funeral car cast from captured cannon, and other trappings of mourning used at the Duke's funeral, are close by. There is much interesting history connected with this church. Near it once stood the celebrated cross of St. Paul, where sermons were preached, papal bulls promulgated, heretics made to recant, witches to confess, and where the Pope's condemnation of Luther was proclaimed in the presence of Wolsey.

The noted *Westminster Abbey* in many respects is perhaps the most interesting of all London's many attractions. We could scarcely realize on that beautiful September morning that we were approaching this famous pile, the Walhalla of England, or Temple of Fame, about which we had heard and read so much. It is not possible to describe it so as to give the reader an adequate conception of it. As a building, it is of vast proportions and of untold richness in historic interest. It is of Gothic design, built of fine stone in the form of a cross, and is four hundred feet long by two hundred feet wide. It was originally founded in A. D. 658, the first building being destroyed by the Danes, and afterwards rebuilt in A. D. 958, nearly one thousand years ago. In this venerable structure all the coronations have taken place since the days of Edward the Confessor. Here it is

"Where royal head receives the sacred gold;
It gives them crowns, and does their ashes keep—
There made like gods, like mortals there they sleep."

Besides being a place set apart for regular divine services, it is England's Temple of Fame, containing the royal burial vaults and long series of monuments to celebrated men. Interment within its walls is considered the last and greatest honor which the nation can bestow on the most deserving of her offspring. Time, that wonderful revealer of so many men's real character, has however disclosed the fact that this honor has been conferred on some now believed to have been scarcely worthy of it. The tombs, monuments and chapels in the Abbey are almost innumerable. In one of its most beautiful chapels—Henry the Seventh's—we stood by the tomb of the late Dean Stanley, yet freshly adorned with an exquisitely beautiful wreath of *immortelles*, the tribute of her Majesty, the Queen, to the memory of the great and good man whose mortal remains sleep within the inclosure of this celebrated structure.

In the transept and *Poet's Corner* we viewed the tombs of Milton, Shakespeare, Southey, Campbell, Spencer, Ben Jonson, Dryden, Dickens, Addison, and many other distinguished poets and writers. These attract more attention than the tombs of kings and queens, being men distinguished for their great intellect rather than the accident of birth, and mostly unstained by the crimes which mar the characters of so many of those who lie in close proximity to them. Our own poet Longfellow has a memorial tablet placed in the group of the *Poets' Corner*, showing in what distinguished honor he is held by the men of letters among the English people.

It would require many weeks and even months to inspect, with any degree of minuteness, all that is contained in this interesting place. It is the spot to which may be traced much of England's proudest history, and the place will ever continue to make eloquent the ages with the lives of those who sleep within this sacred inclosure. As you stroll about, the spaciousness and gloom of the vast edifice produce a profound and mysterious awe. We step cautiously and softly as if fearful of disturbing the hallowed silence of the tombs; while every footfall whispers along the walls, and chatters among the sepulchres, making us more sensible of the quiet we have interrupted. It seems as if the awful nature of the place presses down upon the soul, and hushes the beholder into noiseless reverence. We feel that we are surrounded by the congregated bones of the great men of past times, who have filled history with their deeds, and the earth with their renown.

Contiguous to Westminister Abbey are the *Houses of Parliament*, or Palace of Westminister. It is a great Gothic building, covering eight acres of ground. It is not a handsome structure. It is built of a reddish sandstone, blackened by the smoke of London. It has a frontage on the river Thames of nine hundred feet, with a beautiful terrace. The whole cost is over $8,000,000. It is surmounted by three towers —the Victoria Tower being the highest, rising to a height of three hundred and fifty feet. The entire building has a sort of disjointed appearance about it, lacking symmetry and beauty. It reminds one somewhat of the Smithsonian Institute in Washington, which has been styled "a convention of pepper-boxes." In entering the building you pass into a series of narrow passage-ways and small chambers, which lead into the House of Lords. This is the principal apartment, and is a room one hundred feet long, forty-five feet wide, with a ceiling of the same height. At one end of this chamber is the magnificent throne from which her Majesty, the Queen, delivers her annual message, and opens or prorogues Parliament. No expense has been spared in attempting to make this the most splendid chamber in the world. While it contains much that is of rare beauty and splendor, its pavement consisting of fine mosaic work, its ceiling pannelled and gilt, and everything adorned down to the minutest details with lavish magnificence; yet the architect, it is apparent, has failed most signally in doing his part. The extreme height of the ceiling makes the chamber appear much smaller than it really is. Everything seems profusely piled together. The Lords sit like boys in a country school-house of olden times, on long and broad benches, with backs covered with purple morocco and stuffed, one rising above the other, whilst the Lord Chancellor sits on a crimson sack, called the "Woolsack," without back or arms, and covered with red cloth. For a few moments' rest, we peacefully usurped the Chancellor's place. The Lords have no desks nor anything to hoist their heels upon like our members of Congress, unless it be on the shoulders of the noble Lords sitting in long rows on the benches below them. There is a small gallery into which are packed the aristocracy, and a smaller space for other folks, who may sit there by special permission. The House of Commons is the same in size and structure, gaudily decorated with paintings and statues, but not much larger and not half so comfortable as that occupied by any one of our State legislatures. And this is the great House of Parliament in England! Neither externally nor internally does it in anywise compare with the Capitol at Washington and its legislative halls.

The *Tower of London*, supposed to have been commenced by Julius Cæsar, was next visited. It stands on the banks of the Thames, and covers twelve acres, within which are numerous buildings or apartments, including the barracks, the armory in which are kept sixty thousand stand of arms, the Jewel House, the White Tower, the Bloody Tower where Richard III. murdered his nephews, the Brick Tower in which Lady Jane Grey was imprisoned. We passed through all these, and many other departments. In addition to the Tower's original use as a fortress, it was the residence of the monarchs of England down to the time of Elizabeth, and a prison for state criminals. Numerous are the kings, queens, warriors, and statesmen, who have not only been imprisoned, but murdered within its walls. The histories of Lady Jane Grey, Catharine Howard, Anne Boleyn, Sir Walter Raleigh, Lord William Russell, Sir Thomas More, William Wallace, and King John of France—do they not live in the memories of every reader of history? Immediately in front of the Tower is marked the spot where the scaffold was erected upon which Lady Jane Grey and Anne Boleyn, and a number of other female prisoners were executed. The White Tower was the prison of Sir Walter Raleigh, and here is exhibited the veritable block upon which he was beheaded. The inscriptions cut in the stone walls in all these towers by the prisoners are most curious and interesting, and are religiously preserved. That attributed to Lady Jane Grey was traced on the wall with a pin as follows:

> "To mortals' common fate thy mind resign.
> My lot to-day, to-morrow may be thine."

Many of these gloomy dungeons are consecrated spots—consecrated with the tears and prayers of the righteous

—and are still eloquent with devotion to the principles of our holy Christianity.

The most interesting place, especially to the ladies, is the *Jewel Tower*, containing a circular iron cage, about twelve feet in diameter, in which are exhibited all the crown jewels and royal regalia. It is a splendid sight; the whole collection is worth over twenty millions of dollars. Prominent among the jewels is the crown made for the coronation of Queen Victoria, which, the custodian assured us, cost one million of dollars. The great Koh-i-noor diamond is also among the collection, and is the property of the Queen. It is about as large as an English walnut. There is also the crown made for the coronation of Charles II., and worn by all the sovereigns of England since his time; the crown of the Prince of Wales; the crown made for the coronation of the Queen of James II., also her ivory sceptre; St. Edward's staff of solid gold; the royal sceptre of solid gold, ornamented with precious stones; the state salt-cellar, the coronation spoon, and the baptismal font for christening the royal children, with numerous swords and other valuable relics. The crown of her majesty Queen Victoria is a cap of purple velvet, inclosed in hoops of silver, surmounted by a ball and cross, all of which are resplendent with diamonds. In the centre of the cross is the "inestimable sapphire," and in front of the crown is the heart-shaped ruby said to have been worn by the Black Prince. These crowns will all fade, but not so the crown which Christ gives to his followers.

CHAPTER XXVIII.

LONDON—THE BRITISH MUSEUM—SYDENHAM CRYSTAL PALACE—BUCKINGHAM PALACE—ST. JAMES'S PARK—ST. JAMES'S COURT—MADAME TUSSAUD'S WAX WORKS—DRUNKENNESS IN LONDON.

AMONG the most interesting and instructive places to visit in London is the British Museum. It is a rich store-house of treasures, especially for the student and scholar. Its zoological collection is considered the second best in the world. Its library numbers nearly one million of volumes, and its Egyptian antiquities are unsurpassed. Its marbles are very extensive, comprising the famous Elgin, Phigalean, and Townley collections, with a large assortment of modern works. The number of MSS., prints, relics and antiquities, and drawings, is immense. Among the autograph writings of celebrated men, we noticed one of Luther, Calvin, Melanchthon, Byron, Washington, Michael Angelo, and numerous others; and besides these, the last letter that Charles Dickens is known to have written. It is written with blue ink, and fully sustains the reputation of distinguished men for a miserable handwriting. We also noticed the original *Magna Charta* of King John (1215). In another case is preserved the prayer-book of Lady Jane Grey, and the will of Mary, Queen of Scots.

It was a satisfaction, as well as a matter of much interest, to examine the typographical specimens in illustration of the history of printing, and to see, among the earliest German printed books, the Mazarin Bible, the first printed Bible, printed by Gutenberg and Faust (Mayence, 1455). Among the books bearing the autographs of the authors or early owners is the Wittenberg Bible of 1541, with Luther's signature. Among these collections are included Luther's ninety-five theses against the Indulgence of 1517. Near these is a case containing a volume of the Codex Alexandrinus and the books of Genesis and Exodus according to the Syriac version. This Syrian MS. was written in A. D. 464, and is believed to be the oldest dated MS. of any portion of the Bible now extant. But we cannot detain ourselves to name even the smallest portion of this wealth of collections in art, literature, and science.

From the Museum we go to see the *Crystal Palace* at Sydenham. This magnificent building is four hundred feet long and one hundred and twenty-five feet wide, with numerous transepts, and consists entirely of glass and iron. The view from this palace is one of the most lovely in Great Britian. The gardens are most delightful; their beautiful walks, serpentine streams, statues, fountains, and lawns, render it unsurpassed in beauty. Here one can purchase almost everything that is of utility, manufactured on the spot. It is, in fact, a vast manufacturing emporium of the highest order. A portion of the building is appropriated to tropical trees and plants; to courts of Egyptian, Greek, and Roman sculpture; courts of Assyria, Alhambra, Germany, and Italy. Copies of the masterpieces of all the great sculptors of both ancient and modern times are here, so that those who cannot visit Florence and Rome to see the works of Michael Angelo and other great masters may here see their reproductions. If Italy holds the originals, the best thing England can do is to have almost perfect copies. There are also immense halls filled with the productions, both natural and mechanical, of Asia, Africa, and America; picture galleries, museums and refreshment saloons; in short, everything to please the eye and gratify the appetite. It is a good place to which the weary and tired Londoner, as well as tourist, may resort with profit for rest. There is ample provision made for all kinds of amusements, concerts, and picnics. Children's concerts are very common; as many as three and four thousand little ones often sing here, and thirty thousand persons attend. In the central part of the building is the great Handel Orchestra, which can accommodate four thousand persons. In the middle stands a powerful organ with 4,568 pipes. An excellent orchestra plays here in the afternoon and evening, and concerts are given every Saturday under the leadership of distinguished musicians. In every respect this palace is a place of great beauty, of many attractions, and of decided comfort.

But we did not forget to go and see at least one of the many palaces of her Majesty, the Queen, and for want of time, selected the *Buckingham Palace*. This has been the Queen's residence since 1837 during her stay in the city. Admittance could not be gained, and therefore we cannot, from personal knowledge, describe the internal beauties of this palace. It has the appearance, externally, of genuine royalty, in its exquisite beauty and solid, massive construction. The park (the St. James) in which it stands, with its beautiful clump of trees, its winding expanse of water-fowl, and the charming views it affords of the stately buildings around it, combine to set forth its tranquil charms, and make this one of the most lovely and attractive places in London. To the north, between Buckingham Palace and Piccadilly, lies the Green Park, which is seventy acres in extent—a lovely picture of rest, calm retirement, and smiling plenty, to the lambs that skipped in joyful glee on the rich green, in the golden haze of that beautiful September morning.

Near by is *St. James's Palace*, an irregular brick building, which was the residence of the sovereigns of England previous to Victoria's occupation of Buckingham Palace. The Queen still holds her drawing-rooms here. This palace is rich in historical associations, not all honorable to royalty. George IV. was born here; so also was the son of James II. by Mary of Modena. 'Tis said the child, who was the old Pretender, was conveyed in a warming-pan from his mother's bed to that of the Queen, who occupied the great bedchamber. Here died Queen Mary I.; also Henry, the son of James I.; here Charles I. took the last leave of his children. On the north side of the palace is the *Chapel Royal*, in which the queen and some of the highest nobility have seats during divine services on the Lord's day. The marriage of Queen Victoria with Prince Albert, and those of some of their daughters, were celebrated in this chapel. Down to the death of Prince Albert, in 1861, the Queen's *levées* and *drawing-rooms* were always held in St. James's Palace. Since then, however, the drawing-rooms have taken place at Buckingham Palace, but the levées are still held here. A levée differs from a drawing-room in this respect, that at the former, gentlemen only are presented to the sovereign, while at the latter it is almost entirely ladies who are introduced. Richly dressed ladies; gentlemen, magnificent in gold-laced uniforms; lackeys in gorgeous liveries, knee-breeches, silk stockings, and powdered hair, and bearing enormous bouquets; well-fed coachmen with carefully curled wigs and three-cornered hats; splendid carriages and horses, which dash along through the densely-packed masses of spectators; and a mounted band of the Life Guards, playing in front of the Palace;—such, so far as can be seen by the spectators who crowd the adjoining streets, windows, and balconies, are the chief ingredients in the august ceremony of a "Queen's Drawing-Room." A notice of the drawing-room, with the names of the ladies presented, appears next day in the newspapers.

In the group of many stately, say *royal*, buildings here, we had pointed out to us by our Scotch friend, are the residences of the Prince of Wales, the Duke of Sutherland—the latter being considered the finest private mansion in London—and that of the Grand Duchess. In the Court of St. James, we were favored with the finest instrumental music of our life. Here the bands of the Grenadier, Coldstream, or Fusilier Guards, play for a quarter of an hour daily at 11 a. m. The Grenadiers played the morning we were there. There were fifty performers. They compose the Queen's band. In connection with this performance, the guard of the palace paraded, which is a body-guard of magnificent soldiers, of most striking uniform. In this body of men are representatives from all parts of the British dominion. The parade connected with the band of music was the most brilliant military display we ever witnessed. In the Wellington Barracks, near by, are quartered a battalion of Royal Foot Guards, who paraded the same morning. These soldiers all measure six feet and over in height, and look as if they might be a formidable foe in time of battle.

One of our evenings in London we spent in seeing *Madame Tussaud's Wax Works*. The spacious halls were full of curious visitors, and among these not a few from the States. From morning until 10 o'clock at night there is a constant throng of visitors to this popular resort, and it would be a great oversight, as well as an unpardonable deviation from common custom, for an American to visit London and not go to see this fine collection of wax works on Baker street. One is greatly astonished at the perfection in expression of countenance, likeness, and dress of the distinguished persons represented, so that at first sight the effect is peculiarly pleasing. In our verdancy, upon our entrance, we were about to address an inquiry to one of these figures, who happened to be a representation of a policeman. We *think* to this day yet that we corrected ourselves in time, so as not to incur the smiles of the many who saw us entering the hall. These figures are all life-size, and of great numbers, embracing many of the most distinguished characters in history, kings and murderers of both sexes, of many generations. The whole royal family are here in court dress—the infant children of the Prince of Wales among them; these look angelic. The late Czar of Russia, with his weeping family around him, lies in state here. The scene is truly impressive, and very natural.

The group that attracts the attention of Americans most, perhaps, is that of Abraham Lincoln, Gen. Grant, and Andrew Johnson. The latter is a good likeness, but the other two are rather poor. Near these stands the lamented Garfield, which is far from being as good a likeness as many others. Martin Luther looks well in the group of Knox, Calvin, and Mary, Queen of Scots. If a visitor happens to take a seat on one of the ottomans interspersed among the "figgers," it is sometimes difficult for a moment to decide "which is which." Mrs. Jarley is certainly distanced by Madame Tussaud.

In closing this chapter, we cannot refrain from recording our great astonishment both at the extent and daring boldness of the unblushing drunkenness one sees in London. Drinking and its consequent disturbances of the peace, are not confined to the small and out-of-the-way places in the city, but are practiced to an alarming extent in many of the most fashionable and finest streets. In a few hours' walk, within half a mile of Trafalgar Square, on Saturday afternoon and evening, we passed great numbers of reeling drunkards of both sexes,—women with little children in their arms, dancing and carousing in the middle of the street. The "gin mills" and rummeries and "corner groceries," are as numerous as in some of our narrow thoroughfares, and both men and women could be seen in great crowds at the counters, imbibing, and engaged in noisy controversy. If such was the aspect of affairs in the middle of the day, it is not difficult to imagine what it must be after night-fall. It is an alarming fact to every thoughtful Englishman that, at the present rate of drinking and drunkenness, their people are fast becoming a nation of drunkards.

CHAPTER XXIX.

SPURGEON—LONDON'S GREAT PREACHER—HIS CHURCH—THE SERMON—OUR IMPRESSION—THE HOME OF INDUSTRY—MISS MCPHERSON—THE DARK SIDE OF LONDON—ECUMENICAL CONFERENCE OF METHODISM—BUN HILL FIELDS—BUNYAN—JOHN WESLEY—DANIEL DE FOE—SOME REFLECTIONS ON ENGLISH CHARACTER.

EVERY foreigner who comes to London, of course goes to hear London's great preacher, the Rev. C H. Spurgeon. One must go early if he expects to get a seat, or even standing-room. It was a pleasant Lord's day morning in September, when we attended service at the Tabernacle. Having been favored with a ticket by an English friend, we were at once admitted into the church, though not to a permanent seat. All pew-holders have a first right, and their seats are reserved until ten minutes before the service begins. Up to this time all visitors who have gained an entrance within the building are seated on benches along the wall, when, at a given signal, the ushers proceed to seat the strangers. We were fortunate in being invited to a choice seat, being within thirty feet of the celebrated preacher, and at the same time also had a good view of the great congregation.

As to the church edifice, it is an immense structure, plain, substantially built of stone, having seats for seven thousand people. The front is ornamented with a row of Corinthian columns which supports a portico, under which you pass into the Tabernacle. There are two tiers of galleries going entirely around the audience-chamber, and extending far into the building. At the front of the first tier is the pulpit or platform. The preacher stands sixty feet from the rear wall, and his hearers by the thousands above and behind him, as well as in front and on his side. There is no "great gulf fixed" between him and his hearers. He is entirely surrounded by his vast audience. Under the platform from which he speaks, and extending beyond it, is the choir, composed of one hundred persons, fifty being boys, of possibly fourteen years of age. The chorister stands by Mr. Spurgeon's side during the singing. There is no organ, but there *is* rousing singing, for every one is supplied with a book, and *all* sing. It would be difficult *not* to join in. The choir does no fine performing to the edification (?) of the audience. *All* join in worship. It is hardly necessary to say that the vast Tabernacle was full, for is is *always* full, and that in "*all weathers.*"

Promptly at 11 a. m., Mr. Spurgeon entered by the first tier of galleries, and took his seat at a small table containing a hymn-book and a Bible. Mr. Spurgeon is ungraceful in appearance, short and thick-set, with high shoulders and short neck. His head is large and round, his face full and set with short brown whiskers. His eye is very striking, small, but penetrating and full of fire. He reminded us somewhat of Joseph Cook. Perhaps at first sight the impressson is one of disappointment, as it would seem impossible to reasonably expect anything ex-

traordinary from so ordinary and "material" looking a
man. In his manner of conducting services he is energetic, earnest, and impressive. Two hymns are sung and
two prayers offered before the sermon. The reference to
President Garfield in the second prayer was very touching. The old custom of lining out the hymns is still adhered to. In his prayers, Mr. Spurgeon is as remarkable
as in his sermons. During prayer we felt that we were
in the presence of a man who felt that he was in the presence of God. Many of his utterances are not only touching, but marvellously striking. Here is one: "May the
thunder of thy power make us ashamed of the littleness of
our faith!" In reading the Scriptures before the sermon,
he commented on each verse, making practical application
of its meaning. This was a pleasing and edifying part of
the service. His text was 1 Cor. xiii. 7: "Charity beareth all things, believeth all things, hopeth all things, endureth all things." His theme was: *Love's labors.*

1. *The multitude of love's difficulties.*
2. *The triumphs of love's labor.*
3. *The sources of love's energy.*

It was a great sermon in every respect, and at once
fully explained to us how it is that this man has for thirty
years preached with unabated interest and signal success
to the largest congregations of any living preacher. He
speaks without notes, and becomes sublimely eloquent.
He is not a sensationalist, as some have averred, but a
great, grand, glorious gospel preacher. He is tender,
direct, plain, striking in his utterances, fluent, original,
bold, incisive, and eminently scriptural. He has what

some might call peculiarities, but nothing to detract from the dignity of the sacred desk, or the Christian ministry. It certainly is a blessing and a pleasure to hear such preaching. There evidently is much earnest Christianity in Mr. Spurgeon's congregation, for his preaching will of necessity produce it. We expected much, and were not disappointed. As the preacher closed we could scarcely believe that we had been listening forty minutes. We were also present at the Thursday evening lecture, which was nearly as largely attended as the Sunday service. The Sunday morning sermon is printed and offered for sale at a penny per copy by members of the church after the Thursday evening service.

After the benediction on Sunday morning we felt some one touching us on the shoulder, and on looking round were approached by a middle-aged lady, who at the same time apologized for her freedom. "I presume," she said, "you are a clergyman, and from the States." My reply was, "Yes, madame, but I hardly think I look like one." (After the wear and tear of a tour over the Continent, it seemed to us that least of all did we have the appearance of a clergyman.) "But I infer that you are," said the woman, "from the deep interest you took in the sermon, and the notes you were taking at times." This woman proved to be the good Miss McPherson, so well known in London and in Canada as an eminent Christian worker among the lost and outcast of that great city. She invited us to visit her institution, the Home of Industry, in East London, at four o'clock that afternoon. We consented, and found the place at the time appointed. We were cordially welcomed and conducted to an upper room on the second floor of the building, where we found this good Christian woman engaged in talking to a large number of co-workers in the cause of reclaiming poor and lost waifs of society from the slums of sin and infamy in East London. After hearing Miss McPherson talk, we concluded there *were* meetings in which women had a right to speak, for surely no one can speak like this woman did without help from God. It was a blessing to us to hear her, and we do not see how it could be otherwise to all present. After her eminently biblical talk, she presented in the most touching manner two little girls who knew no home and no parents, picked up that day (in the streets) and received them into the Home, where she had already a large number of such. These poor creatures are gathered into this Home during the summer and winter and formed into classes for religious instruction, and in the month of May Miss McPherson brings hundreds of them over to America and Canada, where homes have previously been provided for them in good families. It is a blessed work, and this good woman will have many stars in her crown out of the multitude she is gathering from the snares of the evil one. We were urged to remain and take tea at the Home with the corps of missionaries engaged with this Christian lady. This will always be a pleasant reminiscence in our life in London. In the evening we accompanied, by invitation, several of the young men to a number of London's lodging-houses, where they held religious services. The sights in these places no pen can picture, and few strangers coming to London ever see. One would not think that man could sink to such depths of infamy as come to view here. They are the hives of thousands out of every grade of society, reaching every stage of crime and sin possible to degraded beings. They pay a few pennies per week for lodging here. They live by theft and murder. Yet these missionaries give them not up as lost, but go among them with the gospel, and do reclaim some.

Later on in the evening, in company with Miss McPherson and several young men, we visited ten of the mission stations under her charge. These mission-points are in the very worst parts of East London, a very refuge for those who can be induced to forsake the ways of infamy. In one mission house ten different languages are employed in teaching the gospel. There are but few places of sin to which this Miss McPherson and her band have not access, and they have no delicacy in improving every opportunity. To all, they hold up Christ as the Saviour of sinners. To any one else, not in company with these Christian workers, an entrance into this part of London, by day or night, would be sure misfortune if not death itself. But Miss McPherson and her band move among the vile and degraded with perfect impunity, and as veritable angels of light. This woman accomplishes great good. Her work is acknowledged by all Christian people as marvellous. It is the power of God. The Queen contributes largely in support of this work. What we saw and heard that night was the *other* side of London, which is not the bright side.

During our stay in London the Ecumenical Conference of Methodism was holding its sessions in City Road Chapel, erected by John Wesley, and where he preached to the end of his life. We attended parts of several sessions. It was a large and interesting assembly. Papers were read on various subjects previously assigned. To a Lutheran some of its proceedings were anything but edifying. To hear of the persistent missionary operations carried on by the Methodist church in Sweden and in parts of Germany, where least of all missionary work, in the true sense of the word, is needed, was the next thing to a vexation. To one who knows how well supplied those parts of the world are with gospel privileges of every kind, it is a mystery how any Christian denomination can, with a good conscience, busy itself in making converts, not to Christianity, but to its own sectary. Such a spirit is not a genuine missionary spirit according to the gospel. It is well known that there is no country in the world, that in every way approaches nearer the high standard of New Testament Christianity than Sweden; yet the great Methodist Episcopal church feels itself called upon to send large numbers of missionaries among this people. If the object is to proselyte good material from another *greater* church, then the Methodist Episcopal church has wisely selected. We greatly prefer her taste to her zeal. The primitive Methodists in England, with but a slight variation, retain the entire service of the Church of England. This did not suit the delegates from America, and at home they would not submit to it. The delegates, too, from this side, were not a little shocked to have wines and even stronger drinks freely handed round to them by their hosts; and not only did the lay, but also the clerical, indulge in this luxury(?) of treating their guests. This we were told by one of the regular clerical delegates from the States. It would seem again from this that the Germans are not the only people in the world who have to bear the sin of using " a little wine (and beer, too,) for their stomach's sake and their often infirmities."

The colored delegates from America to this conference really were the lions of the day. A colored gentleman is quite a curiosity in London, and a little *more* so in a large ecclesiastical assembly. Some of the more ambitious delegates from America did not greatly relish this state of things; but the Englishman being about as fond of novelty as the American, the gentleman of color many times received the preference.

In the rear of this church (City Road Chapel), lie the remains of John Wesley, under a plain marble monument, surrounded by a plain iron fence. On the side of the tomb is inscribed the following: " Reader, if thou art constrained to bless the instrument, give God the glory." By the side of the church stands the three-story parsonage in which Wesley died. The church is substantially built of brick, well furnished, with gallery, and has a seating capacity of about one thousand.

On the opposite side of the street is the Bun Hill Field Cemetery. It is a quaint but beautiful and inviting spot. Here we stood by the grave of John Bunyan, the immortal dreamer, and author of " Pilgrim's Progress." It is a plain tomb; his age is inscribed on the side of it, as having been sixty years. Here also sleeps the mother of the Wesleys, and the flat tombs of stone and marble are still pointed out on which John Wesley stood and preached. In the same cemetery are buried Daniel De Foe, Isaac Watts, Adam Clark, Richard Wattson, and a host of other worthies whose dust awaits the voice of God, but whose spirits dwell with the redeemed.

But we must get ready to take our departure even from lovely England and enjoyable London. We greatly enjoyed our visit among the English people, who are always pleasant, polite and intelligent. At the English inns we enjoyed also the cleanliness, but not the dinners so much, nor the solemn silence; and were so besieged by chamber-maids, waiters and "boots" for a sixpence, that we resolved to show our gratitude for freedom from such annoyances in this country by a generous contribution to every good cause at home.

Among the many things we admired among the English is their independent spirit, and their respect for all who indulge the same feeling. The American, for instance, who believes he can win English esteem by sinking his Americanism, knows little of the English. If they themselves conform to nobody, they expect nobody to conform to them. Aping English manners, or paying court to English prejudices, is the last way in which a foreigner may expect to conciliate English good-will. They like above all things, though they don't always know it, an exotic flavor. They respect above all things genuineness of character. They expect a man to be himself, and not somebody else—an American if he is lucky enough to be born under the Stars and Stripes, or a Turk if he owes allegiance to the Crescent. The American accent, as they call it, is heard with pleasure in England. The most frivolous society is of one mind on this point with the most serious. What society wants above all things is to be interested, and the surest way to interest is to be novel.

If we are allowed another reflection on English character before closing this chapter, we remark that one of the strongest instincts of the English character is the instinct of permanence. It acts involutarily, it pervades the national life, and, as Pope said of the universal soul, it operates unspent. "Institutions seem to have grown out of human nature in this country, and are as much its expression as blossoms, leaves and flowers are the expression of inevitable law." A custom in England once established is seldom or never changed. The brilliant career, the memorable achievement, the great character, once fulfilled, takes a permanent shape in some kind of outward and visible memorial, some absolute and palpable fact, which thenceforth is an accepted part of the history of the land and the experience of the people. England means stability—the fireside and the altar, home here and heaven hereafter; and this is the secret of the power that she wields in the affairs of the world, and the charm that she diffuses over the domain of thought. Such a temple as St. Paul's Cathedral, such a palace as Hampton Court, such a castle as that of Windsor or that of Warwick, is the natural, spontaneous expression of the English instinct of permanence; and it is in memorials like these that England has written her history.

CHAPTER XXX.

FROM ENGLAND INTO SCOTLAND—EDINBURGH—THE SIR WALTER SCOTT MONUMENT—CALTON HILL—THE NELSON, BURNS AND NATIONAL MONUMENTS—HOLYROOD PALACE AND ABBEY—MARY QUEEN OF SCOTS—HIGH STREET—JOHN KNOX'S HOUSE—ST. GILES' CATHEDRAL—PARLIAMENT HOUSE—MID-LOTHIAN—MANUSCRIPT OF SCOTT'S WAVERLEY—THE CASTLE.

IN a gloomy London drizzle we made our way to King's Cross Station on the Great Northern Railway, to take our final leave of London and to go over into Scotland. There stood the splendid express known as the "Flying Scotsman." Its reputation is far-reaching and well deserved. It leaves King's Cross terminus at 10 a. m., stops half an hour for dinner at York, and reaches Waverley Station in Edinburgh at 7 p. m. The rate of speed being seldom less than fifty, and often more than sixty miles per hour, makes this one of the quickest runs of which we have any record. In our journey we passed through many beautiful and historic towns, as well as some fine country scenery.

As we approach Stevenage we are reminded that here the abbots of Westminster had their manor lands, and also of the place where Charles Dickens found the original hermit described in one of his Christmas tales—Mr. Mopes. And now we are in the fen country, some seventy miles from London, and soon reach Peterborough. In an hour more we come to Scrooby, where a little Christian community of Independents was gathered long ago, who went from Scrooby to Boston, from Boston to Holland, from Holland in the Mayflower to the New World, and founded the Pilgrim Father Church. Presently York is reached and we look upon its stately minster. It was here that Constantine the Great was proclaimed Emperor. York minster has probably an older and wider reputation than any Cathedral in England. It was founded in the seventh century, erected in its present form in 1171, but not completed till three hundred years afterwards. It was the centre from which Christianity spread through the country north of the Humber. The day is now far advanced, and the rainfall has greatly increased. The harvest just cut suffers from the wet, and many shocks of wheat are green with a second growth.

We must hasten on and pass by unnoticed many places of interest. Evening is now upon us, and as we skirt along the coast of the German ocean, we hear the boom and melancholy roar which remind us of other days. At Berwick on Tweed we cross over into Scotland. This place was for many centuries the military key of Scotland. It was frequently taken by assault, and there is scarcely a foot of ground in the neighborhood that has not been the scene of terrible conflict. Some time after dark, Edinburgh was reached, and we found a pleasant home at the "*Crown Hotel.*"

Edinburgh is a grand city. It has not undeservedly received the title of the "modern Athens." It consists of the old and new towns. They are separated by a deep valley, formerly occupied by water, and called the North Loch. Now it is a great railway terminus, standing amid pleasure-grounds in the heart of the city. The architecture of the old town is characterized by what has been justly called picturesque disorder; that of the new, by chaste design, massive outline, and symmetrical proportions. It is decidedly a solid city, and the modern portions of it very beautiful, built mostly of gray sandstone. Its streets are wide, well paved, and remarkable for cleanliness. There is, however, a singular absence of shade trees. The city has many massive public buildings of elegant architecture, and is renowned for its monuments and charitable institutions, evincing among its people a degree of patriotism and public spirit of which few cities in Europe can boast.

Among the points of special interest and most worthy of being seen, we mention the monument to Sir Walter Scott. It stands within East Princess street gardens. It bears a general resemblance to the most admired examples of monumental crosses, of the largest proportions, being one hundred and ninety feet in height. A stair of two hundred and eighty-seven steps conducts to the top; and from its thirteen different galleries fine views are obtained of Sir Walter's "own romantic town." In the niches are statues of the most familiar characters in his novels and poems—such as Prince Charles, Meg Merrilies, The Last Minstrel, The Lady of the Lake, and Rob Roy. Under its canopy is the marble statue of Sir Walter Scott, attended by his favorite dog Bevis. For architectural beauty there is nothing even in Paris to compare with this monument; and yet, strange to say, the design was made by a self-taught architect, Mr. Kemp. It was erected in 1844, and cost nearly one hundred thousand dollars.

But now we go to the top of Calton Hill, from which, perhaps, the most comprehensive view of Edinburgh and its surroundings is obtained. From it both the old and new town are seen at a glance, the former with its dense masses of lofty houses—some ten stories high—crowning the ridge leading up to the castle. In the distance tower the highlands and "King Arthur's Seat." The latter derives its name, as is known to the student of history, from the fact that tradition designates it as the spot from which King Arthur looked down upon the scene of his victory over the Saxons.

Calton Hill is studded with monuments and public buildings. Here is Burns' monument, an elegant structure, forming a small temple, surrounded by twelve burnished marble pillars. The circular tower, one hundred feet in height, on the summit of the Hill, is Nelson's monument. It is built of massive brown stone, and whilst very fine, looks somewhat like a lighthouse. It is used as a time-signal. Near by stands the National monument, an unfinished structure, which was intended to commemorate the Scotchmen who fell in the battles consequent on the French Revolution. The design is after the Parthenon at Athens, and it was commenced in 1822. To the left of this are Playfair's and Dugald Stewart's monuments.

But let us now pass from the new over into the old part of the city, and go to see Holyrood Palace. This

Palace, by reason of its connection with the career of the beautiful Mary, Queen of Scots, is perhaps the greatest attraction in the city of Edinburgh. Queen Mary's apartments are here shown, with her bed in the same state as when last occupied by her. Here is her furniture, all faded and moth-eaten; tables, work-stands, and the work-basket she used, and also some specimens of needle-work executed by her during her imprisonment. A melancholy sadness invests the place. The bed-chamber is possibly twenty feet square, with rather low ceiling, of carved oak, and the walls are hung with decaying tapestry. One is keenly impressed by these surroundings with the story of sorrow and crime which connect them with the olden time. The small closet adjoining the bed-chamber was the favorite retreat of the Queen, and it was in this room that the slaughter of David Rizzio, her secretary, took place, despite the prayers and commands of the Queen. The secret stairway in the wall by which Darnley and the rest of the conspirators gained access to the Queen's apartments, is also pointed out, as well as the spot at the head of the stairs where the body of Rizzio was placed after the tragedy had been enacted. The faded window-curtain is pulled aside to show you the blood-stain in the oaken floor where Rizzio lay dead—if you have faith to believe that part of the story—for three centuries have passed since that fatal night of lawless love and relentless vengeance. A fine staircase on the southwest corner of the piazza of the palace leads to the royal apartments, which have been elegantly fitted up, and in modern times are honored by the presence of her majesty Queen Victoria and the royal family, who make it their stopping-place on their way to the Queen's private country-seat in the Highlands of Scotland. The room, called the Presence Chamber, in which Queen Mary met and had an interview with John Knox, is still pointed out.

Connected with Holyrood, is the Abbey, the old chapel royal. It is impossible to look at this venerable ruin without intense interest. Within its now crumbling walls Queen Mary was married to Darnley; in it Anne of Denmark, Queen of James IV., was crowned in 1590. Here Charles I. was crowned, and here in the royal vault repose David II., James II., James V. and his queen, and Henry, Lord Darnley.

From Holyrood we pass up High Street to the Castle. Though this street is now occupied by the poorer inhabitants, its houses were at one time the residences of the nobility and gentry; and some of them have very interesting associations connected with literary men. There is no place in the city so full of old associations as this long street, which, under various names, reaches from Holyrood up to the Castle; every step of the way is full of interest; the wonderfully tall old houses, with their dark winding stairs, and peaks and gables, all have a history.

Out of those same windows, the high-born beauties of long ago looked on bonny Prince Charlie, on gallant Montrose dragged to his death, on lovely, hapless Queen Mary, and on staunch John Knox. Down some of these narrow "wynds," or alleys, reeking now with every kind of evil odor, you may find traces of green grass and stunted bushes, the remains of ancient gardens. In these gloomy courts, the houses rising story upon story, slatternly women screaming to each other out of their windows, dirty children at play in the gutters or on the filthy stairs, lived the lords and ladies of generations past.

Some of these Closes, as they are called, keep their ancient names in the midst of the dirt and squalor, bringing back a whiff of long ago. There is "Lady Stair's Close," where the countess of Stair lived for many years when at the head of the fashionable society of Edinburgh. "James' Court," where Boswell lived, and where Johnson used to roll in to have a cup of tea with him. In "Baxter's Close," Burns had a room. David Hume wrote a great part of his history in the Canongate. Now we pass the Moray House, the old mansion of the Earls of Moray, and the Canongate Tolbooth. We go into the grave-yard of the Canongate church, and stand by the graves of Dugald Stewart, Adam Smith, and the poet Ferguson, whose tombstone was erected by Burns.

What stories the ancient houses on this street could tell us of love and murder, of plots and treason, of the wit and beauty of long ago! But these eventful times have gone by, and we must confine ourselves to the present. On this same street stands the house of John Knox, the great Scotch reformer. It is situated in the Netherbow, and is a good specimen of an old Scottish house. The rooms as now shown are three, a sitting-room, bedroom, and study. Here Knox lived from 1560 to 1572, when he died in the sixty-seventh year of his age, a brave defender of a sturdy Christianity. He was buried in the churchyard of St. Giles, and over his grave the Regent Morton pronounced his eulogium in the well-known words, "*Here lies he who never feared the face of man.*" Above the door of Knox's house is the inscription, "Love God above all, and your neighbor as yourself."

On a high point of this street stands St. Giles Cathedral, dedicated to the saint of that name, and one of the most noted of the eclesiastical buildings in Edinburgh. It is interesting both from its antiquity and historic associations. It dates from the ninth century. Here John Knox preached. Near the front entrance, you see in the pavement the Heart of Mid-Lothian, made famous in one of Sir Walter Scott's novels. The church was undergoing repairs, and we saw but little of its interior. We walked into the churchyard of St. Giles to the spot marked with the letters "J. K.," on a small iron plate, designating the spot where John Knox is buried. We also went in to see the old Parliament House with its great hall, its carved oaken roof and its statutes and portraits. In the library we looked upon the original manuscript of Sir Walter Scott' Waverley, well preserved under a glass case. In passing we noticed St. George's, the church where the celebrated Dr. Guthrie so eloquently preached the gospel, to the great profit and delight of the Scotch people.

Now we have reached the castle. This is built on a rock rising three hundred feet out of the plain, and its position is both commanding and picturesque. It is associated with many stirring events in Scottish history. Within the walls of this castle are exhibited daily the ancient Regalia of Scotland; also Queen Mary's room, in which James VI. was born; Queen Margaret's chapel, one of the oldest chapels in Scotland, recently restored. It is exceedingly small. Here is also Mons Meg, a gigantic cannon used at the siege of Nordham castle in 1847. No better specimens of soldiers are anywhere seen than here. They were untiring in their kindness to us. The University, Museum, National Picture Gallery, and other places of interest we visited, we must pass by unnoticed here.

CHAPTER XXXI.

SOMETHING ABOUT EUROPEAN HOTELS—LANGUAGES—PATIENCE AND GOOD TEMPER—EATING—THE TABLE D'HÔTE—SERVANTS AND WAITERS—FEES AND CHARITIES—IMPROVING OPPORTUNITIES.

THE average hotel charges are cheaper, in most parts of Europe, than they are in our own country. The sleeping apartments are generally excellent, with good beds and fairly good attendance even in second-class establishments. Persons who do not deviate much from the usual track of travel find the English language spoken at nearly all the hotels, and in many of the large stores. It is true, in many cases you see large cards in the show windows of stores, informing you, "English spoken here," but when you go inside you fail to find it. Some knowledge of French and German is very useful, and adds much to the enjoyment of travel.

One of the chief ingredients necessary to a pleasant as well as profitable tour over the Continent of Europe, is a large amount of patience and good temper. We met and were in company with a few Americans who signally failed in this particular. They grumbled and growled and found fault with everything and everybody. They scolded the waiters and the cooks, and tried not to relish their meals. One of the amusing scenes frequently was to witness a war of words between guest and waiter in two different languages. From the general slashing round of dishes, and the frowns on the faces, it was very apparent that both parties were in bad humor; and in the effort to explain matters and state the true ground for complaint, things were fearfully mixed. Persons indulging in such bad temper make themselves unhappy, disgust other people, and fail to enjoy the trip, as those of a more equable temperament always do. The tourist should always go with the determination to take things as they come, and then the probabilities are that he will have a profitable and good time.

It is true there are many things to annoy you if you will allow them, but it is even so at home—yet when abroad, it is still more so. Just let us refer to the time and manner of eating regular meals. Breakfast means only bread and coffee at nine o'clock. There is no use to be in a hurry, for you will not get your breakfast earlier unless you make a special arrangement with *positive* orders, the evening before, and then you will pay extra. The *table d'hôte* (dinner) at the hotels is, to most Americans, an abomination. This meal is usually served at 6 p. m., an hour when the day's work is over, and the meal can be taken at leisure. It is the social meal of the day, and all the guests at the hotel are expected to meet at the table. It requires never less than an hour, oftener two, and unless your company is entertaining, it is a long and dreary process.

Perhaps you have been told that there will be ten or fifteen courses, and if uninitiated you have your mind made up that for once you will have your usual "square meal"; but when the waiter, with swallow-tail coat, with white necktie and shirt front of immaculate whiteness, brings you a small piece of bread and a dish of slightly colored water called soup, you proceed with quiet resignation with the belief that you will have the dinner presently; but your curiosity is only the more aroused when the plates are changed, and after a long dreary waiting you receive a very small bit of fish. Then the table is cleared again, and you are served with a bit of chicken; like a true American, you have dispatched your bread long enough since, and you take chicken and "play it alone"; but you think it "passing strange" when you learn that this is the manner you are to be served these "ten or fifteen courses." So you continue for an hour or two in patient expectation of the meal that is always *coming*. There is a mouthful to eat and then a dreary silence, giving plenty of time to cultivate the grace of patience. We yet have a distinct recollection of the fellow-coutryman who, when he had borne it patiently until the meal was half over, thundered out to the waiter: "Good gracious! Life is too short to be wasted in this manner, sir; for heaven's sake bring me something to eat."

If slow eating is conducive to health, and it certainly is, then nearly all Europeans ought to be very healthy. The manner of serving the dinner is said to be on gastronomic principles, the courses being so arranged as to be most conducive to digestion and to avoid astonishing the stomach by any violent changes in the food to be deposited therein.

It is really very difficult to know exactly what you

are eating. You must have confidence that you are going to enjoy your meal, or close your eyes and go it blind. If you should happen to call for ice-water at dinner you will be gazed at in perfect astonishment, and if you get it at all, you must wait a long time for it. The European considers wine the only beverage proper to imbibe whilst eating. This is used as freely as we use coffee. It is served in large long-necked bottles, placed on the table generously at the disposal of the guests—and they generally *do* dispose of it. If your breakfast at nine and lunch at twelve were not the most satisfactory, you will almost invariably be favored with a splendid repast at *table d'hôte*, the six o'clock meal. By taking meals in the restaurants the cost of living is but little more than half the hotel charges, and generally the quality of the food is much better.

Another thing that might be named as among the annoying things is, the ordeal through which you must pass when about to leave your hotel. It is next to impossible to get your bill until the moment you want to start away. Then there is presented to you a huge sheet of paper containing a long array of items, among which there are sure to be a number of improper charges. If you have time to read it all over and call attention to these errors, they are stricken off with profuse apologies for the *blunders* of the stupid (?) clerk. The best way to do, if at all possible, is to settle all bills the evening previous to your departure the next morning.

The next thing to do is to run the gauntlet of chambermaids, waiters, porters and "boots." To have a string of these individuals bowing at you all the way from your room-door to the carriage-steps, and looking beggary without exactly soliciting alms, gives the traveler some idea of his importance, and he tries to persuade himself that "it is always pleasanter to give than to receive." However, begging is the business of most of these for a livelihood, as they receive little or nothing for their services but what is gathered from the guests.

There was an amusing scene at one of our hotels one day. A party who traveled with the Cook tourist tickets, had printed instructions from Cook not to give even the smallest fee to any one unless as a charity, because their tickets embraced all manner of service at the hotels where they were stopping. As they were about leaving the hotel, the entire household was bobbing and smiling around them, but the tourists persisted in not understanding what it all meant, and quietly shook hands, bidding them all an affectionate adieu. They had no sooner left than the smiles changed to frowns, and all hands were abusing Cook and his people. Fifty Americans passing through a hotel and leaving no money with the servants was not to be borne. This time, however, the thing had to be endured. As a rule the porters receive fees for their attention to guests. Generally the porter is a polite gentleman, and some of them are well educated, speaking various languages with fluency. Regarding these well known annoyances as among the things which necessarily belonged to the tour we were making, we did not look upon them as *really* annoying, and are sure we fared all the better.

Although we discovered that Europe has much to learn from America, we also finally came to the conclusion that we have still much to learn from those old countries. It is undoubtedly true that the great majority of American tourists enjoy the sights and scenes and life in Europe, and come home wiser and better; but it is equally true that many fail to make good use of their opportunities. We know one gentleman who may be safely classed among the latter. He traveled over a large portion of Europe, and on his return home gave all that he saw and felt worth mentioning, in a four-column newspaper article. Nearly everything over the sea disgusted him, and we should not wonder if, by this time, he had become disgusted with himself. One has well said:

> "Nature, through all her works, in great degree,
> Borrows a blessing from variety."

Variety has been called the spice of life, that gives it all its flavor—hence some people use so much spice, that everything becomes artificial, and nature no longer borrows blessings from variety. Too much spice, especially when peppery, spoils the flavor of our pleasure and enjoyment.

CHAPTER XXXII.

THINGS VIEWED IN THE CONTRAST—THE CONDITION OF THE WORKING CLASS IN EUROPE COMPARED WITH OUR OWN—THE WORKING WOMEN—THE OPPRESSED POOR AND LABORING CLASS—ROYALTY—THE INEQUALITIES OF LIFE—AGRARIANISM—SOLUTION OF THE LABOR TROUBLES.

IN making a tour through foreign lands, it is natural for one to view things in the contrast. Whether it be the form of government, the condition of the people, or the state of morals, you judge these in comparison with the same at home. We are well aware that we have not yet attained the highest and purest form of government; that society needs purifying, and our Christianity to become more practical; but even in these vital matters we are certainly far in advance of possibly all the European countries. The crowned heads of Europe are watching with an Argus eye every advance we make in the science of good government. Every year our prosperous existence endangers their power. The story of our liberty is reaching and enrapturing their subjects. The tenure by which they hold their crowns is becoming more frail as time rolls onward; and, if we are true to ourselves, if virtue predominates, if the voice of wisdom is obeyed, if patriotism, discretion and honesty guide our rulers, our government will go on increasing in strength, beauty and grandeur.

By our example we will conquer the world more effectually, and by far more gloriously, than Alexander did with the sword—by regenerating the minds of the people. But we must practice upon the principle that eternal vigilance is the price of liberty. We are more in danger from internal foes than from foreign enemies. If we would be truly great, we must be truly good. Virtue, wisdom, prudence, patriotism, and sterling integrity, must actuate, guide, and fully control our leaders, and the great mass of our increasing population. The towering waves of political intrigue and demagogue influence must be kept back, and the purity of motive and love of country that impelled the sages and heroes of '76 to noble and God-like action, must pervade the hearts of our rulers and the people of our nation. Animated by such a spirit and governed by such principles, our country will always stand in happy contrast with all the monarchies of Europe, and our people be happy and prosperous.

The contrast between the common people or *masses*, and those of better worldly fortune, is infinitely greater in the old country than in our own. This difference is most marked among the female population. The women, in many parts of Germany and Switzerland, perform the hardest kind of labor-work. It is nothing unusual to see more women than men in the harvest-field, and the former generally do the hardest part of the work. Where the barrow and hoe are used, you usually see the woman pushing the former and the man carrying the hoe. If the two are seen sawing and splitting wood, the woman generally does the sawing and the man the splitting. In the many such instances which came under our observation, we always had the impulse to go and *reverse* matters.

It is nothing uncommon to see women making and carrying mortar in buckets on their heads up ladders to the workmen, and handling the brick. It is remarkable, too, to see how these poor working-women wheel wheelbarrows and handle the shovel and pick with all the muscular agility of men. Let us quote the language of another, so that in "the mouth of two or three witnesses every word may be established."

"We found the same proportion of women at work on all the buildings, and there must be thousands of them to-day doing this species of laboring work in Vienna. They comprise young, middle-aged, and old, but seem to be strong and healthy. At dinner-time they swarm into the shops to purchase a piece of brown bread and fat bacon and a mug of beer, and eat their dinners sitting on the curbstones. Their wages are one florin, or forty-eight cents, per day; and we were assured by a gentleman resident in Vienna, that most of them sleep about the buildings on shavings, or in barns or sheds, having no homes. Amidst all the splendor and wealth of this great city, with its millions of inhabitants, there is perhaps more destitution, want and suffering, than in all the cities of America. Still we frequently hear some of our countrymen praising and preferring the governments of Europe." Why do not such go and see? "While viewing this scene, the Emperor and Empress, with his staff and outriders, glittering in gold and precious stones, dashed along the Ringstrasse, on the way to the palace, whilst a short distance off stand the royal stables, an extensive establishment covering at least four blocks of ground each, the meanest animal in which is better cared for than these women."

How much better off and infinitely more happy the working-women in *our* country! In contrast with the same class in Europe, ours are truly queens, in the possession of their own homes and in the affections of their husbands and children.

The poor, and people of humble origin in Europe, have no opportunities to lift themselves from poverty into affluence, or reach the highest place among their fellows, like we have in this country. There "blood will tell," no matter what its quality. Royalty bars the way to many who are worthy.

Shakespeare has said:

> "'Tis better to be lowly born
> And range with humble livers in content,
> Than to be perk'd up in a glistening grief,
> And wear a golden sorrow."

But the sorrow among the masses, especially among the poor working class in Europe is not a "golden sorrow;" it is often the deep and keen sorrow of hunger, produced by faithful labor unrewarded. They work hard and receive a mere pittance for their toil. The laborer there is more a slave than ever our colored "chattels" of the South were. Twelve hours is a day's work over there for the day laborer and the mechanic, whilst the banker and business clerk and all lighter labor are content with six to eight hours. Many parts of Europe are delightful to the tourist, and inviting to foreigners, as places for permanent residence, but only such as are independently rich could enjoy them. The man who must earn his livelihood by the sweat of his brow, cares not to make such a country his home.

The condition of the laboring classes in Europe is the full explanation for the hundreds of thousands who annually throng our shores. While they love their Fatherland, they love freedom more. They want to go to America. Whilst many come to us, yet it is only *poverty* that keeps many more from coming. The laboring class seem to regard America as the haven of all their hopes; and if there were three thousand miles of desert instead of water rolling between them, there would be a regular stampede for these shores. And we think it is safe to say that every industrious foreigner who comes to our country is an argument in favor of ours being the best country the sun ever shines on.

We recognize the fact that differences in condition of life exist not only in Europe but also amongst ourselves; but we have them in a much milder form—they are not so oppressive by any means. These differences, too, have always existed in the human race, and will exist until the perfect redemption comes. Some one has said, " You may dig out the inequalities of life, but they will come again." These seem to rest on strength, talent, wealth, and rank. The first two produce inequalities among savages in the dense forest, in all the rudeness of nature ; the last two produce it in most refined society.

Absurd as it is, riches often give a man more consequence than talent, which, joined with virtue, is the only thing that should place one man above another of inferior capacity.

These inequalities of life, however, are often made so oppressive by the abuse of wealth and rank that there is great ground for complaint; and there is complaint. It would seem when one sees the condition of the masses in parts of Europe—how miserably labor is rewarded, just enough wages given to prevent actual starvation, and the consequent wretchedness this produces—that the right to combine for the regulation of wages would be justified there. But certainly there is far less ground for such a course in our country. Yet, with all the improved condition of our laborers and mechanics in homes and wages received, how rife and dangerous the spirit of agrarianism is becoming amongst us! History is repeating itself in the labor troubles of to-day. It is the same spirit that reigned at Rome two thousand years ago. At the present day, as in former times, we have many restless spirits among us, who set themselves up for reformers of society, proposing to change the whole order of things, and bring about an equality in the human family. We admit the need of reformation in many things and persons, and know of none who need to be reformed more than some of these modern pretenders. Many of them are destitute of moral principles, infidels in heart and practice, agrarians, levellers, too indolent to pursue a laudable calling, and too well known to impose upon the well-informed around them. With such, artificial wants and false pride, indulgence in idleness and vice, a discontented disposition, and a longing after the flesh-pots, are the real sources of misery—not the deprivation of riches, rank, or talent.

Yet at the same time candor and fidelity to the truth force us to say, that the fault of strife between capital and labor is not all on one side. It is a problem not easily solved; it claims the profound attention of both the church and state, the statesman and theologian. The only solution of the impending danger and threatening ruin, we think, is to be found in the spirit of a loving Christianity; by adopting the doctrine of Christ, that men are brothers, and the faithful and conscientious practice of the Golden Rule.

CHAPTER XXXIII.

GLASGOW—MELROSE ABBEY—LIVERPOOL—HOMEWARD BOUND—STORM AT SEA—SHIP ON FIRE—THE GREAT PERIL—DEATH AND BURIAL AT SEA—HOME AGAIN.

EDINBURGH proved to be one of the most delightful cities it was our privilege to visit in the Old World; it was therefore with much reluctance that we took our departure for Glasgow. The Scotchman takes special pains to show you the most interesting objects in his city, and that, too, without a fee. The gentleman who offered to point out to us the places of historic interest in Edinburgh gave us to understand that he would accept of nothing in that way. It gave him pleasure, he said, to do a kind office for an American. A striking characteristic of the Scotch people is that they all know their own history and historic characters. From the highest to the humblest in position, you cannot go amiss for correct information on any subject pertaining to their city, or distinguished men. Any one of them will discourse eloquently, and with becoming pride, about their literary men, statesmen, and warriors. This speaks well for their early training, no doubt in the family and school.

But now we are *en route* by rail for Glasgow, a distance of forty-five miles. The country between these two great cities is well cultivated, and interspersed with neat cottages, and there is evidence of industry and prosperity. Though being in the middle of September, it was harvest time, and from all appearances the crop was a heavy one. Grain is cut in this part of Scotland as late as October. In our approach to Glasgow we observed what is so common in the neighborhood of our own cities, large and beautiful country villas, surrounded with many proofs of refinement, wealth, and taste.

Glasgow is the chief city of Scotland, and one of the greatest commercial centres in the world. It has a population of six hundred thousand people. It is bustling with energy and activity. Parts of it are very beautiful. It is solidly built. The motto upon the city arms is: "Let Glasgow Flourish," and the people seem determined that it *shall* flourish. Among its many industries, the building of iron ocean and river steamers is one of the most important. It affords many other extensive manufactures, as brewing, dyeing, and bleaching. The shipping interests of the city are immense. Glasgow was the cradle of steam navigation, and the first steamer in Europe was launched there in 1812, Henry Bell being the projector. James Watt, a native of Glasgow, first applied steam as a motive power. Beautiful monuments have been erected to both of these inventors.

The cathedral and necropolis afforded us much interest; the latter containing many chaste and magnificent monuments, chief among which is that of John Knox. In the same neighborhood stands the church of the late and distinguished minister, Dr. McLeod. It is not very large, and neither externally or internally especially attractive. It presents a dilapidated appearance. But it was here where one of God's most distinguished sons preached with great power and rich fruits the gospel of peace. Near this church we noticed another church edifice with the following label, in large and attractive letters on its side wall: "*A church where people can attend divine service in their every-day clothes.*" Here certainly is the expressed desire upon the part of somebody to accommodate a class of people who can not afford to parade a "Sunday go-to-meeting" suit. Thousands of people, no doubt, are kept away from God's house because they can not profusely decorate their bodies so as to make a show. Then thousands more of our Christian people, by their extravagant dressing, keep many away from divine services.

But we must hasten. In the evening of the same day we retraced our steps to Edinburgh, where we spent the night. The next morning found us on our way to Liverpool, a distance of two hundred and fifty miles. On the way we stopped off to see Melrose Abbey, so famous in romance and poetry, and the noblest ecclesiastical ruin in Scotland. It is all in ruins, with the exception of the church; yet its ornaments and edges are as sharp as when newly cut. No description, not even the famous one in the "Lay of the Last Minstrel," can give an adequate idea of its beauty. Within its walls are the graves of kings, nobles, and priests of the olden time—among them Alexander II. of Scotland, and a number of the renowned Earls of Douglas. Before the high altar the heart of Robert Bruce is said to have been deposited; a small tablet marks the spot.

We continue our journey on the next train for Liverpool, and we really begin to feel that we are going home. The country is beautifully picturesque along the Tweed, whose banks we skirt. The vale of this river is everywhere beautiful. Villages and hamlets nestle in wooded slopes that rise from the verge of the winding river, and wide-spread pastoral hills and plains present a diversity of quiet beauty seldom surpassed. Later in the day we arrived at Carlisle, where we changed cars. After another long and tedious ride, we reached Liverpool at 5 p. m., and soon found ourself in Clayton Square, at the *Feathers' Hotel.* It proved to be a good, soft place.

We are here, a few days in advance of sailing, and the chief thing to do is to get ready to leave the " Old Field" for home. If we were even to attempt to tell you with what alacrity and delight one does such a thing as getting ready to sail for home, you might conclude we had been home-*sick;* but we were not. Sight-seeing had now about come to an end; and we had little time for looking about in Liverpool, the solid, sombre, and ponderous appearing city. The last Lord's day we spent on British soil, we attended divine services at St. Andrew's church, where we heard an excellent sermon from Canon Le Froy (2 Cor. x. 5). So well were we pleased that we attended service at the same place in the evening, and heard the second part and conclusion of the sermon on the morning text. Canon Le Froy is evidently what we would call, in this country, a low Churchman. In his sermon, speaking of the Church, he said, "Not the Church of England, but *all* churches." " Christ," he said, "came to do two things; one to die for our sins, the other to establish a church—not the Church of England, but *a Church*." The congregations, morning and night, were very large. From the manner in which the preacher handled the common sins of the day, he certainly showed himself a brave, earnest, and true herald of the cross. It was good to be there. The Lord was in that place.

On Tuesday, the morning of the day we sailed, while passing up one of the streets of the city, we noticed the British flag floating at half-mast, and soon also our own flag. Upon inquiry, we learned that President Garfield had died. The expressions of sorrow were apparent among all classes of the English people. They spoke of Gen. Garfield as "the President." We saw men and women weeping as if one of their own household had died. The sympathy was deep, genuine, and universal. It so happened that President Garfield was shot on the day we sailed for Europe, and died on the day we took ship to return.

On a bright September afternoon we took ship at Liverpool, in the vessel *The City of Montreal*, bound for New York, Captain Land commanding—the same brave Captain who subsequently was transferred to the ill-fated vessel, *The City of Brussels*. We had a pleasant company, among them a dozen clergymen of almost as many different schools. All were anxious to reach home, and especially to escape from the "life on the ocean wave," which is much more irksome on the return than on the outward voyage. Next to solitary confinement, there is nothing more wearisome than a homeward trip across the Atlantic, and nothing more trying to patience, nerves and the stomach, when tossed in almost constant storm, as we were. The next afternoon found us in the harbor at Queenstown, and that evening we put out into the broad Atlantic, full of hope and with bright visions of home and loved ones. The sea, however, begins to rise, the waves roll high, the winds pipe through the rigging, the ship rolls and rocks, the elements riot in the fury of the tempest. There is a storm at sea. But there is a storm within as well. We think we are going to die, and after being afraid we would, we get into such distress that we are sorry we can't. We are tossed and pitched and rolled; now our vessel being on the side, then on the steerage, seeming to be after spearing whales. After receiving sundry bruises on our craniums, alternately against the door and wall of our contracted apartment, we sank down hopeless and prostrate, a few moments serving to obliterate all anticipations of escape from that most prostrating of all the trials and tribulations of the stomach with which poor humanity can be beset. For eight days and nights the storm continued with almost unabated fury. At times its violence was much increased. Sleep was out of the question, for it required all our remaining strength to keep ourselves from pitching out of our little beds. At last, however, we got " our sea-legs on," and managed to encounter the storm somewhat. At meals the soup, the coffee, the plates, everything, came flying into our laps; and there goes your next neighbor pitching over the table, and another under it, as if shot out of a catapult.

Amid all our tribulations in our little rooms, we could not help being touched as well as amused by the sincere sympathy our kind steward expressed for us, and the earnest desire he had to afford us all possible relief. He would come to us frequently and say, " Mr. ——, we must get you hup on deck to get some fresh hair; for if you don't get hup on deck and get some fresh hair, you will 'ave an *hagonizing* time of it."

But at midnight, in mid-ocean, when the storm is at its greatest fury, the most thrilling of all scenes yet is suddenly upon us. We are startled with the cry of *fire! fire!* And it was no false alarm. Awful to realize, we find our ship is on fire! Our hearts almost faint within us at the horror that stares us in the face. Now go up the cries of the women and children, and pitiful are the beseechings for "help! help!" Others make preparations to take to the life-boats. But what are these for safety, in such a storm and for such numbers? There were seven hundred and ninety-five souls on board, and boats enough for possibly one-third of this number. Hither and thither rush the seamen (as if on wings), in flying obedience to the word of command by the anxious Captain. The smoke now rolls in dense volumes through the whole aft of the ship; here and there the flames leap up and give a glare of vivid light. Oh, how long were those two hours on which our lives poised for a happy welcome home, or a watery grave in the deep, deep sea! But hope is borne to our troubled hearts; the good and brave Captain tells us the danger is past, and the fire under control. Our anxious ears catch the sound of the life-giving throbs which the great engine sends through the entire vessel. We recover from the fears of our apprehended fate, and joyfully greet every assurance that contributes to our deliverance. We feel that we are safe, for the Captain assures us that the fire is entirely subdued, and our ship not seriously damaged. The Lord heard our prayers and delivered us out of our distress. "He maketh the storm a calm, so that the waves thereof are still." "Then were we glad because we were quiet; so He brought us into our desired haven." The origin of the fire we never could ascertain, but we suspect that carelessness was the prime cause..

On the morning of the same day we had a burial at sea. One of our female passengers died of *delirium tremens*. Her body was wrapped in a sheet, and securely tied with ropes to a heavy plank, at the foot end of which was suspended a heavy iron weight. The body was placed near the open port of the ship. The Captain then read the burial service, and as he pronounced the words, "earth to earth," the seamen shoved the remains off into their watery grave.

Shortly after this sad ceremony, we were startled by the ravings of a drunken man who threatened with death one of our cabin passengers. Memorable, indeed, will ever be that Lord's day morning on the sea! A fire, a burial, and an attempt at murder—truly, it was time, we thought, for us to be getting home.

The last three days and nights were the most charming, as well as beautiful, of all our trip abroad. As if wishing to compensate for eight days and nights of almost constant storm, the sea put on its greatest calm and beauty, and we were reminded of the sea of glass which St. John beheld in his apocalyptic vision from the island of Patmos. The joy of getting home to our own native shore and family was sincerely great, and can only be appreciated by those who have realized a similar experience. How solid and beautiful seemed the hills on which we looked from the deck of our vessel that Lord's day morning, as we lay in the bay off New York! How supremely thankful to our divine Lord for bringing us safely "home again from a foreign shore," and into our "desired haven," and into the midst of our loved ones! Then were we glad and thanked the Lord that there "was no more sea."

www.ingramcontent.com/pod-product-compliance
Lightning Source LLC
Chambersburg PA
CBHW022107230426
43672CB00008B/1312